GRACE AND REASON

Oxford University Press, Amen House, London E.C.4

GLASGOW   NEW YOUK   TORONTO   MELBOURNE   WELLINGTON
BOMBAY   CALCUTTA   MADRAS   KARACHI   LAHORE   DACCA
CAPE TOWN   SALISBURY   NAIROBI   IBADAN   ACCRA
KUALA LUMPUR   HONG KONG

GRACE AND REASON

A STUDY IN THE
THEOLOGY OF LUTHER

BY

B. A. GERRISH

OXFORD
AT THE CLARENDON PRESS
1962

© *Oxford University Press 1962*

PRINTED IN GREAT BRITAIN
AT THE UNIVERSITY PRESS, OXFORD
BY VIVIAN RIDLER
PRINTER TO THE UNIVERSITY

TO MY MOTHER

In fulfilment of a promise

PREFACE

NEXT to 'antinomianism', the charge most frequently brought against Luther by his critics is, perhaps, 'irrationalism'. Many champions have come forward to defend the Reformer's ethical principles, and the import of his assault upon 'the law' has been adequately explained. Fewer discussions have been made of his assault upon 'reason', and the need for drastically qualifying the charge of irrationalism is not sufficiently felt. In actual fact, the assaults on reason and on the law, properly understood, arise from the same basic motive and are expressions of the same fundamental theological standpoint. The opposition between Gospel and law in Luther's theology could equally well be stated as an opposition between grace and reason. Luther's 'irrationalism' is not to be interpreted simply as a call for the theologian to abandon the demands of disciplined thought. Reason, as he understood it, constitutes a threat to the freedom of divine forgiveness, and his polemic is maintained chiefly in defence of the notion of God's 'grace'. How this is so, it is the purpose of the following chapters to make clear.

The present essay is a shortened and revised version of an academic dissertation submitted in the spring of 1958 to the Joint Committee on Graduate Instruction of Columbia University, New York. At that time the author had been unable to trace any monograph devoted wholly to Luther's understanding of reason, despite the many incidental allusions to the topic both in the 'Luther-Literature' and in other studies of Western thought. Wilhelm Link's learned study, *Das Ringen Luthers um die Freiheit der Theologie von der Philosophie*, contains some valuable discussions of Luther's attitudes towards the philosophical theology of the Schoolmen; and Bengt Hägglund, in his recent work, *Theologie und Philosophie bei Luther und in der occamistischen Tradition*, has offered an extremely useful essay on the difficult subject of Luther and the Nominalists. At several points Hägglund in particular addresses himself to the problem of reason in Luther, but, of course, neither of these two works claims to be a comprehensive discussion of the place of reason in Luther's theology.

After the present writer had already completed his manuscript, he received a copy of Bernhard Lohse's admirable work, *Ratio und Fides. Eine Untersuchung über die ratio in der Theologie Luthers* (Göttingen, 1958), the most comprehensive and satisfactory treatment of the problem that has yet appeared. Had this study been available to me during my own research, I would certainly have made extensive use of it: in revising my work for publication, however, I have contented myself with occasional references to Lohse's essay, where his discussions parallel or supplement my own. As one would expect (despite the fact that the two studies were made independently), many of the same sources have been treated by each author and many similar conclusions have been reached. It is equally to be expected, in view of the vastness of the subject, that dissimilarities of approach and of emphasis should appear. In particular, it will be noticed that, whilst Lohse builds upon a developmental study of the 'Young Luther', the present essay adopts what Regin Prenter (in the prefatory remarks to his *Spiritus Creator*) calls a 'systematic-exegetical' method, proceeding by intensive analysis of a crucial text from the 'Mature Luther'. And even though each of our essays has in addition a purely 'systematic' section, there also the reader will discern some variations of approach. Lohse, for instance, does not concern himself greatly with Luther's historical relationships (with the Schoolmen, for instance); and it does, perhaps, constitute a real difference that our own topic is not 'reason and faith', but '*grace* and reason'. The aims and methods of the present study are more fully explained in the Introduction.

It is the writer's firm persuasion that the subject of 'grace and reason' in Luther's theology will be of concern, not only to specialist scholars, but to all who have an interest in the Protestant Reformation, since our theme proves to be by no means peripheral, but brings us to the heart of the Protestant case against the medieval Church of Rome. It is to be hoped, therefore, that our essay will not only help to show the groundlessness of many accusations of 'irrationalism' levelled against Luther, but may also do something towards clarifying the basic significance of Evangelical Protestantism.

With more general readers in mind, the writer has done his best to restrict technical scholarship (which the specialist will rightly demand) chiefly to the footnotes. Since it would be utopian to presuppose a knowledge of Luther's own languages in every reader, English translations are offered from the Latin and German. The translations are our own, but where there are already-existing English versions, which the reader could consult for context, references are occasionally given to them also in the notes.

Finally, one who stands in the Reformed, rather than the Lutheran, tradition may perhaps be pardoned if he suggests that the discussion of Luther's views on reason be compared with the *Institutes* of Calvin, Book II, chapter ii. The chapter is misleadingly titled, since it seems to promise a discussion on the bondage of the will. In actual fact, Calvin here devotes more space to a succinct statement on the capabilities of the 'intellect' in fallen man. (The capabilities of the fallen will are taken up more fully in the following chapters.) Calvin's presentation in some respects amounts to a summing-up of Luther's own, and yet it should be noted that Calvin's conversation is, not with his fellow Reformers, but with Augustine and the Schoolmen.

The writer wishes to record his indebtedness to Professor Wilhelm Pauck, of Union Theological Seminary, New York, his adviser during the writing of this essay, and to Professor Leonard J. Trinterud, his colleague in the Church History Department of McCormick Theological Seminary, Chicago: to both he owes valuable counsel on several points.

B. A. GERRISH

McCormick Theological Seminary
January, 1961

CONTENTS

INTRODUCTION   I

PART ONE

REASON AND PHILOSOPHY

I. Luther's Attitude towards Reason   10

II. Luther's Attitude towards Philosophy   28

III. Luther and Scholasticism   43

PART TWO

REASON AND THEOLOGY

IV. Luther's *Commentary on Galatians*   57

V. The Limits of Reason   69

VI. Reason and Law   84

VII. Reason and Religion   100

VIII. Luther against Scholasticism   114

PART THREE

REASON AND SCHOLARSHIP

IX. Reason and the Task of the Scholar   138

X. Humanism and Scholasticism   153

CONCLUSION   168

BIBLIOGRAPHY   172

INDEXES   181

INTRODUCTION

THAT Luther on more occasions than one fiercely attacked the capacities of human reason, is known well enough; and his critics have made good use of the knowledge. The last sermon preached by Luther in Wittenberg before his death (in 1546)[1] has acquired the status of *locus classicus* for his invective on reason. Here (by no means for the first time in Luther's utterances) 'Reason' appears personified as 'the Devil's Whore', and Luther's animosity towards it is expressed in violent, indeed coarse and vulgar, abuse, which many of his critics are too genteel to reproduce or, at least, to translate. The sermon is not the most informative of Luther's discussions on reason, though probably the most extreme. Neither, however, is it exceptional; so that Luther's customary manner of describing reason has always been a stumbling-block to his friends and a ready-forged weapon of offence in the hands of his enemies. In another passage Luther bids Reason depart (*procul absit ratio*), for all the world as if it were a malignant spirit, which must be frightened away by the theologian's apotropaic incantations. Reason is a 'beast', an 'enemy of God', a 'source of mischief'. It is 'carnal' and 'stupid'.[2] Small wonder that even John Wesley was shocked as he read these words, though he was by no means initially prejudiced against the Reformer.[3]

To these direct tirades against reason we must add Luther's assaults on Aristotle, whose name was, for Luther, almost synonymous with philosophy (one of the activities in which reason is characteristically expressed). Aristotle is the 'destroyer of pious doctrine', a 'mere Sophist and quibbler', an 'inventor of fables', 'ungodly public enemy of the truth'.[4] He is abusively

---

[1] W.A. 51. 123–34. The initials 'W.A.' are used throughout to refer to the definitive *Weimarer Ausgabe* of Luther's works, which is cited by volume, page, and (generally) also by line. Where the vol. no. is obvious (as, for instance, in a catena of refs.), it is omitted. 'W.A. Br.' designates the *Briefwechsel* in the Weimar edn.; 'W.A. TR.' (or simply 'TR.'), the *Tischreden*; 'W.A. DB.' (or 'DB.'), the *Deutsche Bibel*. Occasionally, the TR. are cited by the number of the entry, rather than by page and line.

[2] W.A. 40¹. 362. 15, 22; 365. 18; 275. 17; 344. 23 (CDE).

[3] P. S. Watson, *Let God Be God*, p. 86.

[4] W.A. 8. 127. 20 (cf. *perdens et vastator ecclesiae*: 7. 739. 24); 1. 611. 33 (cf. ibid. 307. 18 and 611. 40, also 2. 704. 9); 9. 23. 7; 6. 186. 14. In the last citation I have

described as 'the stinking philosopher', 'the Clown of the High
Schools', 'trickster', 'rascal', 'liar and knave', 'the pagan beast',
'blind pagan', 'triple-headed Cerberus—indeed, triple-bodied
Geryon', 'lazy-ass', 'billy-goat', &c.[1] This catalogue is scarcely
less impressive than the other one (on 'reason'), and it could,
no doubt, be extended.

As a typical example of the use which Luther's critics have
made of his vituperation against reason, philosophy, and
Aristotle, we may take Jacques Maritain's *Three Reformers*, the
first section of which is devoted to Luther. Maritain's study
relies mainly upon the massive polemics of the Catholic histor-
ians, Denifle and Grisar,[2] as he himself informs us,[3] and this
alone is enough to put us on our guard: the enthusiastic vili-
fications of these two learned, but scarcely impartial, researchers
have been largely outdated by more sober Catholic critiques.
But on this particular problem of Luther's attitude towards
reason, it is doubtful whether Luther's critics have moved very
far beyond Denifle and Grisar.[4]

Maritain's thesis is that the story of Luther marks the 'advent
of the self'. In him the human subject becomes of more concern
than God, and the self usurps the place of Jesus Christ. Luther
is accordingly displayed as the corrupter of religion by 'ego-
centrism'. The accusation is remarkable, since the Swedish
interpreters of Luther completely invert the charge, alleging
that the essence of Luther's achievement was to substitute a
God-centred Christianity for the man-centred religion of the
Schoolmen, this being Luther's 'Copernican Revolution'.[5]

Luther's theology, with its strange emphasis on 'faith without
works', was born (according to Maritain) out of a sense of
failure. 'Unable to conquer himself, he transforms his neces-
sities into theological truths, and his own actual case into a

followed the reading given in the index-volume: presumably the reading *publici*
(for *publicus*), found in the volume cited, was an error.

[1] W.A. 9. 43. 5; 10¹, ². 101. 1; 2. 704. 25; 5. 645. 12; 7. 282. 15; 1. 509. 13;
2. 422. 31 (and 10¹, ². 96. 25, 116. 11); 7. 739. 30; W.A. TR. 2. 456. 32; W.A.
1. 291. 17 (and 10². 329. 15). The index vol. of the Weimar edn. contains a comprehensive list of *charakterisierende Bezeichnungen*.

[2] Heinrich Denifle, *Luther und Luthertum* (2nd edn., 1906); Hartmann Grisar,
Luther (Eng. trans. in 6 vols., 1913–17).   [3] p. 6.

[4] Cf., for example, Arnold Lunn, *The Revolt against Reason* (1950), pp. 51 ff.

[5] See, for instance, Watson's account, op. cit., pp. 33–38; E. M. Carlson,
Reinterpretation of Luther, pp. 77 ff.; Anders Nygren, *Agape and Eros*, pp. 681 ff.

universal law.'[1] Luther's heresy was not a 'deviation of the intelligence', for: 'Lutheranism is not a system worked out by Luther; it is the overflow of Luther's individuality.'[2] And so Maritain builds up his picture of a man whose greatness was mere 'animal greatness', the sheer violence of hurricane, buffalo, or elephant. He was not a great *person* but a great *individual*. He was a man 'wholly and systematically ruled by his affective and appetitive faculties'.[3]

We are, of course, not at all surprised to hear that this monster of Maritain's was an anti-intellectualist. Luther was, indeed, the first great Romantic, 'and that attitude of soul would naturally go with a profound anti-intellectualism, which was besides helped by the Occamist and nominalist training in philosophy which Luther received'.[4] Luther was, in fact, an enemy of philosophy, lacking force of intellect, 'strong summoner of the great undefined powers which lie dormant in the creature of flesh'.[5] Luther's progressive degradation, as he more and more yielded himself to the forces of instinct, can even be traced in the series of portraits of him, 'the last of which are surprisingly bestial'.[6]

Three things may perhaps be distinguished in this critique. First, Maritain has no difficulty whatever in producing citations (mostly borrowed from Denifle's collection), in which Luther condemns himself out of his own mouth; the repeated disparagements of reason uncover Luther's fundamental anti-intellectualism for all to see. Second, Luther's explicit repudiation of reason is worked into an elaborate portrait of the man himself as a creature of passion, self-willed and obstinately indifferent to the niceties of logicality. Third, the assault on reason is traced, at least partially, to Luther's education in the *via moderna* of the Nominalists. On all three points Maritain has given us the kind of picture which has passed into 'textbook' accounts of Luther's place in the history of Western thought. Even writers who are not by any means hostile to the Reforma-

[1] Op. cit., pp. 10–11.   [2] Ibid., p. 15.
[3] Ibid., p. 28.   [4] Ibid., p. 30.
[5] Ibid., pp. 4 and 5.
[6] Ibid., p. 11. Here again Maritain is, of course, following the methods of Denifle, who illustrated his thesis with reproductions of selected portraits. One of the reasons why the last in the series was 'surprisingly bestial' was because it was made of the dead Luther after decomposition had already set in.

tion frequently display a not much deeper understanding of the complexities in Luther's attitude towards reason.[1]

Our main concern in this essay will be with Luther's actual utterances on the worth (or worthlessness) of reason. It will immediately become apparent that the real problem is not that Luther's statements exhibit a uniform hostility towards reason, but that they present a strangely ambivalent attitude, alternately heaping upon reason extravagant praise and unqualified opprobrium. Part II, the main section of this study, will accordingly be devoted to the task of elucidating Luther's attitude and trying to lay bare the theological presuppositions which lay behind it. For this purpose a particular text has been selected and closely scrutinized. Luther's own words, rather than the interpretations of secondary sources, must of course be our principal interest; nevertheless, in the conclusion to Chapter VI our own findings are compared with the discussions of some of the Luther-scholars who have touched on our theme.[2] Luther never wrote any monographs on the 'problem of faith and reason', and perhaps this partly explains the paucity of secondary sources on his standpoint within this special area: what can be known of his standpoint, must be gleaned mainly from *obiter dicta*, though occasionally he does enlarge upon the theme in extended digressions. The text which we have chosen, the so-called *Larger Commentary on Galatians* (1535), is rich both in *obiter dicta* and in lengthy digressions.[3]

[1] It is hardly necessary to offer examples; but see, amongst others, John A. Hutchison, *Faith, Reason, and Existence* (New York: Oxford University Press, 1956), p. 99; or H. J. Paton, *The Modern Predicament* (London: George Allen & Unwin Ltd., 1955), p. 119. Both of these writers give a direct citation from Luther, but neither of them pauses to present the many qualifications which would need to be made if full justice were to be done to Luther's many-sidedness.

[2] Bernhard Lohse, in the book referred to in our Foreword, sketches the previous literature dealing (for the most part, only incidentally) with Luther on reason: *Ratio und Fides*, pp. 7 ff. A similar review of the literature appears in Karl Stürmer, *Gottesgerechtigkeit und Gottesweisheit bei Martin Luther*, pp. 11-19. I was not acquainted with Stürmer's dissertation until I found it referred to by Lohse. As Lohse remarks, it has passed virtually unnoticed in the Luther-literature, although it deserves the honour of being regarded as the first comprehensive study of the problem. (I shall have occasion to refer to Stürmer's main thesis below.) Both these two sketches of the literature really serve only to establish the surprising neglect of Luther's views on reason.

[3] The name 'Larger Commentary' is sometimes used to distinguish the published version of 1535 from Rörer's notes of the actual lectures (1531): so, for instance, Aulen, *Christus Victor*, Eng. trans., pp. 121-2. But the same designation serves to

Our second concern has been to counterbalance the picture of Luther as an irresponsible creature of instinct, the picture which, as we have seen, commonly accompanies the charge of irrationalism or anti-intellectualism. Luther, certainly, was no philosopher: he did not claim to be, he did not wish to be. His own understanding of himself was as a 'doctor of the Holy Scriptures'—he was, indeed, not a little vain about his doctorate in theology—and his life's work was expounding the books of the Bible to his students and making them intelligible to the common folk.[1] In his own chosen area Luther was an extra-ordinarily painstaking worker: he certainly compares favourably with Erasmus, who could, on occasion, be a little slapdash. If 'reason' be taken to include, as surely it must, the skills of the scholar no less than the speculations of the philosopher, then Luther was pre-eminently a 'reasonable' man. In Part III, then, another portrait of the Reformer is presented, which shows him as a dedicated scholar, passionately devoted to the demands of accuracy and honesty, who shared in a general shift of interest away from Scholastic philosophy and towards the 'learning' of the Humanists. Luther's 'revolt against reason' must, in fact, be seen in its proper historical context if we are ever to evaluate it with any depth of understanding. Here, of course, is an area of Luther-research which has been much better explored.[2]

The third question, Luther's relation to Occamism, also belongs to the matter of 'historical context'. At present, however, the entire question is a highly controversial one. Indeed, part of the problem lies in our relative ignorance, not merely of Luther's debt to the Nominalists, but of the views of the Nominalists themselves. In this matter Grisar showed admirable caution, and even went so far as to suggest that perhaps growing interest in this problem of Luther's relation to the Occamists might prove a valuable stimulus to Occamist studies themselves.[3] Somewhat more recently, Gordon Rupp has bluntly said: 'The

distinguish the later exposition from Luther's early Lectures on Galatians (1516–17) and the Commentary of 1519.

[1] Part of the subtitle of Kooiman's *Martin Luther* appropriately describes him as *Doktor der heiligen Schrift*. See also Karl Holl, 'Luthers Urteile über sich selbst', *Luther*, ch. 6.

[2] Especially valuable are: M. Reu, *Luther's German Bible*, and W. Schwarz, *Principles and Problems of Biblical Translation*.

[3] Op. cit. I. 140, n. 1.

nature and extent of Luther's debt to Occamism cannot be
clarified in the present state of studies of late scholasticism.'[1]
But, fortunately, the problem with which we are concerned can
be approached from other angles than by way of hunting for
origins. After all, Luther's actual usage of the term 'reason'
(*ratio*, *Vernunft*) can only be elucidated by a direct lexical study,
and to enter the discussion through the doorway of Nominalist
theology is as likely to mislead as to illuminate. Luther's meaning must be clarified in the light of what he says, not in the
(supposed) light of how he was educated. This is not to deny
categorically that a study of the origins of Luther's thought
may illuminate our problem; but such a study must be secondary.
And in view of the difficulties attending any account of Luther's
relation to Occamism, we have been content, in Part I, to offer
no more than a brief survey of some of the things that are being
said in this area: it is, after all, a full problem in itself, and it is
only touched on here for the sake of completeness in enumerat-
ing, if not in solving, all the problems which my subject involves.
The conclusion to Part II will, in any case, make it quite clear
that the principal force of Luther's assault on reason, so far
from being explicable in Nominalist terms, is directed precisely
against the *via moderna* and its tendency towards Pelagianism.
However, in certain respects, Luther's severe curtailing of
reason's scope in theological matters does bear some resemblance
to Occam's religious epistemology. Accordingly, the first two
chapters of Part I present a preliminary sketch of Luther's
attitude towards reason and philosophy; chapter three points to
the parallels with Occamism; and not before Part II, Chapter
VIII, is it shown how Luther struck out on a line of his own
which eventually ranged him, not with, but against the champions of the *via moderna*.

Primarily, this essay is a study in the history of ideas: its
aim is not to criticize—much less to advance our own view of
the place of reason in the theological task—but to explain. It is
neither apologetic, nor merely descriptive. It does not seek to
defend or recommend Luther's opinions, nor simply to string
illustrative texts together with no effort at organization. It is,
in short, interpretative, seeking to discern the pattern in Luther's

[1] *Luther's Progress to the Diet of Worms*, p. 17. Cf. the same writer's larger work,
The Righteousness of God, pp. 87 ff.

thought and to make explicit his fundamental presuppositions. Such a purpose does, to be sure, demand that the historian try to see Luther's contemporaries through Luther's own eyes; and admittedly the sixteenth-century scene would look very different through the eyes of Erasmus or of Luther's Nominalist professors. But the historian who wishes, for the moment, to understand the mind of just one man is obliged to adopt for the time being that one man's (no doubt, very limited) perspective.

Especially in the first of our three concerns (the elucidation of Luther's actual utterances), the main task of an interpretative study will be to show how the Reformer's views on reason harmonize with his total conception of Christianity. It could, indeed, be stated as a general rule that none of his religious ideas can be grasped in isolation: each must be seen in relation to the basic structure of his thought and to what he himself regarded as the centre of the Christian Faith. What is needed in dealing with Luther's views on reason is the kind of approach which Gustaf Wingren employed so successfully in interpreting the Reformer's teaching on 'vocation'. (In his own words, Wingren's aim was 'to integrate Luther's statements about vocation with his basic theology, that is, to present expressions concerning *Beruf* in the context of his fundamental concepts. . . .')[1] Of course, the results of such an inquiry may only prove that the scholar is examining a notion of no more than marginal significance in Luther's theology—a notion which exhibits no necessary connexion with the centre of his thinking. But with the concept of reason exactly the opposite is the truth: a systematic study reveals that the problem of reason carries us back to the heart of the Lutheran Gospel.

The very mention of a 'systematic study' may arouse the suspicions of those who see no orderly structure in Luther at all. Luther's friends, as well as his critics, have claimed that his thinking cannot be reduced to any discernible systematic pattern. R. H. Tawney's familiar description of Luther's social thought as 'the occasional explosions of a capricious volcano'[2]

---

[1] *Luther on Vocation*, Eng. trans., p. vii.

[2] 'Luther's utterances on social morality are the occasional explosions of a capricious volcano, with only a rare flash of light amid the torrent of smoke and flame, and it is idle to scan them for a coherent and consistent doctrine.' In his next sentence Tawney goes on to claim that Luther gives the impression of 'an impetuous but ill-informed genius, dispensing with the cumbrous embarrassments

might seem applicable to his utterances on other subjects also—
not least, on reason. Even so sympathetic an interpreter of
Luther as Heinrich Boehmer insisted on the futility of seeking a
strict consistency in the Reformer's thought, warning against
the attempt to bind his views forcibly into a logical structure.[1]
The very fertility of Luther's intellect, according to Boehmer,
robbed him of the capacity for organization. Conversely, Calvin,
the genuine systematist, was no creative thinker.

Now, no one would deny that, however diligently we try
to weave Luther's astonishing variety of ideas into an obvious
pattern, loose ends will always remain. It is not hard to cull a
few flat contradictions from his writings. (One could perhaps
perform the same service for any theologian.) Nevertheless, it
would be a serious failure should the scholar overlook the fact
that organizing principles really are there in Luther's thinking,
which often explain apparent inconsistencies and show how the
great variety of his theological ideas are bound together. In
particular, recent Luther-research has stressed the manner in
which the entire structure of the Reformer's theology is determined by the doctrines of the 'two kingdoms' and of the forgiveness of sins. It is these two fundamental conceptions which give
Luther's thinking such inner harmony as it has, and it is these
same two conceptions that bring order into his apparently incompatible utterances on reason.[2] It already appears in the

of law and logic'. *Religion and the Rise of Capitalism* (New York: Harcourt, Brace and
Company, 1926), p. 88.

[1] *Luther in Light of Recent Research*, p. 250.

[2] The literature on these two themes is, of course, enormous. (1) The best
studies on the two kingdoms are perhaps: G. Törnvall, *Geistliches und weltliches Regiment bei Luther*, and F. Lau, *Luthers Lehre von den beiden Reichen*. A good recent study
is Heinrich Bornkamm's article, 'Luthers Lehre von den zwei Reichen im Zusammenhang seiner Theologie', in the 1958 number of *Archiv für Reformationsgeschichte*.
In English there is a brief article by E. M. Carlson, 'Luther's Conception of Government', *Church History*, xv (1946), 257 ff. (largely dependent on Törnvall). See also
the recent book of F. E. Cranz, *An Essay on the Development of Luther's Thought on
Justice, Law, and Society* (an excellent study, relating the doctrine of the two kingdoms
to Luther's theological 'reorientation'). For the most part it is the political implications of Luther's teaching on the two kingdoms that has aroused most interest. (2) The
classic statement of the structural significance of forgiveness in Luther's theology
is certainly that of Einar Billing, *Our Calling*, Eng. trans., p. 7: 'Anyone wishing to
study Luther would indeed be in no peril of going astray were he to follow this rule:
never believe that you have a correct understanding of a thought of Luther before
you have succeeded in reducing it to a simple corollary of the forgiveness of sins.'
Further reference is made to this 'rule' in Ch. IV, below.

preliminary sketch of Chapters I and II (in Part I) that the doctrine of the two kingdoms provides the framework for Luther's observations on reason: and in Part II it is further shown how close the assault on reason stands to the cardinal doctrine of forgiveness. It is in order to stress this remarkable association of 'reason' and 'forgiveness' that our essay bears the title '*Grace* and Reason' rather than '*Faith* and Reason'. For the problem of human reason, according to Luther, is that it cannot comprehend the Gospel's message of free forgiveness by grace alone.

'Luther on reason' is a vast subject—perhaps, surprisingly so—and even when the ground to be covered has been carefully mapped out, it would not be difficult to lose one's path. Our subject touches on many of the controversial themes of present-day Luther-research, and it is tempting to stop and argue on the way. In one fashion or another, Luther's views on reason could be linked to topics as diverse as civil government and the *deus absconditus*,[1] natural law and justification by faith, original sin and monastic vows. And Rudolf Otto (perhaps we should only expect it) finds a connexion between the 'devil's whore' and the 'numinous'.[2] It is hardly too much to say that a textbook of Lutheran dogmatics could be written from the stand-point of this single term 'reason'. However, it is our resolve to keep strictly within the limits of our three principal concerns, and within these limits to concentrate on the crucial task of showing how Luther's various attitudes (on reason, Scholasticism, and Humanism) arise out of his central religious convictions.

[1] On the interpretation of the *deus absconditus* in Luther see the survey by John Dillenberger, *God Hidden and Revealed*. Some remarks on reason, speculation, and the 'naked God' will be found in Ch. V, below; but this is really a subject in itself.
[2] *The Idea of the Holy* (Eng. trans., London: Oxford University Press, 1936), p. 104.

PART I

REASON AND PHILOSOPHY

———

I

LUTHER'S ATTITUDE TOWARDS REASON

THE essentials of Luther's attitude towards reason and philosophy are not difficult to piece together, in spite of the lack of any systematic treatise on the subject from his own pen. All that is required is a careful examination and organization of some of the allusions (both the briefer, and the more extended, ones) scattered throughout his writings. The only insurmountable hindrance would be a hopeless inconsistency, if Luther were really as muddled as some of his opponents have alleged. But such proves not to be the truth: in actual fact, Luther's thinking in this area, as in so many others, falls into certain constantly recurring patterns, which can readily be discerned by a careful and sympathetic reader.

Many of the most important allusions to reason are to be found in the *Church Postils* of 1522.[1] The *Table-Talk* also seems frequently to have centred around problems of reason and philosophy.[2] The so-called *Larger Commentary on Galatians* contains the most important passages, but these will be held over for Part II. Two other works are worthy of special mention in connexion with Luther's attitude towards reason. Oddly, perhaps, the *Lectures on Genesis* (published in four parts, 1544–

[1] W.A. 10¹, ¹. Many of the postils may be found translated in J. N. Lenker, *Luther's Church Postil* (*Gospels* in 5 vols., *Epistles* in 3 vols.).

[2] W.A. TR., 6 vols. For translations see Smith and Gallinger, *Conversations with Luther*. The old translations of Hazlitt and Henry Bell are not without interest; see Bibliography. In his book, *Luther's Table Talk: A Critical Study*, Preserved Smith evaluates the *Tischreden* as historical documents.

54) have several crucial passages.[1] More important, no doubt, are the references in the Weimar edition of the *Disputations* (W.A., vol. 39, two parts), a collection covering the years 1535–45.

It is hard to evaluate the relative importance of these five works for our own special purposes. The *Church Postils*—and, indeed, though to a lesser extent, the *Lectures on Genesis*—present Luther mainly as a homilist, and they scarcely give him occasion for the expression of his opinions on philosophy. The same holds for the *Table-Talk*: no man could wish his dinner-table conversation to be taken (or mistaken) for the most serious or most profound reflections of which he is capable. At first glance, the *Disputations* might seem to present the requisite kind of source. But here, too, there are snags. For, in the first place, the purpose of a disputation, as a strictly academic exercise, did not necessarily require the faithful expression of genuine convictions; and, in the second place, many of the disputations associated with Luther's name were not actually prepared by his hand. Still, the difficulties are, perhaps, largely imaginary. For, as a matter of fact, fundamentally the same position is presented in all five of the sources named, and there are no large contradictions to puzzle over. We will, then, proceed, without further evaluation of the sources,[2] to our 'preliminary discussion' of Luther's attitude towards, first, reason, second, philosophy; and under the second topic will be included some remarks on Luther's attitude towards Aristotle, who was, in his eyes, the very incarnation of philosophy.

[1] W.A. 42–44. The early chapters will be found in Lenker's translation (see Bibliography). The new 'American edn.' of Luther's works has recently commenced a fresh translation of the *Genesisvorlesung*. In his *Die Genesisvorlesung Luthers*, Peter Meinhold raised serious doubts concerning the authenticity of this work, arguing that in several respects the editor, Veit Dietrich, revised Luther's lectures in the direction of Melanchthon's outlook. (See, for instance, pp. 332–41, where Meinhold maintains that the number and accuracy of the classical quotations suggests the hand of the editor.) As Jaroslav Pelikan rightly points out in his introduction to vol. 1 of the 'American edn.', Meinhold's argument is weakened by the fact that he tends to make the 'Young Luther' normative for his critical judgements on the *Genesisvorlesung*. Nevertheless, care has to be exercised not to attach much weight to statements in this work which are not paralleled in others of Luther's writings.

[2] One more word should perhaps be added, albeit only in passing, on the question of sources. The so-called *Lutheri Dialectica* (included in the old 'Walch edn.', xiv. 1309 ff.) is certainly not from Luther's own hand and cannot be taken into consideration in discussing his attitude to philosophy. Cf. Jaroslav Pelikan, *From Luther to Kierkegaard*, p. 13.

Luther's attitude towards reason

In a single extremely informative passage Luther both states
and answers the problem with which we are concerned, namely:
What does he mean by slighting reason?[1] He has been saying,
in his explanation of Isaiah lx. 1–6, that the prophet rejects the
natural light of reason, showing it to be mere darkness: for,
if we had light within ourselves, the Gospel need never have
shone upon us. 'Light illumines, not light, but darkness.' There
is no intermediate light (the light of reason) between Christ and
darkness, as the Schoolmen wrongly suppose. Indeed, the more
'reasonable' men are, the further they generally are from the
True Light. But suppose somebody objects:

How can everything that natural reason teaches be darkness?
Isn't it clear enough that two and three make five? Again, isn't a
man who wants to make a coat wise if he takes cloth for it, foolish
if he takes paper? Isn't he a wise man who marries a godly wife, and
isn't he a fool who marries an ungodly wife? And there are countless
other examples in all of mankind's life.

As the objector is made to point out: Christ himself commends
the wisdom of the man who builds upon rock. Luther's reply
to the imaginary objector sums up in a single sentence the crux
of his standpoint on the place of reason: 'That is all true; but
you must here distinguish God and men, things eternal and
things temporal.' He proceeds to explain his meaning as follows:

In temporal affairs and those which have to do with men, the
rational man is self-sufficient (*da ist der mensch vornunfftig gnug*): here
he needs no other light than reason's. Therefore, God does not teach
us in the Scriptures how to build houses, make clothing, marry,
wage war, navigate, and the like. For here the light of nature is
sufficient. But in godly affairs, that is, in those which have to do with
God, where man must do what is acceptable with God and be saved
thereby—*here*, however, nature is absolutely stone-blind, so that it
cannot even catch a glimpse (*eyn harbreytt anzeygen*) of what those
things are. It is presumptuous enough to bluster and plunge into
them, like a blind horse; but all its conclusions are utterly false, as
surely as God lives.

[1] Postil for Epiphany, on Isa. lx. 1–6; see esp. the passage beginning W.A.
10¹, ¹. 527. 11 ff. (In referring to the *Kirchenpostille* I have generally identified the
passage both by its Biblical text and by its place in the Christian calendar.)

Underlying this statement of his position is Luther's fundamental dualism of an Earthly and a Heavenly Kingdom.[1] It
remains now to enlarge a little on the main features of this
dualism, so far as they affect our main theme.[2]

Reason's sphere of competence, the area within which it
may legitimately be exercised, is the 'Kingdom of Earth' (das
irdische Reich). Now and again, Luther offers lists of the kinds of
activities which reason supervises within this specified area,
and the lists do not greatly vary. Reason is able to do many
things: it can judge in human and worldly matters, it can build
cities and houses, it can govern well.[3] The world[4] knows how
to build, how to keep house, how to manage estate and servants, how to be outwardly pious and to lead a decent, honest
life.[5] In the main, Luther seems to be thinking precisely of
those human activities which we, too, would describe as 'mundane', that is, such activities as we need to perform in order to
exist at all. But he does extend the list far enough to include
'government' (in the political sense). Reason is able to found
kingdoms and commonwealths, to fence them in and make them
firm with useful laws, to direct and govern them with good
counsel and sound precepts, to prescribe many things indispensable for the preservation of commonwealths and of human
society (societatis humanae—virtually, 'civilization'). Reason, in
fact, is the 'soul of law and mistress of all laws'. The philosophy
of government rests upon the principle that reason (in a sufficiently liberal amount) is the possession of the few, whilst laws
prescribed by reason must serve for the many.[6]

---

[1] See Introduction, p. 8, n. 1, above.

[2] This paragraph has condensed several pages of Luther's postil. The main
passages I have used are: W.A. 10[1, 1]. 527. 14, 529. 4, 529. 7, 530. 13 ff., 531. 5,
531. 6 ff.

[3] Postil for 4th Sunday after Easter, on John xvi. 5–16; W.A. 12. 548. 14 ff.

[4] For Luther 'world' and 'reason' are in many passages interchangeable, and he
switches from one to the other without any difference of meaning. So, for example,
in the postil for Epiphany Sunday, cited above.

[5] W.A. 21. 389. 21 ff. (Ascension, on Mark xvi. 14–20.)

[6] W.A. 40[3]. 612. 35 ff. (on Isa. ix. 1). 'Leges pertinent ad vulgus, ratio ad
singulares. Ideo illi reguntur et ei regunt legibus, et quia desunt vere sapientes per
rationem, ideo oportet uti legibus, quas statuerunt ratione sapientes' (W.A. TR. 2,
no. 2629a; cf. 2629b). See also TR. 6, no. 6955, where reason is called 'the heart of
law'. Cranz correctly sums up Luther's teaching at this point when he remarks that
for the Reformer reason is 'the all-embracing term which best refers to man's
principle of action in the realm of the world of civil justice, natural law, and polity'
(op. cit., p. 109). Cf. Lau: 'Die ratio erweist sich als die allgültige Norm für die

Beyond these 'mundane' affairs, Luther will even allow reason some insight into moral and religious issues, though here, obviously, we are near the border-line of the 'Heavenly Kingdom'. Reason has some respect for the Second Table of the Law, and those who transgress it are sometimes punished; and yet the world scarcely regards as sin at all that which the last two precepts forbid.[1] Reason does, to be sure, see clearly that good is to be promoted, evil avoided, but it can not tell *what is* good or *what is* evil. Natural reason is like a man who wants to go to Rome, knows that there is a right road to get him there, but cannot decide which it is. In other words, reason is only aware of a purely formal sense of moral obligation: it cannot attach it to specific duties or concrete policies of conduct.[2] More particularly, reason cannot decide what is right or wrong *before God*.[3] It is not hard to see how, in Luther's thinking, moral issues lie close to the border of the Heavenly Kingdom: our conduct is directed towards our fellow men (*coram hominibus*), yet always under the eye of God (*coram Deo*). In the last analysis, what reason does not know is the road *to God*; and this is the conclusion to Luther's illustration of the 'road to Rome', although he seemed at the outset to be discussing a purely ethical issue.

The severe limitations upon reason's grasp of more strictly theological issues are closely parallel. If reason stumbles at the doctrine of the Incarnation, that is not because reason refuses to believe in God, but rather that it does not understand who God is; consequently, it invents a God after its own fancy. Reason agrees that God's Word is to be honoured, but arrogantly sets itself up as judge deciding what is, what is not, God's Word.[4] Luther even goes so far as to say in one place: 'Let us

weltlichen Ordungen . . . Das Dominium der *ratio* sind die *civilia*, "*die gubernandae res in Oeconomia et Politia*" ' (*Äußerliche Ordnung und weltlich Ding*, p. 45). As Lau points out, in the sphere of civil government reason becomes a *seltenes Charisma*: not everyone has enough of it to be a ruler (ibid., pp. 54–55). It is at this point that Luther's doctrine of reason is closely linked with his remarkable idea of the *viri heroici*, the *Wunderleute*; see esp. Gunnar Hillerdal, *Gehorsam gegen Gott und Menschen*, pp. 58–66.
  [1] TR. 1, no. 200. Luther followed the Roman practice of reckoning the prohibition of covetousness as containing two separate Commandments.
  [2] W.A. 10[1, 1]. 203. 10 ff. (Christmas, on John i. 1–14).
  [3] W.A. 12. 548. 23 (4th Sunday after Easter, on John xvi. 5–16).
  [4] W.A. 10[1, 1]. 240. 7 (Christmas, on John i. 1–14).

here learn also from nature and reason what to think of God.'
Reason knows that God wants to save from all evil, therefore,
that he is the source of all good. 'The natural light of reason
reaches so far that it regards God as kind, gracious, merciful,
tender-hearted.' But reason falls short at two points: first,
although it believes that God *can* aid, it does not believe that
God *will* do so *for it*; second, though it knows *that* God is, it
does not know *who* or *what* God is. The meaning of the second
charge is, presumably, that reason attaches its notions of Deity
to the wrong object, that is, not to the God who reveals Himself
in Christ; more will be said of the first charge in a later chapter.[1]
In general, Luther is clearly drawing the familiar Scholastic
distinction between the knowledge 'that God is' (*quod sit Deus*),
which is within the reach of natural reason, and the knowledge
'what God is' (*quid sit Deus*), which is beyond natural reason.
In one curious passage from the treatise *On Monastic Vows*
Luther makes the assertion that, though reason does not know
what God is, it knows with the utmost certainty what God is
not. The distinction would, no doubt, prove untenable on
careful analysis, and I only mention it as further evidence for
Luther's basic tenet that reason does not know God's nature
(*quid sit*), though it can certainly know of His existence (*quod sit*).[2]

Reason does, then, have a legitimate sphere of competence,
within which it is autonomous; it only begins to be called in
question when it approaches the boundary-line of the Heavenly
Kingdom. In its own strictly demarcated area man's native
intelligence needs no special word from God—though, of course,
it is itself a gift from God, an endowment bestowed upon man

---

[1] W.A. 19. 206. 7 ff. (on Jonah i. 5).
[2] 'Non enim capit ratio, quid sit deus, certissime tamen capit, quid non sit deus'
(W.A. 8. 629. 26). The argument of the passage is interesting: Luther appeals to
reason against the taking of monastic vows, on the ground that a vow is useless
when we cannot guarantee to fulfil it. The impulses that dwell in our flesh are not
subject to our control, and it would be absurd to offer God something which He
alone could bestow as a special gift. 'Quod ergo huic rationi evidenter adversatur,
certum est et deo multo magis adversari. Quomodo non coelesti veritati non
pugnabit, quod terrenae veritati pugnat?' (629. 31). I think this does perhaps
represent an integral part of Luther's attitude towards reason. Where reason
claims to know, it may be wrong; but where something is obviously wrong, even
to reason, it will even more certainly be wrong 'before God'. Reason errs *in
affirmativis* rather than *in negativis* (629. 25, 26). Lohse evidently considers this
passage as of quite crucial importance, and he has discussed it exhaustively: op. cit.,
pp. 65 ff. and 77 ff.

at his birth. Not all a believer's doings call for some special prompting of the Spirit. Even the Biblical saints and heroes generally acted as reason guided: when Abraham received no certain word from heaven, he did as reason dictated. The 'saints' are like other men in busying themselves in the common routine tasks—and yet, Luther adds in a significant remark, though they do the same things as the ungodly, their works are made acceptable to God by their faith. Genuine saints do nothing out of the ordinary, save when specially commanded by a definite word and the Spirit's promptings. Man was created for domestic and civic (or 'political') occupations. What Luther terms the *communia*, the institutions of social life, were ordained of God: it is here that man finds his calling—be it even in milking the cows and ploughing the fields—not in the monasteries. With admirable common sense Luther advises his flock to imitate the Biblical heroes in their ordinary occupations, not in the special things that they did; for the human mind is affected by a foolish tendency to admire only what is uncommon, strange, extraordinary. The Christian should be dutifully engaged in what the Papists superciliously call 'lay works', though Luther prefers to speak of 'civil works', since, by faith and the word, the works a man does in the social order may be made genuinely 'spiritual'. For the proper performance of these works God has given us 'natural reason'.[1]

As long as reason is exercised within these limits, Luther has nothing but praise to heap upon it. Reason is the 'head and substance of all things'. It is the best thing in this life—indeed,

---

[1] W.A. 43. 104. 37 ff. (*Genesisvorlesung*, on Gen. xx. 2). The passage is of great importance for our theme; obviously, it is too long to cite in full, but here are some of the crucial sentences to which I have alluded; 'Cum enim nullum certum verbum de coelo . . . haberet, facit, quod ratio suadet. . . . Non enim spiritus sanctus semper impellit pios homines: quaedam sinit eos facere suo arbitrio et voluntate' (104. 37). 'Communibus studiis etiam occupantur, seminant, arant, edificant etc. Ad haec recte facienda sufficit ratio et industria . . . quanquam similia impii quoque faciunt, tamen haec in piis Deo grata sunt propter fidem, in qua vivunt' (105. 12). 'Quin instruxit nos ratione naturali, qua regamus ista civilia, ne tentemus Deum, subiicientem nobis terram' (106. 29; the allusion is to Gen. i. 28). Here, of course, the problem of reason touches on another vast area of Luther's thought, 'vocation' and the 'three hierarchies' (Church, household, and the state). But on these questions I must refer the reader to the works of Wingren and Cranz already cited. It should, however, be emphasized that vocation and the hierarchies do belong within the Earthly Kingdom, so that, for example, even many matters pertaining to the life of the Church are subject to reason: see Cranz, op. cit., pp. 147–9; Lohse, op. cit., p. 125.

it is something divine. Reason is personified as the 'inventress
and mistress of all the arts, of medicine and law, of whatever
wisdom, power, virtue and glory men possess in this life'.
Reason is what marks off mankind from the brute beasts, and
the Holy Scriptures themselves have appointed her queen of
the earth (Genesis i. 28). Nor has her rule been taken from her
by the Fall: she remains a kind of 'divine sun' (*sol et numen*),
in whose light the affairs of this life are to be administered.[1]
Reason is the greatest, the inestimable, gift of God.[2] In another
place, Luther concedes that the light of nature (reason) is a
part of the True Light—though here the rider is added, 'when
it recognizes and honours him by whom it has been ignited'.[3]

Of course, reason is not infallible even within its own proper
domain, neither is it omniscient. Sometimes its judgements are
erroneous—for example, in matters of public government and
administration.[4] It is unable to meet the demands laid upon it
even in this present world. For to 'live soberly, righteously, and
godly, in this present world' (Titus ii. 12) is like keeping sober
in the ale-house, chaste in a brothel, godly in a dance-hall,
guiltless in the midst of murderers. Here nature and reason are
lost.[5] Again, reason often displays its ignorance even in the
Earthly Kingdom. The world is full of daily miracles, and it is
only their frequency that dulls our sensitiveness to their wonder.
Luther is particularly fond of illustrating this point (made more
than once in his works) by reference to the 'miracle of birth'.[6]
But reason's fallibility and evident lack of omniscience do not
alter Luther's basic judgement; in the Worldly Kingdom, it is
God's most precious gift.

In the Heavenly Kingdom, on the other hand, reason is
nothing but darkness. The words of Christ could never be
grasped or fathomed by reason, but only as the Holy Spirit
reveals them to simple believers. The apostles themselves were
of this sort: ignorant fishermen, for the most part, who learned

---

[1] *Disputatio de homine*, theses 4–9 (W.A. 39¹. 175). The Disputation will now be
found in English, American ed., vol. xxxiv.

[2] 'Ratio maximum et inaestimabile est donum Dei nec ea, quae in rebus humanis
sapienter constituit et invenit, contemnenda sunt' (W.A. 40³. 612. 31; on Isa. ix.1).

[3] W.A. 10¹, ¹. 203. 8: . . . *ist eyn stuck des waren liechts*. On John i. 1–14; Christmas
postil.

[4] See again the exposition of Isa. ix. 1 (W.A. 40³. 613. 3 ff.).

[5] W.A. 10¹, ¹. 41. 5 ff. (Christmas, on Titus ii. 11–15).

[6] TR. 4, no. 5015; W.A. 43. 374. 11.

to understand the Scriptures, not in the 'schools', but through revelation.[1] The world knows nothing of Christ's doctrine. The message of salvation has to be preached: had it been known before Christ, he would never have needed to descend from heaven or to send his servants into all the world. Of such things as concern God's Kingdom and how to escape sin and death, the world knows nothing.[2] Christ's conversation with Nicodemus shows clearly 'what reason can do'. Reason belongs to the flesh: it is so blind that it can neither see nor know the things of God.[3] Whilst it may properly be called 'light' of a sort (*in suo genere*), it knows nothing of 'spiritual wisdom'. Even if it knows of God's existence, it still does not know 'His will toward us'.[4] The Scriptures must be our guide in the Kingdom of Heaven, not reason. It would be a monstrous piece of frivolity to cast aside the authority of Scripture and follow reason.[5] Human reason has experience only of temporal things, therefore it is ridiculous to introduce it into a controversy on a spiritual issue, such as the supremacy of the Pope. Here it must not be placed on the same level with the Divine Law. 'For the directions of worldly order and reason are far below the Divine Law.' It is futile to defend the divine order by human reason (unless first it be illuminated by faith): this would be like illuminating the sun with a feeble lantern or resting a rock upon a reed. Human reason can only stumble along, like a man on stilts.[6] In short, if we want to find Christ, we must not seek him, as Mary did, 'amongst his kinsfolk', but in his Father's House—that is, in the Word. Mary did not know how to find Christ, and so she sought him in the wrong place; we also seek him in the wrong place, if we look to reason or to the Fathers and the Councils of the Church. All these things belong to the world.[7]

The blindness of reason in matters which properly belong to the Heavenly Kingdom is exhibited in its erroneous judge-

[1] W.A. 21. 234. 30, 235. 5 (Easter Monday, on Luke xxiv. 13–25).
[2] W.A. 21. 389. 21 ff. (Ascension, on Mark xvi. 14–20).
[3] W.A. 10[1, 2]. 298. 5, 12; and 301. 27 (Trinity, on John iii. 1–15).
[4] 'Quae sit Dei erga nos voluntas, certo constituere non potest, quae sit vera pax, quae vera coram Deo iusticia, non novit' (W.A. 40[3]. 613. 14; from the exposition of Isa. ix. 1).
[5] 'Portenta haec sunt et nugacissimae nugae, si seposita scripturae auctoritate rationis iudicium sequaris' (W.A. 42. 92. 33).
[6] *Against the Papacy* (1520), W.A. 6. 290. 27 ff.
[7] W.A. 17[2]. 29. 7 ff. (1st after Epiphany, on Luke ii. 41–52).

ments concerning God. It concludes either that there is no God, or that He is disinterested in human affairs. It is only the Holy Scriptures that give us a true understanding of the efficient and final causes of creation; reason can go no further than the material and formal causes.[1] As John the Baptist did not come of himself, but was 'a man sent from God', so neither the Gospel nor any sermon on the True Light can come of itself or from human reason: they must be sent from God. The doctrines of men will never show Christ.[2] We must not measure the Word by reason: this is the error of the fanatics. Human nature always objects to the way God does things. Luther confesses that he has often tried to suggest to God some possible improvements in the government of the world—sound, well-intentioned advice which would certainly tend towards God's greater glory! No doubt, God laughed at this 'wisdom': 'I am no passive God, but an active God, whose wont it is to command, to rule, to direct.'[3] 'Frau Hulda' (Luther's nickname for reason) blames God for the evil done by men: for why did He make them the way they are?[4] Reason, in the last analysis, is arrogance; therefore, God deliberately finds ways of humbling it. Sometimes He turns away His face, seeming to be the very Devil himself. Sometimes He deprives even His saints of Christ, just as He took Jesus away from Mary for three days. And sometimes He prescribes rites with the intent of humiliating and causing offence.[5] The last of these devices is especially interesting. Luther mentions circumcision as a kind of test case for judging the arrogance of reason, 'that smart woman, Madam Jezebel'. For natural reason could not imagine anything more utterly foolish than the command to circumcise. If Abraham had listened to reason, he would never have believed that the command came from God at all. Circumcision made the Jews a laughing-stock, so utterly pointless did the practice seem. Luther replies that the point of circumcision is precisely to offend reason, to force it to surrender its vanity. If God had given a token which reason could approve, then man's arrogance

---

[1] W.A. 42. 93. 11 (on Gen. ii. 21).
[2] W.A. 10[1, 1]. 216. 20 (on John i. 6; Christmas Day).
[3] W.A. 44. 373 ff., esp. 376. 30 and 377. 7 (on Gen. xxxix. 21–22).
[4] W.A. TR. 6, no. 6889.
[5] W.A. 44. 376. 1 (this is the *initium operationis divinae*, God's *ratio gubernationis*); 12.
412. 12 ff.; 10[1, 1]. 504–19.

would have remained. 'And so God is not interested in circumcision itself, but in the humbling of haughty nature and reason.'
Such, at least, is the 'temporal cause' for circumcision; there is
also a 'spiritual cause', and of this Luther proceeds to give the
meaning. But the main point for our purposes is his view of the
'temporal cause'. He gives further examples of 'articles of faith'
which reason finds silly. 'All this is immeasurably above and
against reason.' 'All God's works and words are against reason.'
'In this God is seeking only that man may have the humility to
bring his reason into captivity and be subject to divine truth.'[1]

   Reason, then, is not the appropriate organ of knowledge in
the Spiritual Kingdom. The only source of spiritual knowledge
is the Word. Hence reason, in refusing to hearken to the Word,
takes on the character of disobedience and pride.[2] It is faith,
not reason, that receives the Word. The distinction between the
two spheres of knowledge, with its accompanying distinction
between two organs of knowing, is rigidly maintained. More
will need to be said in the next chapter concerning the two
spheres of knowledge, for Luther virtually identifies them with
theology and philosophy. But before turning to Luther's attitude
towards philosophy, we ought to ask two further questions:

   [1] See esp. W.A. 10[1, 1]. 506. 7, 507. 14, 506. 14, 506. 21; on the Gospel for New
Year's Day, Luke ii. 21. Both the general statement, that reason stumbles at all the
articles of faith, and the specific examples could be paralleled from other writings
of Luther's. The *Disputatio de iustificatione* says, quite without qualification, *Ratio
adversatur fidem* (W.A. 391. 90. 23); Denifle cites a passage in which Luther claims
'it is impossible to reconcile faith and reason' (op. cit. 1. 609); and the *Tischreden*
state that reason considers all the articles of faith to be foolishness, that all God's
works are past reason's finding out (4, no. 4126; 2, no. 2210). Turning to specific
doctrines, we find that reason stumbles at: the Trinity (W.A. 10[1, 1]. 191. 2, 239.
15); Creation (W.A. 42. 92. 27; TR. 2, no. 2659); sin (TR. 6, no. 6660); the
Incarnation (TR. 6, no. 6645: reason cannot know Christ for Saviour of the world
when it sees him born a little child and lying in his mother's bosom); the doctrine
of Christ's Two Natures (reason cannot harmonize the two statements, that Christ
was Son of David and Son of God: W.A. 45. 155. 35 ff.); the Crucifixion (the
greatest wonder that ever was upon the face of the earth is that God gave up His
beloved Son to be crucified, saying: Go, let them nail you to the gallows; does God
treat Caiaphas, Herod, Pilate, more kindly than His own Son? TR. 6, no. 6618);
the Resurrection (Christ's Resurrection had to be revealed by an Angel, and to
foolish women! TR, 6, no. 6601); the Sacrament of the Lord's Supper (W.A. 42.
117. 16); Baptism (reason is scandalized at Baptism's simplicity, desiring some
greater ceremony: W.A. 21. 541. 23 ff.); the resurrection of the saints (W.A. 43.
373. 35 ff.). The list could be extended, no doubt.
   [2] *Ratio* is explicitly contrasted with *obedientia* in Luther's comments on several
Biblical passages, esp. Gen. xvii. 23–27, 1 Sam. xv. 22, and John xiii. 6 ff. See, for
example, W.A. 42. 669 ff.

(1) Did Luther believe that a proposition could be true in one
of the two spheres, and not in the other? and (2) Did he allow
no place for reason in the domain of theology, even the reason
of the 'regenerate' believer?

In relation to the question whether fallen man is able to do
good, Luther comes close to denying an assertion in philosophy
and accepting it in theology. Here is a point where we have to
'distinguish the worldly from the spiritual, the political from the
theological'.[1] When we say that a man, with his natural reason
and will, can do no good thing, we must add: 'theologically
speaking' (*auf theologische Weise*); for in the 'political' realm
(that is, what we would call 'moral philosophy') the statement
would certainly not be true. But Luther does not seem to be
thinking of a double-truth theory such as we would associate
with some of the later Nominalists. The assertion 'Fallen man
can do no good' really has a different *meaning* in theology from
what it has in philosophy, since it refers to different sorts of
'good' in each context.[2] But Luther does come closer still to
something like a double-truth theory in one of his disputations:
the *Disputation on the Sentence, 'The Word became flesh.'*[3] Here
the question at issue is precisely whether the sentence is true
in theology, yet false in philosophy. It is, then, upon this disputation that we will need to concentrate in the third chapter,
when we turn to the question of Luther's relation to the
Nominalists.

The second question, whether Luther did not find any
place at all for the exercise of reason in the domain of theology,
demands careful consideration, since it is at this point that he
has been most seriously misunderstood. In the main, Luther's
advice to the Christian on how to handle reason is, as we would
now expect: blindfold it, sacrifice it, drown it in Baptism.
When a man is tempted to listen to the seductive voice of reason,
the best thing he can do is close his eyes and hold on grimly
to faith.[4] Fortunately, this is not Luther's only counsel. Occasionally he even seems to speak of faith as continuous with

[1] TR. 6, no. 6682 (esp. 117. 23 ff.).
[2] In addition to TR. 6, no. 6682, see: W.A. 42. 106–7; 10[1, 1]. 326. 7 ff.; 42. 128.
38 (on the corruption of reason by the Fall); 40[1]. 294. 16.
[3] W.A. 39[2]. 3–33.
[4] W.A. 12. 635. 5 ff.; 44. 377. 10.

reason, as though faith merely *added to* the knowledge which we
have already through natural reason. But this is, I think, only
in regard to a specific issue in which, according to Luther,
natural reason does have a certain amount of insight. For when
Paul wishes to defend himself against the charge of antinomianism, he makes his appeal first to 'natural reason' ('I speak after
the manner of men': Rom. vi. 19). Even reason teaches that
we must shun evil and do good, and rulers are following reason's
guidance when they establish laws for restraining wrong-doing.
'Although the Gospel is a higher gift and wisdom than human
reason, it does not alter or tear up man's understanding: for it
was God Himself who implanted reason in man.' But reason
falls short at two points: it cannot understand why laws are not
naturally fulfilled, and it fails to do anything about it. The best
it can do is restrain evil by laws and punishments; but it cannot
uproot it, because it has no control over the inward thoughts
from which evil works proceed. But we have a doctrine not to
be learned from human reason: and this reveals both the source
of evil (i.e. sin) and how to restrain it (i.e. by grace). So then,
we assist reason. Paul makes use of the law and of reason's
teaching on good works, but he goes beyond them.[1]

Of even greater importance are the passages (and there are
many of them) in which Luther makes room for the possibility
of reason's being regenerated. Asked whether the 'tools of
learning (*artium*) and of nature' were of service to the theologian, Luther, mentioning particularly languages, replied:
'A distinction has to be made between the abuse of a thing and
the thing itself.' The value of these tools lies in their ability to
make things clear (this being their proper use). But in themselves they do not guarantee sound results: they do Erasmus
and his sort no good at all, for though the Erasmians have the
linguistic skills, yet they make the most pernicious errors. And
what of the 'light of nature' (reason)? Again, Luther's reply is
'I make a distinction (*distinguo*).' Obsessed by the Devil, reason
is bad; illuminated by the Spirit, it is good. The essence of the
'distinction' lies in a contrast between *ante fidem* and *post fidem*,
between a use of reason 'before faith' and a use of reason 'after
faith'. The result of illumination by faith is that reason begins

---

[1] W.A. 22. 105 ff. (7th Sunday after Trinity, on Rom. vi. 19–23). See esp. 108.
12, the sentence I have translated.

to work with an entirely new set of presuppositions, no longer those derived from experience in worldly affairs, but those which are revealed in the Scriptures. 'Without faith, reason is no use and can do nothing. . . . But, when illuminated, reason takes all its thoughts from the Word.' In short, its value lies in the interpretation and clarification of the sacred text. The substance of reason remains, only the 'vanity' is purged away.[1] If reason before faith is darkness in divine matters, yet in a believer it may become an 'excellent instrument of godliness'. The same holds for all the *naturalia* (endowments of nature): though in the ungodly they may serve in the cause of ungodliness, yet in the godly they may serve in the cause of salvation (*serviunt ad salutem*). An eloquent tongue moves a man to faith; similarly, reason makes discourse clear. Reason, in fact, must be transformed—slain, but raised to newness of life, like our bodies at the Last Day. Reason is not the same after faith as it was before. All things are changed, and this is 'regeneration through the Word': the same faculties remain (*membra*: Luther is still thinking of the parallel with our resurrected bodies on the Last Day), and the same person; but regeneration through the Word transforms the faculties and fashions a different person from the one who was born of Adam.[2]

Sometimes Luther oscillates between two kinds of statement: (1) that the old light (reason) is *extinguished*, and a new light (faith) is kindled; and (2) that the old light is *transformed* into the new light. Partly, the ambiguity is in the concept of regeneration, which may be thought of either as a new birth or as renewal. The metaphors of the snake's sloughing off its old skin and of putting off the old Adam, may seem to confirm the impression that Luther wishes to be rid of reason once and for all. But it seems to me that the metaphor of 'resurrection' expresses his real meaning: you cannot opt out of rationality, but you can undergo a change of mind. You become 'an entirely new man, who sees everything differently, thinks differently, wills differently'—not who ceases to think at all! Indeed, regeneration means the acquisition, at last, of genuine wisdom: 'He *now* understands . . . sees clearly. . . .'[3] Whilst Luther rejects

[1] W.A. TR. 1, no. 439.
[2] TR. 3, no. 2938a (cf. ibid., b); 6, no. 6741.
[3] W.A. 10¹, 1. 231–5 (on John i. 13); 328. 17.

the allegorists' interpretation of the Fall, that Eve stands for the 'inferior reason', Adam for the 'superior reason': he concedes that there *is* a sense in which reason may be divided into two 'parts', higher and lower. The lower has to do with the management of domestic and political affairs; the superior is that by which we contemplate things which pertain to the religion revealed in the Word, where we *do* nothing, but only learn and contemplate. But this, he suddenly remembers, is not actually in his text! And so he concludes, reverting to his normal pejorative usage: 'For what ability or perception does reason have in the matter of religion?'[1]

Clearly, what has happened is that the notion of 'regenerate reason' tends to coalesce with the notion of 'faith' itself. This, doubtless, hardly makes for lucidity. For sometimes regenerate reason seems able to do anything faith could do; sometimes it is severely limited. In the *Commentary on Galatians* we will find passages where regenerate reason does the distinctive work of 'saving-faith'; yet elsewhere Luther tells us that, even when illuminated, reason cannot understand the articles of faith (the Trinity and the Manhood of Christ), though it can sometimes[2] understand the Ten Commandments and the religion of the Jews.[3] For the most part, when Luther is not simply using 'regenerate reason' as another name for 'faith', he is thinking of it as the organ of orderly thought being exercised upon matter provided by the Word. It is in this way, I think, that we should take his repeated correlation of 'Scripture and reason'. When, for example, Luther stood before the Diet of Worms and refused to recant unless 'convinced by the testimony of Scripture or plain reason', he certainly did not mean to set up an independent authority by the side of the Scripture. He meant: 'unless convinced either by direct citations of Scripture or by reasonable inference from such citations'.[4] Charles Beard's interpretation will not do, when he writes: 'It is impossible to doubt that he

---

[1] W.A. 42. 138. 15 ff. (on Gen. iii. 14).

[2] The Weimar edn. reads *aliquando*: on the analogy of other passages (some of which will be examined later) I think the reading *aliquo modo* is to be preferred. But I have nevertheless translated according to the Weimar text.

[3] TR. 4, no. 5015.

[4] Preuss showed (in an article on this formula, published in *Theologische Studien u. Kritiken*, 1908) that *ratio* in Luther may sometimes be understood to mean 'die rein logische Schlußfolgerung aus anerkannten Prämissen'.

here assigns to reason an independent position by the side of Scripture: the words will bear no other interpretation.'[1] Luther is thinking of *ratio* solely in terms of what the Westminster Confession calls 'good and necessary consequence'.[2]

The main features of Luther's teaching on reason are, then, by no means abstruse or hard to determine. To be sure, inconsistencies remain, and it is another question whether Luther's position is defensible. One thing is certain: many of the time-honoured lines of criticism are beside the point. It is not sufficient to say, 'Luther was an irrationalist: he attacked reason', and leave it at that. One must stop to inquire *why* he attacked reason, *in what respects* he attacked reason, and *what he meant* by 'reason'. And a careful scrutiny of the sources makes it plain that the crucial issue concerns Luther's fundamental dualism. To sum up, Luther distinguishes between two areas of human experience, two directions towards which man faces. Man lives in relation with his fellow men (*coram hominibus*) and also in relation with God (*coram Deo*). He has to do both with the created order and with the Creator Himself. His life is lived in two distinct spheres: the one is natural, temporal, earthly; and the other is spiritual, eternal, heavenly. Outwardly, he is related to the world; inwardly, he is related to God. In all his dealings with the world man's guide is reason: the world is the Kingdom of Reason (*regnum rationis*), and by his God-given understanding and wisdom man is able to subdue the earth and have dominion over the beasts of the field. In his dealings with God, however, only faith can be man's guide, specifically, faith in 'the Word'

---

[1] *The Reformation of the Sixteenth Century*, p. 153.

[2] Ch. i, sec. vi, of the Confession does, indeed, express Luther's sentiments exactly: 'The whole counsel of God . . . is either expressly set down in Scripture, or by good and necessary consequence may be deduced from Scripture.' It is, however, possible, as Lohse has argued, that Luther's answer at Worms recognizes the ability of reason to establish the absurdity or self-contradictoriness of a doctrine on which the Scriptures are silent; in this case Luther would have been challenging his opponents at Worms to show either that his position was un-Biblical or that it was absurd (in the sense of self-contradictory). This, of course, would mean that in a certain sense reason really is *neben* the Scriptures, not merely *unter*; and yet this does not allow to reason any 'natural knowledge' which could supplement the revealed knowledge of Scripture. This is the conclusion Lohse reaches by using the passage from the *De votis monasticis* (see p. 15, n. 2 above) to interpret the *Wormser Formel*. (See op. cit., pp. 106 ff., and Lohse's recent article in *Luther*, 1958, pp. 124–34.) Obviously, it is hardly possible to decide whether Preuss or Lohse has more correctly divined Luther's intended meaning at Worms.

or in Christ:[1] The spiritual sphere is the Kingdom of Christ (*regnum Christi*). By judicious use of his natural capacities a man may acquire a certain outward or civil righteousness in the *regnum rationis*; but righteousness in the *regnum Christi* is acquired only by faith—indeed, not so much acquired *by* faith as given *to* faith, for here righteousness is not 'active', but 'passive'. Reason illuminated by faith has some grasp of spiritual matters, and works inspired by faith are pleasing *coram Deo*. But if unregenerate reason presumes to pronounce on divine affairs, it shows itself to be utterly out of place and stone-blind; and if works are performed apart from faith, they are not accepted by God. 'Civil righteousness' can in no wise justify a man before God.

If, then, we are to do justice to the complexity of Luther's thought, we must carefully distinguish: (1) natural reason, ruling within its proper domain (the Earthly Kingdom); (2) arrogant reason, trespassing upon the domain of faith (the Heavenly Kingdom); (3) regenerate reason, serving humbly in the household of faith, but always subject to the Word of God. Within the first context, reason is an excellent gift of God; within the second, it is Frau Hulda, the Devil's Whore; within the third, it is the handmaiden of faith. And if 'we find no more precise discussion of the activity thus attributed to reason in the lives of the regenerate' (reason in the third sense), this is not, as Köstlin seems to suppose,[2] merely because its function has become purely formal, that is, to deal in thought and speech with the material presented to it by faith and the Word; it is also because reason, when regenerate, is virtually absorbed into faith, becoming faith's cognitive and intellective aspects. Because reason belongs to the natural sphere, Luther will not allow that it is competent to judge in matters of faith; and yet, because faith comes through the hearing and understanding of the Word, Luther found himself bound to concede that reason—man's rationality in the broadest sense—was, when

---

[1] Luther uses 'the Word' to refer both to Jesus Christ and to the Scriptures, which bear witness to him. Sometimes (perhaps most characteristically) 'the Word' means for him 'the Gospel concerning Jesus Christ'. See, for example, the *Treatise on Christian Liberty*, Philadelphia edn., II. 315.

[2] *The Theology of Luther*, II. 266. Pp. 215–16 and 263 ff. are a useful, though brief, summary of Luther's attitude towards reason, clearly relating *ratio* to the doctrine of the two kingdoms.

regenerate, faith's indispensable tool. We cannot, I think, deny that Luther's understanding of the place of reason is perfectly intelligible, sometimes well-argued, even if we neither like it nor are willing to accept it.

II

LUTHER'S ATTITUDE TOWARDS PHILOSOPHY

A T many points Luther's critique of philosophy runs parallel
to his critique of reason. And yet it soon becomes apparent
that here he has a very different kind of opponent in
mind. Strangely perhaps, as it will seem to us, if he had any
single group in mind when he spoke against reason, it was the
Schwärmer or fanatics. He sometimes mentions others also, of
course: the 'heretics', for example, such as the Arians and the
(only very dubiously Christian) Manichaeans, and also the
'Papists'.[1] But for him it was the 'fanatics' who most perfectly
exemplified the arrogant attempt of reason to seek knowledge
of God apart from the Written Word. It is this fact which lends
some plausibility to Beard's thesis that Luther, though he once
allowed reason to stand as a parallel authority to the Scripture,
later hardened himself against reason when he became embroiled
in controversy with the Prophets of Zwickau, with Carlstadt,
and with Thomas Münzer.[2] The thesis is, I believe, incorrect
so far as Beard's understanding of the formula 'Scripture and
reason' is concerned, but it does draw attention to the significant association, in Luther's mind, of reason and fanaticism—
a combination which sounds quite extraordinary in *our* ears.[3]

Naturally, however, it is the Schoolmen that Luther has
chiefly in mind when he turns to the question of philosophy.

---

[1] For *ratio* as the source of heresy, see: W.A. 42. 117. 39 ff. (Arians, Anabaptists);
21. 231. 35 (including the Manichaeans); 22. 39. 11 ff. (Arians and Papists). The
source of all heresy is 'measuring doctrine by reason', 'listening to the Devil's
Bride'.   [2] Op. cit.

[3] Julius Köstlin also emphasizes the connexion between Luther's estimate of
reason and his struggle with the fanatics, especially on the problem of the Lord's
Supper. Even the notorious last sermon of 1546, mentioned above, centres around
the 'sacramentarian controversy'. It is not possible to go into this side of our problem in any detail, but one comment surely must be made: Luther's case against the
fanatics is pre-eminently 'reasonable', and one cannot but admire the skill with
which he picks their linguistic arguments to pieces. In regarding their arguments as
the inventions of Madam Reason, Luther does not in the least mean to assert that
they are cogent; he is merely making the negative judgement that they are not
founded upon the Word. But for further details and documentation I refer to
Köstlin, op. cit.

Yet the fundamental criticism of philosophy is the same: it is excellent in its proper place (*in suo loco*), but it cannot be autonomous in theology. The same goes for Aristotle—the 'father of the Schoolmen'—whose philosophical categories and judgements should not be transferred into theology. We will consider, first, what Luther has to say about philosophy and philosophers in general; second, what he says of Aristotle.

Luther's attitude towards philosophy

Once again, many of Luther's most important utterances on our theme are to be found in the *Church Postils* and the *Table-Talk*, and are generally not much more than *obiter dicta*. Yet they present a fairly consistent viewpoint, which is not difficult to discern.

The sharp division between the areas of philosophy and theology is clearly stressed in the *Postils*, whenever occasion presents itself. Philosophy is concerned with the objects of sensory perception, things which can be experienced and conceptualized; whereas the Christian's concern is with invisible things, the 'things which are not', that is, things whose existence men question because they cannot see them.[1] It is the Gospel that teaches us about the nature of God and of ourselves, 'whence we came and whither we are going'. In these matters the philosophers are totally ignorant.[2] It is not the Scriptures that are obscure, as the Papists falsely allege, but the philosophers: there is nothing but darkness in the heathen philosophers.[3] All the glory which philosophers have in the world's eyes is nothing before God.[4]

Similarly, in the *Table-Talk* we find it stated bluntly: 'Philosophy does not understand sacred things.' Philosophy must not be mixed up with theology. 'I do not disapprove its use, but let us use it as a shadow, a comedy, and as political righteousness.' To regard it as the substance of theology (*ipsam rem theologiae*) just won't do.[5] Hence, whilst Luther is willing to use philosophy

---

[1] W.A. 37. 538. 22. Walch reads *wichtigen* for *nichtigen*, but the Weimar reading is perfectly possible—Luther may well be alluding to 1 Cor. i. 28.

[2] W.A. 10¹,². 10. 14.

[3] Ibid. 73. 25.   [4] W.A. 22. 368. 21.

[5] TR. 5, no. 5245. Luther further says: 'Wiewol mirs nicht zu wider ist, das man die Philosophiam lehre und lerne. Ich lobe und billige es, aber es gehöret Bescheidenheit dazu; man lasse die Philosophiam in ihrem Zirkel bleiben, dazu sie Gott gegeben hat' (ibid.).

to back up a point,[1] he will not build upon its foundations:
philosophy is *the heathen's* theology.[2] Philosophers are not (in
the true sense of the word) theologians; and it was not for nothing that Paul warns us beware of philosophy, for it has only
words of human wisdom, which do not, and cannot, agree with
the Gospel.[3] Philosophy should be content to investigate matter,
its primary and secondary qualities, and to distinguish accidents
from substance. It cannot have an adequate understanding of
causes, for it presupposes neither God nor the Devil.[4] Luther's
basic objection is to 'curiosity' or 'speculation', prying into
matters which we could not possibly comprehend and meantime neglecting those things that belong to godliness. It is
interesting to note the topics which are included under the
heading of what cannot be comprehended: people argue,
Luther says, about the after-life, about the Trinity, about the
Two Natures of Christ. 'There's human nature for you! It
insists on doing whatever is forbidden.' It neglects justification,
and pries into 'higher things', asking 'Why? why? why?' That
is the way it goes when philosophy gets into theology, and that
is the way the Devil seduced Eve.[5] All these speculations are
futile without the Word of God. There was a time when we did
not have access to the Word. Now that we have the Word, we
despise it: *praesentia fastidimus*.[6]

Luther's postil on the Gospel for Epiphany (Matt. ii. 1–12)
deserves special mention.[7] It contains a long digression on 'the
natural philosophers'. Something of nature is known to us all;
but human reason is inquisitive and always wants to know more.
Reason begins to speculate beyond what is permissible. Luther's
assault on this enterprise is unqualified. The Fall of Adam has
made it impossible for man to understand more of nature, for
by the Fall man's reason was corrupted. The endeavour is,
therefore, fruitless, and the natural philosophers are divided into
squabbling sects.[8]

---

[1] TR. 1, no. 427.

[2] 'Philosophia est quasi theologia gentium et rationis' (TR. 1, no. 4).

[3] TR. 3, no. 2881 (48. 26).

[4] TR. 5, no. 5228. My interpretation presupposes that the correct reading
should be *cum non praesupponit Deum*, &c. (17. 29). The negation is not in W.A., but
see Smith and Gallinger, op. cit., p. 117, n. 1.

[5] TR. 5, no. 5534.   [6] TR. 5, no. 6064.

[7] W.A. 10[1, 1]. 555–728.

[8] Ibid. 565. 6, 566. 2, 565. 16, 566. 3 and 5.

Now, this certainly sounds like gross obscurantism, an un-
blushing attempt to quell the scientific spirit of investigation.
But a closer look at the text would modify first impressions.
(1) In the first place, what does Luther have in mind when he
speaks of the 'natural philosophers'? Apparently he means
chiefly the astrologers—after all, the text tells of the Adoration
of the Magi. And whilst Luther certainly believed that there
were all kinds of mysterious powers in nature, even that the
heavenly bodies served as 'signs',[1] he thought that the attempt
to read man's fortune in the stars was mere quackery. 'God
help us!' is his exasperated summing-up when he surveys the
fables and lies of the astrologers. (2) In the second place,
Luther's objection to speculation is quite specific: it goes beyond
what can be known by experience or revelation. The repeated
appeal to 'experience' (*erfarung*) indicates a healthy empiricism,
not a narrow-minded obscurantism—though, of course, one
must beware of reading into Luther's terms too much of our
own contemporary meanings. Luther's objection to the study
of the stars is that they are beyond experience, so that there can
be no check upon assertions made about them. 'Those who
lie about far-distant lands, lie with all their might, there being
none with experience to contradict them.'[2]

Luther goes on to criticize Aristotle, 'the great light of nature,
the heathen master who now rules in Christ's stead in all the
universities'. The whole passage is put forward with a gay
irony, and we should remember that it was written in the common tongue, for simple people as well as for students. But again
we notice that Luther comes back to this conclusion: the
sources of knowledge are two, experience (or common sense) and
revelation (or Christ). 'Be content with what experience and
common sense teach you.'[3] 'Everything which is not of Christ
is to be avoided.' 'Whatever more you want to know, is not

---

[1] Luther distinguishes what we may term 'ordinary' and 'extraordinary' signs:
e.g. the sun as a sign that the day's work is to begin and a comet as foreboding
disaster. It is the former sort that he approves.

[2] Ibid. 560. 9, 570. 4, 566. 15 (on astrology); 565. 17, 566. 3, 584. 14, 566. 11,
566. 13 (on experience).

[3] The illustrations of what experience teaches—that fire is hot, water is cold and
wet, that in summer one job must be done and in winter another—concern minding
farm and family, clear indication of the kind of reader Luther has in mind. He also
likes to make allusions to habits of animals, both wild and domestic, when speaking
of 'what we know'.

needful for you: it is idle curiosity.' Sometimes Luther seems to
be saying that speculation goes beyond even reason, for he
certainly regards reason as tied to sense-perception—though
often, of course, he mentions the fact only to belittle reason,
adding that faith is knowledge of things unseen.[1]

Smith and Gallinger have collected some of Luther's table-
talk on 'astronomy and astrology',[2] and the comments which
they have translated present very much the same impression
of Luther's feelings about these subjects. The two are carefully
distinguished: Luther admires astronomy and mathematics
because they have to do with demonstrations, but he has no
respect for astrology. Not even Melanchthon (who liked to
dabble in such matters) could induce him to trust the astrologer's predictions. The difference between the astrologer's
predictions and the physician's is that the physician has 'certain
symptoms and experience to guide' him. Most of Luther's
critics know that he rejected Copernicus' heliocentric universe
on the grounds that Joshua 'commanded the sun, not the earth,
to stand still'; but, on another occasion, Luther expresses wil-
lingness to accept the conclusion of the astronomers that the
moon is the smallest and lowest of the stars, suggesting that
perhaps the Scriptures, in referring to the sun and moon as the
two 'great lights', were simply describing the moon as it looks
to us. In other words, Luther was not in the least disrespectful
towards well-founded scientific conclusions, though he certainly
could not conceive of any contradiction between science and
Scripture.

Luther's attitude towards Aristotle

Many of Luther's utterances concerning Aristotle have been
collected in the Weimar edition's index of persons,[3] and it is,

[1] W.A. 10¹, ¹. 567. 7 ff.; 569. 19, 569. 7, 570. 19 (the three direct citations);
611. 8 ff.
[2] *Conversations With Luther*, pp. 101–4. Bornkamm points out (with reference to
TR. 1, no. 1160) that Luther greeted the new science with enthusiasm and liked
to contrast himself with Erasmus in this respect. In the advance of scientific knowledge Luther saw the gradual recovery of Adam's lost dominion over the creatures.
See Heinrich Bornkamm, 'Faith and Reason in the Thought of Erasmus and
Luther', in *Religion and Culture* (ed. by Walter Leibrecht), pp. 138–9; also 'The
Picture of Nature', in his book, *Luther's World of Thought*, p. 184.
[3] W.A., vol. 58, part one. F. Nitzsch gives a comprehensive list (based, unfor-
tunately, on the Erlangen edn.) at the end of his book, *Luther und Aristoteles*.

I think, possible to discern in them a pattern of thought which frequently recalls his judgements on reason and philosophy. The 'characteristic descriptions' of Aristotle, recorded in the Weimar index, have already been noted in our introduction. It is important to observe that, for Luther, the name of Aristotle is virtually synonymous with reason and philosophy, so that one of Luther's descriptions for the Greek philosopher is 'the light of nature', precisely the same expression which he uses elsewhere in speaking of reason.[1]

There are a large number of passages in which Luther deplores the Aristotelian conquest of the schools: he sounds the call to rebel, and even suggests (in his early lectures on Romans) that his mission is to cry out against philosophy—to learn the philosophy of the schools, as one would witchcraft, only in order to destroy it. Aristotle is the 'father of the Schoolmen', and he rules in the universities. He has become the authority in the place of Christ and the Scriptures. Instead of the Scriptures illuminating the light of nature, it is Aristotle who is used to cast light on the Scriptures, so that theology has been pushed out by pagan sophistry. It was considered damnable heresy to contradict Aristotle: scholars spent all their life studying him, and learning nothing.[2]

Luther evidently regarded the study of Aristotle as a substitute for the proper business of Christians, which is the study of the divine Word. The Church has lost the eyes of Christ because some are preoccupied with their profits, some with their pleasures, some with ambition, some with ecclesiastical law—and not a few with Aristotle's philosophy![3] This is Luther's general picture of Aristotle and the universities. But we must look a little more closely, and in so doing we will find that in at least four ways the Reformer's harsh judgement is considerably modified: he maintains that Aristotle is valuable in his own proper domain; that we must not evaluate all his works alike; that his champions never really understood him; and that, even if Aristotle is to be condemned, there are other philosophers who are to be preferred.

First, then, Aristotle must be kept in his own domain. In

---

[1] W.A. 7. 739. 23; cf. 2. 395. 19, 363. 4; 7. 738. 31; 10¹, ¹. 567. 11; 17². 27. 33.
[2] W.A. 1. 304. 11; 8. 98. 30; 56. 371. 17; 7. 739. 23 ff.; 10¹, ². 10. 23; 17². 27. 33;
TR. 5. 684. 36; W.A. 10¹, ². 74. 9.   [3] W.A. 3. 423. 2.

general, Luther's objections are less to the philosophy of Aristotle itself than to the corrupting influence it has upon theology when the two are confused. The philosophers mix Aristotelian philosophy with theology. It is Aristotle's false metaphysics and philosophy that have deceived our theologians. As soon as they open their mouths they teach nothing but the papal laws and the writings of Aristotle. They teach nothing about Christ, but all about the Pope and Aristotle.[1]

To Luther's mind it was quite astonishing that anyone should fail to see the incompatibility of Aristotle and 'Catholic Truth'.[2] And yet one recalls that it was the special concern of his own teacher, Trutvetter, to demonstrate their harmony.[3] The important thing to note, however, is that he does not deny some validity to the heathen master's philosophy in its own sphere. Aristotle wrote with admirable learning on the problems of ethics. Both his books and Cicero's are extremely useful for the conduct of this life.[4] In other words, Aristotle's moral philosophy is of value in the Earthly Kingdom. This, no doubt, explains the apparent contradiction between the abuse which Luther heaps on Aristotle's *Ethics* in one place and the praise which he bestows upon it in another.[5] When Luther looks at Aristotle's natural philosophy and moral philosophy, weighing them strictly on their own intrinsic merits, he much prefers the latter; but he can conceive of nothing more mischievous than Aristotle's ethics when they are mixed up with the theology of grace and salvation. In any case, he calls it mere philistinism (*barbarum est*) to be ignorant of Aristotle's natural philosophy, even though it may not be universally true. After all, the Greek philosopher's views form an integral part of culture and rest upon sound arguments.[6] Clearly, as long as the distinction between theology and philosophy is kept before the mind, there is nothing to prevent one from passing favourable judgements upon Aristotle— or, at least, giving him a fair trial. Sometimes Luther's praise

---

[1] W.A. 44. 771. 7; 56. 349. 23; 5. 641. 15, 650. 19.

[2] W.A. 9. 27. 22.

[3] Fife, *Revolt of Martin Luther*, p. 58.

[4] W.A. 40³. 608. 15.

[5] 'Aristoteles est optimus in morali philosophia; in naturali nihil valet' (TR. 1. 178. 10). Yet: 'Tota fere Aristotelis *Ethica* pessima est gratiae inimica' (W.A. 1. 226. 10).

[6] W.A. 42. 21. 9 ff. (on Gen. i. 6).

is a little grudging;[1] but he had some enthusiasm for the philosopher's method,[2] and liked the discussion of *epieikeia* in the fifth book of the Ethics.[3] He even allows that both Plato and Aristotle 'knew well from the light of nature: "Do not do to another what you would not have him do to you." '[4] Perhaps Luther was not being entirely ironical when he suggested that Aristotle was safe only for those who had first been made fools in Christ.[5]

As soon as we turn to theology, on the other hand, his whole attitude is changed: here Aristotelian philosophy has no validity whatever, but is mere darkness; and Aristotle himself appears as a seducer.[6] On a number of different points Luther indicates the impossibility of applying Aristotelian opinions to theology without undermining the Truth. Because of these opinions, Aristotle is to be excluded from the *forum theologicum*: they only subvert the understanding of Scripture.[7] It is within this context that we should place Luther's charge that Aristotle has supplanted Christ. 'Instead of Christ and Paul we used to learn Averroes and Aristotle in the schools.' The blind pagan reigns more widely than Christ himself. The man with the highest reputation for learning amongst the Papists was the one who could cite, not Christ and the Apostles, but Aristotle,

---

[1] 'Ethica Aristotelis aliquid sunt' (TR. 3. 451. 23); 'Aliquid dicit Aristoteles, cum ponit hominis finem esse felicitatem' (W.A. 42. 98. 13). Less grudging, but vague, is his commendation of the *Physics, Metaphysics*, and *De Anima* in TR. 1. 57. 41.

[2] '. . . quia methodum exacte observat, diligendus, alioqui non magna tractat' (TR. 3. 451. 18).

[3] TR. 6. 345. 28; W.A. 44. 704. 15. A close connexion between *epieikeia* (*Billigkeit, aequitas*) and reason often appears in Luther; sometimes he seems virtually to equate them. This is really an affirmation of the notion (already referred to) that reason is the 'soul of law', therefore, in a sense, above the law. Luther saw justice most 'reasonably' administered when the prince moderated the strict letter of the law according to personal circumstances, and this is the meaning of *epieikeia*. Reason and law, thus exercised in freedom, become in the truest sense agencies of love. On this see esp. Holl, op. cit., pp. 270 f.; also William A. Mueller, *Church and State in Luther and Calvin*, pp. 49 ff. Aristotle's doctrine is expounded in Book V of the *Nicomachean Ethics*, ch. x (II. 138 ff., in Sir Alexander Grant's edn.; there are, of course, many translations). Luther's use of this doctrine is perhaps the most striking example of his insistence that in the *regnum rationis* the Christian may have something to learn from the heathen. Cf. Cranz, op. cit., pp. 109 and 144-5.

[4] Tr. 6. 250. 22.   [5] W.A. 1. 355. 2.

[6] W.A. 1. 226. 26, 509. 11.

[7] TR. 4. 299. 1 (*de voluntate theologica*); W.A. 5. 33. 7 ff. (*habitus*); 1. 226. 12 (*de foelicitate*; cf. 9. 23. 9); 6. 29. 21 (*de motu infinito*); 39¹. 176. 24 (*de Theologico homine*).

though Aristotle knew nothing of Christ or of God. Indeed, it had become an absolute disgrace (presumably in the sense of *infra dignitatem*) so much as to mention Christ even from the pulpit.[1] Similarly, Luther thought that Aristotle had supplanted the Scriptures. 'The Devil takes the Bible from us, and gives us the accursed fictions of Aristotle.' The universities did not read the Bible, or, when they did, they insisted that it should be understood according to Aristotle.

When I was a monk they used to despise the Bible. Nobody understood the Psalter. They used to believe that the Epistle to the Romans contained some controversies about matters of Paul's day and was of no use for our age. Scotus, Thomas, Aristotle were the ones to read.[2]

The second qualification of Luther's attack on Aristotle is the Reformer's insistence that Aristotle's works must be carefully differentiated. The *Address to the German Nobility* (1520) contains a section on reforming the universities, and here Luther makes proposals which show clearly that he did not evaluate all Aristotle's works equally.[3] His advice is that the *Physics*, *Metaphysics*, *De Anima*, and *Ethics* of Aristotle, previously esteemed to be his best books, should be completely discarded, together with the rest of his books which treat of nature. Yet the *Logic*, *Rhetoric*, and *Poetics* he would be glad to retain, possibly in an abridged form; but they must be read without a mass of commentary and notes.

The reasons for this differentiation are both general and specific. Luther had specific objections to the *De Anima*, which left no room for a doctrine of immortality, and to the *Ethics*, which seemed to him a denial of God's grace (for reasons which will need to be discussed later). But perhaps even more important is the distinction, implicit in Luther's discussion, between those works of Aristotle which put forward a certain world-view and those which only instruct in the art of thinking and speak-

---

[1] W.A. 25. 219. 13; 6. 457. 31; 30³. 500. 15; 45. 704. 7. Cf. also: W.A. 10¹,². 96. 21; 7. 739. 27; 10¹,². 116. 11 ('Nemen den blinden heyden Aristoteles zu hulff, der muß ihnen Christus wort außlegen'); TR. 2. 204. 42 and 3. 145. 28. Luther's own practice is to preach, not Aristotle, but Christ: TR. 4. 561. 9; cf. W.A. 44. 776. 18.

[2] W.A. 4. 554. 34; TR. 2. 203. 1; 4. 610. 22; cf. W.A. 6. 510. 31; 7. 100. 25 ff.; 1. 128. 15.

[3] W.A. 6. 457 f. See esp.: 457. 35; 458. 26.

ing. Hence the *Logic*, *Rhetoric*, and *Poetics* are explicitly said to be more highly esteemed because they could be used as text-books in training young men to speak and preach.

Very much the same view had been maintained by Luther a year before (1519) in a series of propositions on the theme, 'Whether the books of the philosophers are useful or useless to theology.'[1] The first two propositions may be translated as follows:

Sacred theology, although it is divinely inspired doctrine, yet it does not refuse to be communicated in letters and words (*non tamen abhorret literis et vocibus tradi*). Of all the sciences invented by man, the most conspicuously useful for propagating theology is grammar.

This, clearly, is the cause of Luther's sympathy for the 'formal' treatises of Aristotle. But his point is that you do not really need to devote all your energies to Aristotle simply in order to use language correctly. It is true that even 'saintly doctors' sometimes use Aristotelian terms, but this is no ground for studying Aristotle: the same argument would require research in the peasants' ale-houses. Probably Hägglund is right in say-ing that Luther is trying to draw a distinction between the concepts as such and the philosophical world-view from which they are taken.[2]

It is perhaps worth pointing out here (in anticipation of the discussion in our next chapter) that this fondness of Luther's for the methodological disciplines is quite consistent with the Nominalist tradition in which he was trained. It has, indeed, been suggested with some plausibility that the Occamist bias towards 'sermonical disciplines' led to a neglect of the natural sciences. The charge has, of course, been repudiated,[3] but the mere fact that it was ever made is of some significance. As a matter of fact, both Luther's own teachers wrote works on physics—physics, along with ethics and logic, being one of the three disciplines into which Arnold of Usingen divided philo-

---

[1] W.A. 6. 29. 'Conclusions quindecim tractantes, an libri philosophorum sint utiles aut inutiles ad theologiam.' The theses were not printed until the following year.

[2] 'Weiter wird eine Grenze zwischen den Begriffen oder Termini als solchen gezogen und der philosophischen Anschauung, der sie ursprünglich entnommen sind.' Op. cit., p. 10.

[3] For example, by Scheel, *Martin Luther*, 1. 194 ff.

sophy.[1] But still, there can be no doubt of the Nominalists' special love for dialectics.

Luther's belief that the older Schoolmen never really understood Aristotle could also be considered evidence of a distinctively Nominalist training. Part of E. A. Moody's thesis in his work, *The Logic of William of Occam*, is that Occam was especially concerned to restore the original Aristotle, to free him from the opinions of both Augustinian theologians and Arab philosophers. But it is, I think, quite clear that Luther's allegation of misunderstanding is levelled as much against the Occamists as against the Thomists: neither of the two parties really understood Aristotle. The Greek philosopher was a much better man than the Schoolmen allowed him to be, for they twisted his teaching to fit into the patterns of their own false notions about God and religion.[2] It is this charge against the Schoolmen which constitutes the third qualification of Luther's anti-Aristotelianism.

Most often, the grounds for the charge of misinterpretation are not carefully specified. Hence Luther simply says, for example, that although the University of Cologne condemns as a heretic whoever dares to contradict Aristotle, yet they do not understand him. Repeatedly, he simply says of his opponents: 'They do not understand Aristotle', with scarcely any explanation.[3] But there are some specific points on which the charge is more carefully stated. Thomas, he claims, misunderstood Aristotle's teaching on 'accidents and subject', so that the Schoolman is to be criticized, not merely for propounding in theology opinions borrowed from Aristotle, but for misinterpreting the philosopher as well.[4] Perhaps the reason for Luther's frequent failure to specify the doctrines in which Aristotle had been misunderstood by the Schoolmen, is simply that the charge itself was a general one. For it is possible, I think, to maintain that the Schoolmen, according to Luther, misunderstood Aristotle precisely because they applied his opinions to theology: in

---

[1] Physics embraced metaphysics, natural philosophy, and mathematics. Fife, op. cit., p. 57. (Pages 58–59 of Fife's book contain a well-documented discussion of Luther's views on astronomy and astrology in relation to his Aristotelian training.)

[2] Cf. W.A. 5. 414. 25, where Aristotle's theology is said to be *neutralis*: only when mishandled, does it run into conflict with the Spirit.

[3] TR. 5. 684. 36; W.A. 6. 188. 3. Cf.: W.A. 1. 508. 37; 10[1, 2]. 74. 11; 303. 500. 15; 1. 29. 27.   [4] W.A. 6. 508. 22.

other words, our first and third points really are different ways
of stating the same thing, since to misunderstand Aristotle is to
transfer his philosophical categories into the sphere of theology.
As we will see, Luther states quite clearly in the *Commentary on
Galatians* that Aristotle was a better man than the Papists just
because he confined his opinions to his own sphere and made
no incursions into the domain of faith.

Occasionally, the charge against the Scholastics is not only
that they have misunderstood their Aristotle, but that they are
actually ignorant of him.[1] No doubt one should make allowances here for polemical exuberance: it is a pleasant thing to be
able to refute an adversary from his own authorities (this is the
way the Devil himself tried, though without success, to defeat
the Messiah). Possibly, too, we should make allowances for
Luther's undoubted vanity when he claims to know his Aristotle better than any of his opponents.[2] And yet here again we
should not fail to note the passage in which he calls himself a
better interpreter of Aristotle since he portrayed him in his own
colours, not trying to harmonize him with the opinions of others.[3]

The fourth consideration which modifies the harshness of
Luther's judgement upon Aristotle is by no means complimentary to Aristotle himself. But it does indicate that the
condemnation of Aristotle must not too readily be considered a
general condemnation of all philosophy. Frequently, it is true,
the name of Aristotle is a synonym for philosophy or reason.
But not always. For Luther is able, on occasion, to weigh philosophers one against the other (including Aristotle), and to state
a definite preference. His bias against philosophy in general
and Aristotle in particular does not prevent him from making
comparative judgements, and this does seem to indicate that

---

[1] See esp. W.A. Br. 1. 158. 38 ff. (to Egranus; 24 Mar. 1518); W.A. Br. 1. 301.
19 ff. (to Spalatin; 14 Jan. 1519). The second of these two letters recounts an
argument Luther had at Dresden with a Thomist.

[2] He 'understands perfectly' Aristotle's *Physics, Metaphysics*, and *De Anima* (TR.
1. 57. 41); when it comes to Aristotle, he knows what he is talking about at least
as well as his enemies: he understands him better than Thomas or Scotus did (W.A.
6. 458. 17: from the *Address to the German Nobility*; cf. the closely similar passage in
the *Open Letter on Translating*, W.A. 30². 635. 23).

[3] W.A. 1. 611. 37, from the *Resolutiones disputationum de indulgentiarum virtute* (1518).
The whole discussion on p. 611 is important for our immediate problem, since
Luther is there arguing that his opponents 'not only fail to understand Aristotle,
but also disseminate their error and false understanding throughout almost the
entire Church'.

the bias did not utterly blind Luther's perceptiveness in philosophical issues—although, to be sure, his judgements are almost
always made from a strictly theological viewpoint.

Luther evidently had a special affection for Cicero. Whilst
he found himself obliged to acknowledge Aristotle's superiority
in native ability (*ingenio*), he insists that Cicero often had the
sounder viewpoint—on the origin of mankind, for instance.
The Greek was the better dialectician, but for actual content
(*rem*) he cannot touch the Roman. 'If you want real philosophy,
read Cicero.' Occasionally, Luther's enthusiasm for Cicero
betrays him into what most of us would be inclined to consider
mere extravagance: 'Cicero', he somewhere claims, 'is much
more learned than Aristotle.' And he will even defend the
Roman philosopher's apparent inferiority on the grounds that
he was a busy man, for his academic pursuits were considerably
hindered by his pre-occupation with affairs of state.[1]

In one passage, indeed, Luther shows that his respect for
Cicero arises precisely out of the Roman philosopher's 'want of
leisure': he was a man conversant with practical affairs, whereas the Greek was a 'man at leisure and with plenty of money'.
For this reason the *Offices* is a superior work to Aristotle's *Ethics*.
'Cicero's concern was with real life (*res*), whereas Aristotle dealt
with mere logic (*dialecticam*).' Cicero is described as a 'man full
of worries and civic burdens', whereas Aristotle was a 'lazy
ass'.[2] In a similar vein, Luther admires Cicero for his earnest
spirit: 'He didn't fool around and play the Greek the way
Aristotle and Plato did.'[3] But the same passages in which these
remarks appear also betray the severe limitations of Luther's
philosophical criticisms: Cicero is only favoured, in the last
analysis, because his opinions more closely approximate distinctively Christian dogmas.[4] Specifically, Luther mentions the
doctrines of the soul and of God. It was, of course, a standing
problem for the medieval champions of Aristotle that a doctrine

[1] W.A. 42. 408. 34 (cf. 42. 63. 34, where it is said that Aristotle, had he heard of
man's creation, would have burst out laughing and judged it a silly fable); TR. 2.
456. 29; 4. 612. 27; W.A. 42. 408. 19.
[2] TR. 2. 456. 31. Yet Luther did not totally despise Aristotle as a moral philosopher: see, for example, TR. 3, no. 3608d (451. 23).
[3] TR. 3. 698. 13.
[4] 'Ille proxime accessit ad cognitionem multarum rerum Christianarum, quod
testantur disputata eius de anima, de natura Deorum etc.' (TR. 2. 456. 25).

of immortality was only very doubtfully compatible with the identification of 'soul' with the 'form' of a human being.[1] Here is one of the points on which Cicero is supposed by Luther to be superior to Aristotle, and it earns him the honorific title 'best of the philosophers'.[2] The second main point for which Cicero earns Luther's commendation is his concern for the question, not whether God *exists*, but whether God *cares* (*an res humanas curet*). On this point Aristotle, though he certainly teaches the existence of God, is a mere 'Epicurean':

> Aristotle is an utter Epicurean. He does not believe that God cares for human affairs—or, if he does so believe, then he considers that God governs the world as a drowsy nursemaid rocks a child. Cicero, on the other hand, went much further.[3]

Like the question of immortality, this also belongs to 'physics' (in the very broad sense which Arnold gave the term), so that Cicero is ranked above Aristotle both in moral and in natural philosophy.[4]

Basically, the conclusions to our separate discussions of reason, philosophy, and Aristotle are the same. The ambivalence of Luther's attitude towards all three is to be explained by reference to his dualism of an Earthly Kingdom, on the one hand, and a Heavenly Kingdom, on the other. The articles of belief cannot be arrived at by the exercise of natural reason; neither is there any point in the attempt to buttress by reason what is

[1] 'Scriptura sacra pugnat contra Aristotelem, qui negat animam immortalem, sed dicit animam et corpus eandem esse substantiam' (TR. 3. 698. 4; cf. W.A. 1. 355. 6; 6. 458. 7; 20. 70. 27). It is precisely the insistence on the inseparability of form and matter (save in the sole instance of the Prime Mover) that is supposed to distinguish Aristotle from Plato. If the soul is identified with the 'form' of the human being, then it cannot persist after the dissolution of the body (the 'matter'). St. Thomas did, of course, try to salvage the doctrine of immortality by his interpretation of the abstruse passage in the *De Anima* of Aristotle which mentions the *intellectus agens* (Book III, ch. v; the edn. of Edwin Wallace has both text and translation, pp. 158 ff.). Cf. A. E. Taylor, *Aristotle* (revised edn., New York: Dover Publications Inc., 1955), pp. 86–87.

[2] TR. 3. 698. 10.

[3] TR. 5. 155. 1. For the name 'Epicurean' used of Aristotle cf. W.A. 39^2. 255. 11; 40^3. 493. 22 ff.; frequently it means no more than 'sceptic'.

[4] TR. 3. 698. 11. For further comments on Aristotle's shortcomings on the two questions of immortality and God's concern for mankind see TR. 3. 451. 18. A third point in which Luther found Aristotle wanting was the philosopher's teaching on the eternity of the world (e.g. W.A. 1. 355. 6).

already given in faith. The distinction between the two spheres must be rigidly maintained. Philosophy must not be confused with theology, nor reason with faith. 'Philosophy has to do with what can be known by human reason. Theology has to do with what can be believed, that is, with what is apprehended by faith.'[1] A similar division appears in the thought of William of Occam and the later Nominalists. Inevitably one asks the question: How far, if at all, was Luther dependent upon his Nominalist teachers in this particular phase of his thinking? And to this question we must now turn.

---

[1] 'Philosophia versatur circa cognoscibilia ratione humana. Theologia versatur circa credibilia, id est, quae fide apprehenduntur' (W.A. 39^2. 6. 26). From the *Disputatio de sententia*, 'Verbum caro factum est.'

III

LUTHER AND SCHOLASTICISM

ATTEMPTS to explain Luther in the light of his forebears have been legion.[1] Heinrich Denifle's suggestion that Luther was little more than an 'ossified Occamite' can be made to appear more plausible than most, and Hartmann Grisar follows Denifle closely at this point. No doubt, any theory which places exclusive emphasis on just one candidate for the position of Luther's forerunner will be refuted by its own exclusiveness. In naming Occam as Luther's forerunner, one could hardly mean to ignore Augustine, for example. At one stage of his development, Luther certainly was profoundly moved by the Mystics; and almost all his life he carried on his work in close relation to the Christian humanists, as we shall see. However, it can hardly have been without significance for Luther's thinking that, both in the University of Erfurt and in the Augustinian monastery, he was subjected to Nominalist teaching; and, as a matter of fact, the evidences of his training appeared again and again in his opinions even after he had become the leader of the Reformation. Both these facts— Luther's training in Nominalism and his use of distinctively Nominalist doctrines—make us willing to believe that his understanding of the specific issue of 'faith and reason' may, to some degree, have been learned in the school of Occam's disciples.

Luther's training in Nominalism

Little need be said of Luther's education in the university. Not that the facts are particularly well known. We know that he matriculated at the university in 1501 (at the age of 18), that he took the bachelor's degree in 1502 and the master's in 1505. But virtually all that we know concerning the lectures he attended is by inference from attempts to reconstruct the university's curriculum: in other words, we can only surmise

---

[1] A list of Luther's alleged 'helpers and guides' is given in Boehmer, *Luther in Light of Recent Research*, p. 86.

what he *must* have learned, direct evidence being very scanty.[1]
Still, the curriculum of a medieval university was rigidly fixed,
so that the indirect evidence on Luther's studies at Erfurt does,
no doubt, give an accurate enough picture. The emphasis
would have been mainly upon the *trivium* (grammar, rhetoric,
logic) until he took his bachelor's degree; then upon the
quadrivium (geometry, mathematics, music, astronomy). And
the curriculum would have culminated in a close scrutiny of
Aristotle's *Ethics* and *Metaphysics*.

But concerning the content of the lecture-courses, or the way
in which Aristotle was taught, we can know very little. It is,
however, generally agreed that Luther's main instructors,
Jodocus Trutvetter and Bartholomaus Arnold von Usingen,
were both convinced Occamists.[2] And when, not later than the
autumn of 1507, Luther began serious study of theology, it was
again two Nominalists who were his teachers: Johann Paltz
and Johann Nathin.[3] Even before he became a serious student
of theology, Luther had read Gabriel Biel's *Canon of the Mass*,
for this was the prescribed preparation for his ordination to the
priesthood.

Luther must, then, have been thoroughly grounded in the
philosophy and theology of Nominalism; and although he
acquired his knowledge of the *via moderna* only through those
who were by no means slavish disciples, he more than once
owns Occam himself as his 'beloved master'.[4] He claims to be

---

[1] The main sources for Erfurt's undergraduate programme are: (1) the *Acten
der Erfurter Universität*; (2) a manuscript of an Erfurt M.A., Herbord of Lippe, which
gives the requirements for graduation to the first degree some eighty years before
Luther; (3) a discussion of the logic courses by one of Luther's own teachers,
Jodocus Trutvetter. See esp. Otto Scheel, *Martin Luther*, I. 152 ff.; and Fife, *Revolt
of Martin Luther*, pp. 39 ff. Fife himself apparently leans heavily on Scheel's work
in this area. Also valuable for Luther's student-days (both in the university and in
the monastery) are: Henri Strohl, *L'Évolution religieuse de Luther;* Rupp, *Luther's
Progress to the Diet of Worms* and *The Righteousness of God*. Many important original
sources are collected in Scheel's *Dokumente* (revised edn., 1929; Strohl cites the
earlier edn. of 1911).

[2] Fife, op. cit., pp. 49 ff.; Rupp, *The Righteousness of God*, p. 87; &c.

[3] Fife, op. cit., pp. 107–9, 112; Rupp, *The Righteousness of God*, pp. 87–88. Johann
Paltz left Erfurt in 1507, so that if Luther did not begin to study theology until after his
ordination in May of the same year, then Paltz could only have taught him for a very
short while—possibly, not at all. Johann Nathin was certainly Luther's principal
instructor, and we know that Nathin had studied under Biel himself at Tübingen.

[4] *Magister meus* (TR. 2. 516. 6; W.A. 39¹. 420. 27); *mein lieber Meister* (W.A. 30².
300. 10); *mein Meister* (W.A. 38. 160. 3).

of Occam's party;[1] he spoke of Occam's dialectical skill with
profound respect,[2] and even calls him 'without doubt the most
eminent and the most brilliant of the Scholastic doctors (*princeps
et ingeniosissimus*)'.[3]

Luther's debt to Occamism

In spite of the fact that Luther was already calling the
Nominalists 'hog-theologians' in 1515,[4] we should not be surprised to find elements of real continuity in his later thinking.[5]
Several of Luther's distinctive doctrines have been claimed as
Nominalist in origin; and there is good reason for accepting at
least some of the suggestions, although mere verbal resemblances may be misleading and Luther was seldom so unoriginal
as to leave his borrowings untouched by the stamp of his own
peculiar genius.[6] There is, in short, both truth and error in
Denifle's blunt assertion: 'He remained an Occamist.'[7]

On (1) the problem of 'universals' Luther did, apparently,
always remain a convinced Occamist. He expressly owns his
allegiance to the 'Terminists', who argue that the term *human-
itas*, for instance, names all men individually: it does not refer
to a 'common humanity existing in all men ("ein gemeine
menschheit, die in allen menschen were"), as Thomas and the
others held.[8] This is an accurate statement of the difference
between Thomists and Nominalists, and Luther clearly meant
to acknowledge his own adherence to the Nominalist party,

---

[1] *Sum Occanicae factionis* (W.A. 6. 600. 11). Cf. *meae sectae* (W.A. 6. 195. 4); also:
'Terministen hieß man eine secten in der hohen schulen, unter welchen ich auch
gewesen' (TR. 5. 653. 1).
[2] *Summus dialecticus* (TR. 2. 516. 6).
[3] W.A. 6. 183. 3. Further refs. to Occam will be found in W.A. 58[1]. But see
Rupp, who suggests (following Holl) that 'many of Luther's apparently deferential
remarks about Occam prove to be ironical': *Luther's Progress*, p. 17.
[4] Boehmer, *Luther in Light of Recent Research*, p. 87.
[5] Vignaux has stressed the continuity in Luther's thought, illustrating it from
his earlier and later utterances concerning the Trinity: *Luther commentateur des
Sentences*, pp. 25, 29.
[6] 'These influences, however, are of a kind to be reflected in subtle undertones,
to be detected by deep and sympathetic study. They are in no wise, as in some
recent polemic, to be apprized on the strength of superficial verbal similarities, or
on what Milton called "the ferrets and mouse-hunts of an index".' Rupp, *Luther's
Progress*, p. 19.
[7] Op. cit. 1. 591. See also pp. 638 ff.
[8] TR. 5. 653. 1. Cf. 4. 679. 9 and W.A. 39[2]. 11. 36.

'the very newest sect, and the most powerful one even at Paris'. Luther's statement of the controversy is not, to be sure, a complete one: it was, for instance, the *terminus conceptus* (or 'natural sign'), not the *terminus prolatus* (or 'conventional sign'), which constituted the 'universal' for Occam. But Luther says enough for an 'informal statement'.

Secondly (2), Luther always retained a fondness for the sermonical arts, in which the Nominalists excelled.[1] It is at least possible that he taught 'Little Logic' for a time before completing the requirements for the master's degree, since one of the conditions for attaining the rank of bachelor was a promise to teach for two years in the faculty of philosophy, unless excused.[2] 'Dialectics' occupied Luther frequently even in casual conversation. In the *Table-Talk* he distinguishes between the 'old logic', which is concerned with definition, and the 'new logic', which is concerned with inference.[3] He shows a profound respect for dialectic as the art of plain speaking, carefully separating it from rhetoric, which 'adorns speech'.[4] Dialectic instructs, rhetoric is only an ornament.[5] Rhetoric's business is to persuade the will; dialectic teaches the intellect.[6] Luther considers correct speech (*proprietas sermonis*) a 'singular gift of God'.[7] Of course, the dialecticians also stood for a kind of petty quibbling which only infuriated Luther.[8] He always retained sufficient independence of judgement both to suggest improvements even where he commends and to concede, where he criticizes, that the dialectician's art *can* be performed well. Greek terms, being

---

[1] Occam's logical theory was surprisingly advanced, though it suffered from the lack of any system of symbols. To give only one illustration, he was quite familiar with the logical equivalences which are known in the modern sentential calculus as 'DeMorgan's Laws': i.e. that the negation of a conjunctive proposition is equivalent to a disjunctive proposition in which the disjuncts are the contradictories of the corresponding conjuncts; and the converse. Symbolically: $-(p.q) \equiv (-p \lor -q)$ and $-(p \lor q) \equiv (-p.-q)$. Cf. Boehner, *Occam: Philosophical Writings*, pp. xxxvii ff.

[2] Fife, op. cit., pp. 45 and 48. 'Little Logic' meant the introductory course based on Books I and IV of the *Summulae Logicales* of Petrus Hispanus.

[3] TR. 4, no. 4570 (see esp. 383. 7). The *vetus dialectica* possessed only Aristotle's *Categories* and *De Interpretatione* (plus Porphyry's *Eisagoge*); to these were added in the twelfth century (thus making the *nova dialectica*) the *Prior* and *Posterior Analytics*, the *Topics*, and the *Sophistic Refutations*. Fife, op. cit., p. 41, n. 56.

[4] TR. 3, nos. 3237a (230. 25) and 3237b (231. 3).

[5] TR. 2, nos. 2139-40.

[6] TR. 2, nos. 2629a (555. 16, 26) and 2629b (556. 33, 557. 10).

[7] TR. 4. 402. 26 (no. 4612).

[8] TR. 2. 354. 25 (no. 2191); 4. 624. 9 (no. 5033).

'foreign', should be done away with. But Luther still is willing to retain the distinction between the four kinds of cause, and he explains 'faith' by means of it.[1] Indeed, one of the reasons why he wishes to abolish Greek terminology is perhaps contained in his explicit insistence that dialectic is not the purely professional concern of academics. It can be made far more generally serviceable.[2] It is indispensable in dealing both with Sacramentarians and with Papists.[3] Besides, Luther evidently enjoyed it for its own sake: he had, according to Melanchthon, a natural aptitude for it,[4] and he mentions on one occasion that he would like to write a treatise on the subject for his son.[5] Indeed, there is, so he claims, Biblical warrant for the distinction between 'dialectic' and 'rhetoric', and St. Paul uses both.[6]

Thirdly (3), many scholars have endeavoured to maintain that Luther's cardinal doctrine of justification owes much to Occam's theories of 'acceptation' and 'imputation'. Grisar no doubt goes too far in asserting that Luther drew up his doctrine of justification 'entirely on the lines of a scheme handed down to him by his school'.[7] Resemblances, however, may certainly be discerned. Occam was perhaps impressed, as Luther was, with the inadequacy of medieval notions of grace. But instead of revising the old notion, he set a new one side by side with it. He contented himself with saying that God *could, if He wished,* grant eternal life without sanctifying grace or works of merit: man could be justified simply by God's 'accepting' him (*a sola divina acceptatione*), his sins no longer being imputed. Occam 'understood forgiveness of sins no more to mean the infusion of the substance of righteousness into man, but held that it signified merely the non-imputation of sin to man'.[8] But we should not

---

[1] Again, see TR. no. 2191; also 3. 230. 21, 30. In 4, no. 5082b, the definition of faith by means of the four causes is extremely interesting, for Luther did not often give a formal definition of this, or any other, basic soteriological term.

[2] TR. 2. 555. 28, 557. 13; cf. 4. 647. 21: even the simple 'rustic' can understand a definition by means of the four causes!

[3] TR. 2. 556. 4, 557. 19; 4. 383. 1.

[4] TR. 2. 556. 1, 557. 16.

[5] TR. 4. 647. 9 (no. 5082b). The whole of this *Tischrede* is of interest for Luther's attitude towards dialectic, since he both describes its content and illustrates its use.

[6] TR. 4. 648. 3: the allusion is to Rom. xii. 7–8, where Paul distinguishes the gifts of 'teaching' and of 'exhortation'. 'There's dialectic and rhetoric for you!'

[7] Op. cit. 1. 155. I am indebted to Grisar for his account of Occam's views on justification.

[8] Boehmer, *Luther in Light of Recent Research*, p. 90.

forget that according to Luther, though *man* needed to do nothing for justification, this was only because *Christ* had already done all. The basis for Occam's (and Scotus's) theories of acceptation was 'voluntarism', God's power to do anything He chose, save what would involve a contradiction. Luther's understanding of justification, on the other hand, rested upon 'atonement'; hence he can speak, not only of 'non-imputation', but also of the 'imputation of Christ's righteousness', a notion quite foreign to Occam. Besides, Occam never did actually throw out the medieval conception of justification by grace, though he hardly knew what to do with it.[1] Again we are impressed with Luther's capacity to modify whatever he received.

Luther expressly acknowledges his debt to Nominalist teachings on (4) the Sacrament of the Lord's Supper.[2] It was from reading D'Ailly rather than Occam himself that Luther became convinced of the error of 'Transubstantiation'. But D'Ailly closely followed the master at this point.[3] Once more, Luther went beyond the Nominalists in embracing an opinion which they *would* have preferred *if* it were not contrary to the plain teaching of the Church (*nisi Ecclesia determinasset contrarium*). The elements are not transformed into Christ's body and blood: rather the body and blood are present in and with the bread and wine.[4]

In the same passage of the *Babylonian Captivity* in which Luther acknowledges his debt to the Nominalist understanding of the Sacrament another debt goes unnoticed, namely (5), to the Nominalist stress on Biblical authority. Here Luther pens the celebrated words: 'Whatever is asserted without Scripture or approved revelation may be held as an opinion, but need not be believed.'[5] Yet, once more, it is not hard to discern how far Luther here goes beyond the Nominalists; for the limiting factor of ecclesiastical authority is swept away, and the Bible rules alone.

---

[1] Luther 'quotes Occam in such a way as to represent him as teaching as a fact what he merely held to be possible'. Grisar, op. cit. 1. 157. But is 'quotes' strictly accurate? Cf. esp. W.A. 10[1, 1]. 468 f.

[2] *De Captivi ate Babylonica*: W.A. 6. 508. 7 ff.

[3] See Birch's preface to the *De sacramento altaris* of Occam, pp. xxiii ff.

[4] A doctrine of 'impanation' is, of course, found as early as the eleventh century: the suggestion was not new in the Nominalists. Seeberg, *Textbook of the History of Doctrines*, II. 75.

[5] W.A. 6. 508. 19.

Even this select list of parallels between Luther and the
Nominalists is impressive, though by no means exhaustive.[1]
Strangely perhaps, there is no evidence that Luther was influenced by Occam's anti-papal writings: apparently he did not
even read them until after the Reformation had begun.[2] The
brand of Nominalism in which he was originally trained came
through the 'Gabrielists', and Gabriel Biel is claimed as soundly
orthodox in his attitude towards the Papacy.[3] With these
parallels in mind, we can now turn to the question: How far
was Luther a debtor to the Occamists' understanding of 'faith
and reason'?

Faith, reason, and twofold truth[4]

The confidence of the Schoolmen in the capabilities of reason
was at its height in the eleventh and twelfth centuries. Anselm
(1033–1109) seemed sure of his ability to demonstrate, by appeal
to reason alone, the truth even of the Church's belief in the
Incarnation and the Atonement.[5] But in the thirteenth century
we find Albert the Great (1193–1280) drawing a distinction
between what may be known by reason without faith and what
may be known only by faith. The separation between faith and
reason, widened in St. Thomas,[6] really contains in embryo the
Nominalist doctrine that a statement may be true in philosophy
and false in theology: Thomas's 'twofold way of truth' made
possible Holcot's 'double truth', though, of course, the latter is
not logically inferable from the former. Once the distinction
between the spheres of faith and of reason was established, the
tendency was to reduce the overlap until the two were almost

[1] Further possible borrowings of Luther from Nominalism will be found in
Boehmer, *Luther in Light of Recent Research*, p. 88, and Rupp, *The Righteousness of
God*, pp. 88 ff.
[2] Rupp, op. cit., p. 88: see the refs. to the *Table-Talk* in n. 3.
[3] C. Ruch, article 'Biel', *Dict. théol. cath.*, vol. II[1]: Biel was a model of 'doctrinal
orthodoxy' (col. 817), and he was never 'anti-papal' (col. 818).
[4] In the following discussion I am especially indebted to Heim's 'Zur Geschichte
des Satzes von der doppelten Wahrheit' (see Bibliography); also to Hägglund, op.
cit., pp. 87–102. Cf. Heim, *Das Gewißheitsproblem*, ch. xi.
[5] See esp. the preface to *Cur Deus Homo?* 'Leaving Christ out of view (as if nothing
had ever been known of him), it [sc. the first book of the *Cur Deus Homo?*] proves,
by absolute reasons, the impossibility that any man should be saved without him.'
S. N. Deane's translation, p. 177.
[6] For Thomas's views on faith and reason the *locus classicus* is, of course, chs.
iii–viii of the *Summa contra Gentiles*, Bk. I. In Pegis's translation, pp. 63–76.

completely self-contained and the truths of faith were totally
inaccessible to reason: they could, indeed, even be opposed to
reason, since their certainty rested solely upon the authority of
the Church and the Scriptures. This is the point at which Occam
(c. 1280–c. 1349) arrived in the fourteenth century.

Our concern here is not, of course, with Occam's philosophy
as a whole, but only with his teaching on the competence of
reason in matters of religious belief. For Occam, without doubt,
the sole adequate ground for belief is authority. His faith is the
Catholic Faith: whatever the Roman Church explicitly believes,
this alone, and nothing else, he believes either explicitly or
implicitly.[1] It is certainly rash, indeed dangerous, to hold a
belief which reason judges false, but not if the belief rests upon
the authority of Scripture, the Roman Church, or the 'approved
doctors'.[2] But this cannot be construed as a fundamental distrust of reason. On the contrary, the famous principle which
we call 'Occam's razor' was, rightly understood, a powerful
affirmation of reason's capabilities. For essentially it is a
'principle of sufficient reason'. We must not affirm the truth
of a statement or the existence of an object unless we are forced
to do so by reason, observation, or authority.[3] The principle is
epistemological rather than ontological.

This perplexing attempt to exalt reason without undermining
authority underlies Occam's discussions on the possibility of
natural theology. He loses no opportunity to criticize Duns
Scotus's proof for the existence of God, since the impossibility
of an infinite regress is not easily demonstrated.[4] The existence
of one God is beyond the kind of demonstration which affords
scientific knowledge in the strictest sense. This does not mean
that His existence is at all improbable. Such articles of belief as
the existence of one God and the immortality of the soul are
certainly more probable than their contraries. Occam's point

[1] De sacramento altaris (ed. Birch), p. 164.
[2] Ibid., p. 126. Note the phrase (line 5), 'probare per rationem evidentem vel per
auctoritatem sacrae scripturae', which is so reminiscent of Luther's utterance at
Worms.
[3] Ibid., p. 318.
[4] In I. Sent., d. 11, q. 5. Cited in De Wulf's History of Mediaeval Philosophy, II. 184.
Cf. the passage from the Centiloquium translated in Tornay's Ockham, pp. 188–95.
Philotheus Boehner argued in the Franciscan Studies for 1941 that the Centiloquium is
spurious: see pp. 58 ff. Boehner gives the Latin text in several instalments; ibid.,
1941–2.

simply is that they cannot be proved demonstratively. Fundamentally, the distinction made is between two kinds of argument,
the strictly demonstrative and the merely probable (or persuasive
or dialectical). In two places, indeed, Occam does appear to
offer what purports to be a demonstrative proof of God's
existence.[1] But, in the main, as Boehner observes, Occam 'seems
to have been interested rather in showing how much it is *not*
possible to demonstrate'.[2] God's unity, for instance, is beyond
demonstration, although it may be shown to be probable. The
question whether it can be demonstrated that God exists,
depends partly on what you mean by 'God': if Occam does
sometimes seem convinced of the existence of God by unaided
reason, he makes it quite clear that he means by 'God' only the
First Cause of the cosmological argument.[3] The 'One Lord' of
the Christian Faith he asserts without any ambiguity to be
beyond proof. 'An article of faith cannot be proved demonstratively.'[4] And, of course, the doctrine of the Trinity is still further
removed from reason's competence, whilst God may, if He so
will, act even *against* reason.[5]

Occam's views on the indemonstrability of God are closely
bound up with his general epistemological position, and into
this wider question we cannot here inquire in detail. Suffice it
to say that the denial of the philosopher's ability to prove
evidently or demonstratively that God exists followed inevitably

---

[1] In the *Ordinatio* and *Questions on Physics*; see Boehner, *Ockham: Philosophical
Writings*, p. xliii; the proof from the *Questions on Physics* is given on pp. 115 ff. in
Latin and English.

[2] *Ockham: Philosophical Writings*, p. xlv.

[3] And even the notion of 'First Cause' is modified, for reason says that we must
argue from conservation to Conserver rather than from product to Producer.

[4] *Quodlibeta*, I, q. 1; text and translation, in Boehner's *Ockham: Phil. Writings*,
pp. 125–26. In the light of this passage it seems clear that both de Wulf (op. cit.)
and Gilson (*Reason and Revelation*, pp. 86–87) are misleading in their unqualified
assertion that the existence of God is, for Occam, beyond demonstrative proof. De
Wulf, indeed, commits the academic sin of citing out of context: 'Non potest sciri
evidenter quod Deus est'. Occam immediately adds the words (omitted by de Wulf):
sic accipiendo Deum; and he goes on to show that we can prove God's existence
demonstratively if we understand by 'God': 'that than which nothing is more noble
and more perfect'. Gilson's account in *Christian Philosophy in the Middle Ages* does
take note of the two sides of Occam's teaching on the demonstrability of God (see
esp. p. 497). Also valuable is Copleston's discussion, *Hist. Phil.* III. 80 ff. Other
works dealing with Occam's views on faith and reason are mentioned in Guelluy,
Philosophie et théologie chez Guillaume d'Ockham, pp. 17 ff.

[5] See Birch's introduction to the *De sacramento altaris*, p. xxvi.

from Occam's fundamental epistemological premisses. All knowledge, he believed, is based on experience. What he calls 'intuitive knowledge' embraces only immediate sense-perception and introspection: it serves only as the basis for judgements concerning the existence or attributes of sensible particulars. Experience, in fact, is defined too narrowly to serve as foundation for a religious apologetic, so that the only way to a 'natural' (that is, not revealed) knowledge of the Creator lies through knowledge of the creatures, and Occam was a sharp enough logician to see the weaknesses of this sort of argument.

To sum up, Vignaux is apparently right when he finds in Occam's teaching on the knowledge of God three 'zones' which are removed progressively farther and farther from reason's competence.[1] (1) The world is a totality of things, of which some are dependent for their existence and preservation upon others. To avoid an infinite regress, we have to posit a finite number of causes and a first cause which is itself uncaused. This first cause is the most perfect being in the world, but we cannot prove that it (or he) is one. Thus far reason goes with its natural capacities. (2) That there is only one God, is a matter of belief. But by building upon the God of faith reason can, by inference, make further statements about His nature.[2] (3) But as for the Trinity, here reason is perplexed. Once it has appreciated the simplicity of the divine nature, reason in no wise comprehends the possibility of the plurality of Persons: left to itself, it declares such a thing absolutely impossible.

The broad similarity of this position with Luther's is not difficult to perceive. Occam's slogan (if we may call it such) is the sentence: 'An article of faith cannot be proved demonstratively.' Articles of faith are beyond natural reason. But did Luther teach the doctrine of 'double truth', attributed to Robert of Holcot, Occam's disciple?[3] According to Denifle, Occam prepared the way for the thesis which was formulated in his own lifetime by Holcot: 'A proposition may be false in theology and true in philosophy, and *vice versa*.'[4] Holcot even began a search

---

[1] Article 'Nominalisme' in the *Dictionnaire de théologie cath.* XI[1], col. 782.

[2] 'Posé le Dieu de la foi, voici ce que la raison conclut en le considérant. . . .'

[3] For Robert Holcot, the Cambridge Dominican, see esp. Gilson, *Christian Phil. in the Middle Ages*, pp. 500 ff.; Copleston, op. cit. III. 122 ff.; Hauréau, *Hist. de la phil. scholastique*, II[2]. 434 ff.

[4] '. . . Es könne etwas theologisch falsch und philosophisch wahr sein und

for what he called a *logica fidei*—a new 'logic of faith'—apparently believing that the rules of philosophical logic simply did not apply in matters of theology. It is impossible for us to form any notion of the content of such a logic, since Holcot's quest never took him very far.

In his disputation concerning the proposition, 'The Word was made flesh', Luther clearly defends a position very close to Holcot's 'double truth'.[1] It is not necessary to discuss the disputation in detail.[2] Luther's intention is, indeed, quite clear in the first half-dozen theses alone. Although it is to be held that two truths never contradict each other (*omne verum vero consonat*), yet the same proposition is not true in different disciplines ('idem non est verum in diversis professionibus'). Hence, the proposition, 'The Word was made flesh', is true in theology, but quite impossible and absurd in philosophy. The Sorbonne, therefore, 'that mother of errors', is disastrously mistaken in asserting that the same thing is true in philosophy and theology: this would be to enslave the articles of faith to the judgement of human reason. And in thesis eight Luther goes on to say that, according to Paul's teaching, it is the intellect (including philosophy) which must be brought into captivity in the service of Christ. Rational inferences from theological premisses may be dialectically valid, and yet theologically the conclusions may be false.[3] Even within philosophy itself ('philosophy' being taken as the inclusive name for all rational disciplines) what is true in one science may not be true in another.[4] Strictly speaking, Luther sees no *contradiction* between the deliverances of philosophy and of theology:[5] it is simply that philosophical categories and techniques are not *applicable* in theological matters. To confuse the two is like asking the weight of a line or the length of a pound; it is to put new wine in old wineskins.[6]

---

umgekehrt' (op. cit. 1. 609). Denifle also mentions Petrus Pomponatius of Padua (who was tainted with Averroism) as an advocate of the 'double truth' theory. Heim traces the notion of 'double truth' back to Averroes—and even earlier, to Neoplatonism (op. cit.).

[1] 'Disputatio de sententia: Verbum caro factum est' (W.A. 39². 3–33); Jan. 1539.
[2] Both Heim and Hägglund make much of it. Cf. also the remarks of Cranz on the Promotion-Disputation of Palladius and Tilemann, op. cit., pp. 66 f.
[3] This is illustrated by various arguments, couched in syllogistic form, in theses 16–26; e.g.: 'Omnis caro est creatura. Verbum est caro. Ergo verbum est creatura' (no. 24).   [4] Theses 29–39.   [5] Cf. thesis 21.
[6] Theses 31–32, 41. It is in this sense that we should understand the assault on

The resemblance of this viewpoint to Holcot's is apparent, without our going into the disputation which Luther based upon these theses, and it can hardly be accidental that both Luther and Holcot stood in the Occamist tradition. Luther even seems to suggest (in thesis 27) that theology needs 'another dialectic', which reminds us of Holcot's *logica fidei*; but, for Luther, the other dialectic 'is named the Word of God and faith'. It would, however, be a mistake to lay too much emphasis upon this side of Luther's thought. It is, indeed, the logical outcome of the divorce between theology and philosophy, succinctly expressed in the words cited already from the disputation which follows the theses: 'Philosophy and theology are different. Philosophy has to do with what can be known by human reason. Theology has to do with what can be believed, that is, with what is apprehended by faith.' But, as will be shown in Part II, Luther's thought also takes another line which owes nothing to Occamism, unless by reaction against it.

In conclusion, what we know of Luther's education, both in the university and in the monastery, inclines us to suppose that his own thinking must have been strongly influenced—at least, in the beginning—by the distinctive doctrines of Nominalism; and this supposition can, in some measure, be confirmed by noting several of Luther's opinions which show close resemblances, sometimes even verbal resemblances, to opinions of Occam, D'Ailly, and Biel. There is, then, no need for surprise if Luther was also influenced by the *moderni* in the special area of thought which immediately concerns us. The sharp division between the spheres of faith and of reason had certainly been made by Occam, and Luther may have inherited the master's general attitude at this point. But two words of caution need to be added before proceeding.

First, even if we allow the possibility of Occam's influencing Luther's attitude towards faith and reason, just how illuminating is this conclusion supposed to be? Without doubt, the question is of historical interest; but if we merely conclude that Luther was an 'ossified Occamite', we are still left with the

mathematics which appears later (in the disputation proper: W.A. 39². 22. 1). Luther would not have us jettison mathematics: his point is that the doctrine of the Trinity is inaccessible to the mathematician. 'Mathematica est inimicissima omnino theologiae, quia nulla est pars philosophiae, quae tam pugnat contra theologiam.'

problem why Luther was the man who started a Reformation, not Occam, or D'Ailly, or Biel. It will surely be more important, in the long run, to see where Luther *differed from* Occam. J. Paquier suggests that Occamism manifested two fundamental characteristics: concerning everything that had to do with intelligence, it was pessimistic, sceptical, destructive; concerning all that is related to the will, it was optimistic and semi-rationalistic.[1] Very roughly, it was the former characteristic which influenced Luther positively; against the latter he reacted violently, as the theses *Against Scholastic Theology* (1517) and the *Heidelberg Disputation* (1518) make particularly obvious.[2] For in the matter of soteriology Occam's 'optimism concerning the will' led him into what the Roman Catholics, no less than Protestants, consider semi-Pelagianism. Suppose, then, that we grant Luther's debt to Occam in epistemology: it would still be absurd to call him an Occamite, for in the questions which most deeply concerned him he was vehemently opposed to Occam.[3]

Second, even in the problem of faith and reason Luther is not an Occamite *simpliciter*, so that to draw attention to the similarities may be thoroughly misleading. For what happens in Luther's own distinctive theological development is that his acceptance of Occam's limitations upon reason and his attack on Occam's exaltation of free will tend to merge in a single charge which places him squarely against the advocates of the *via moderna*. The epistemological problem ('How do we know God?') becomes subordinate to the soteriological problem ('What must I do to be saved?'), and the repudiation of reason is transformed into a flat denial of one kind of answer to the

[1] Article 'Luther', in *Dict. théol. cath.* IX[1], col. 1251.
[2] As Vignaux points out, it was the *Disputatio contra schol. theol.* that enabled Holl to protest against Denifle's understanding of Luther as an Occamite: see Vignaux, 'Sur Luther et Occam', *Franziskanische Studien*, XXXII (1950), 21. Vignaux's article is mainly a detailed discussion of theses 57 and 94.
[3] In his recent article, 'Was Luther a Nominalist?' (*Concordia Theological Monthly*, 1957), Hägglund points out that, although the Nominalists drastically reduced the number of theological propositions that are accessible to reason, they still believed that the truths of revelation, once established, become fitting objects for the scrutiny of reason. In so far as this was the supposition behind the Nominalist *logica fidei*, Luther opposed it. 'The idea of a logic of faith assumes that the mysteries of faith can be enclosed within the rules of rational thinking' (p. 451). The point is that for Luther the problem of reason was basically theological: he is concerned, not merely with the fact that natural reason cannot reach certain supernatural truths, but also that 'human reason is blinded by original sin' (p. 449).

question of man's salvation. 'Reason', in fact, is identified with just that attitude of mind which seeks to exalt the moral and religious capabilities of the human will as the instrument of man's salvation, so that by a strange turn in the argument Luther finds himself attacking reason in characteristic Nominalist style precisely in order to destroy the other characteristic of Nominalist thought, its optimism concerning the powers of the human will. In short, Luther's attack on reason, even if it began as an inheritance from Nominalism, finally ended as an assault upon the Nominalists and all who shared with them a vain reliance upon man's natural capacities. How a Nominalist doctrine came to be pressed into the service of Augustinianism, is the question to which we must now turn.

PART II

REASON AND THEOLOGY

IV

LUTHER'S *COMMENTARY ON GALATIANS*

I N this section (the central part of our essay) the same problem
will be approached by a somewhat different method.
Hunting up incidental references to 'reason' from works
written by Luther at many different periods of his life and on
widely different topics is, to be sure, an indispensable part of the
inquiry. But it cannot be the whole of it. What is required now
is to set Luther's understanding of *ratio-Vernunft* within the
framework of his religious thought as a whole. Of course, this
does not mean that every little corner of his theology has to be
explored. But it does mean that we must try to relate Luther's
concept of reason to his dominant interests, to his most characteristic ideas—in fact, to those fundamental *motifs* which organize
his several teachings into a unity. It is often alleged that Luther
was unsystematic to the point of muddle-headedness, so that
the task which I have set myself may seem impossible. It is
true that he was not a system-builder in the same way, or to the
same extent, that Calvin was: like Paul, Luther was an 'occasional' writer. Yet there is without any doubt a certain pattern
of thought which recurs again and again in Luther's writings—
'frequently and almost *ad nauseam*', as he himself admits. It is
the notion of 'justifying faith' which holds his diverse utterances
together. Luther's thought is (as Sydney Cave has rightly
observed) an 'immense reduction, a concentration on the one
article of saving faith in Christ'.[1] Frequently Luther speaks of

---

[1] *The Person of Christ*, p. 139.

the regulative importance of the *iustificatio sola fide*: 'The article
of justification is master and head, lord, governor, and judge
over all the various branches of doctrines: it preserves and
directs all the church's doctrine, and it raises up our conscience
before God.'[1] And this is really the same as to say that the
conception of justifying *faith* is the regulative factor, since it is
(in Luther's own judgement)[2] the character of faith that determines the understanding of justification. Luther's diverse
teachings, then, do have a certain kind of unity, just as (so
Einar Billing suggests) the petals of a rose grow out from a
common centre. It is with this 'common centre' that we have
to do: Billing calls it the 'forgiveness of sins', and Luther's own
term was 'justification by faith alone'. As Billing rightly insists,
we have not fully understood a Lutheran idea until we have
shown it as 'a simple corollary' of this central doctrine. This is,
as we will show, not less true of 'reason' than of any other
Lutheran idea.[3]

Our problem, therefore, is the 'problem of faith and reason'.
And yet it will immediately appear that in many respects the
associations which this expression brings before our minds are
utterly remote from Luther's own thinking: at most, they are
secondary. For Luther's concern was with *justifying* faith—
faith, not as a mode of cognition, but as the *organon leptikon* of
salvation. True, he relates faith to reason, just as we do, but
when his thoughts are moving (as they generally are) within
the circle of ideas associated with justification, both his notion
of faith and his notion of reason are quite different from what
we ourselves usually have in mind when *we* speak of the
'problem of faith and reason'. His notion of faith transfers
us from the critical and epistemological sphere (in which for
years past theological and philosophical inquiries into the
problem of religious faith have commonly moved) into the
sphere of soteriology (which virtually circumscribed Luther's
own thinking).

Luther's *Commentary on Galatians* of 1535 (revised, 1538) has
been selected as a text on which to base the argument. The text

---

[1] W.A. 39¹. 205. 2 ff.

[2] 'Quod autem aliqui non intelligunt, quomodo sola fides iustificat, in causa est,
quod quid fides sit non cognoverint' (W.A. 6. 94. 7).

[3] See Introduction (above), p. 8, n. 2, where reference has already been made to
Billing's 'rule'.

is to be found (in Latin) in volume 40, parts one and two, of the Weimar edition.[1] An English translation appeared in 1575, with a foreword by the Bishop of London, and in 1577 it was 'diligently revised, corrected, and newly imprinted againe'. It went through many printings and revisions. One, however, virtually superseded all others: the so-called 'Middleton edition', which took its name from 'the Rev. Erasmus Middleton, B.D., Rector of Turvey, Bedfordshire', who furnished biographical and historical prefaces to a version published in 1807. Concerning the translators of the original sixteenth-century version—'certaine godly learned men', as the Bishop of London calls them in his foreword—we know very little.

They refuse to be named, seeking neither their own gaine nor glorie, but thinking it their happinesse, if by any meanes they may releeue afflicted minds, and do good to the Church of Christ, yeelding all glorie to God, to whom all glorie is due.

In 1845 'the Rev. John Owen' produced an entirely new translation, which, however, failed to compete with the older work and was never reprinted. In 1939 Th. Graebner tried to make Luther 'talk American' in a modern 'streamlined' version; but even those who fall for the racy style will regret Graebner's free use of the editorial knife. The best translation available, no doubt, is P. S. Watson's recent revision of the Middleton edition.[2]

The original Middleton edition was in many respects an unsatisfactory translation. It is sometimes inaccurate, usually verbose, and occasionally selective (according to the translators' own sympathies). On the last matter the translators confess to a little 'sponging out', mainly where Luther 'differeth somewhat from Zuinglius'. But they are big-hearted enough to add: 'Let us not be so nice for one little wart to cast away the whole bodie.' Some of the other omissions in the English translation are interesting. That the translators decided to leave out the curious digression *de fascino* ('concerning witchcraft'), is understandable: however entertaining to the sophisticated modern, it hardly

---

[1] *In Epistolam S. Pauli ad Galatas Commentarius ex praelectione D. Martini Lutheri (1531) collectus, 1535*, edited and revised by A. Freitag and with a foreword by R. Drescher.

[2] 'A revised and completed translation based on the "Middleton" edition of the English version of 1575' (London: James Clarke and Co. Ltd., 1953).

shows Luther at his best.[1] Understandable also is the refusal to
include the comment on Gal. ii. 6: 'It is a light fault in the Holy
Spirit if he offends a little against the grammar.'[2] And the
translators must have considered it not far short of blasphemous
when they found: 'If the devil scourge me, I have a stronger
devil [sc. Christ], who will scourge him in his turn.'[3] Most
allusions to previous commentators are cut out—possibly
because nearly all of them are disparaging, not to say con-
temptuous.[4] One passage is left out because it seems to doubt
the inerrancy of the Scriptures.[5] Other omissions are extremely
hard to explain, and this has led Watson to suggest that the
translation may have been made from a defective version.[6] It
is not necessary for our purposes to speak further about this
here. But there are other objections to the translation also. It
is not always strictly accurate, partly because of its very wordi-
ness. Its language is, naturally, antiquated.[7] Sometimes it is
very free, to say the least; as, for instance, when *missis, vigiliis,
&c.* is rendered by 'masses, diriges, trentals *and such trash*'—a
translation which Luther himself might have approved on the
grounds that the 'sense' is in the original, but which would
certainly strike the rest of us as an unjustifiable reflection of the
translators' prejudices.[8] And, of course, more serious departures
from the Latin could be pointed out.[9]

The omissions are translated in P. S. Watson's revised version,
and some corrections are made. Further, Watson offers a new
rendering of Luther's own preface. Nevertheless, in spite of
Watson's case for 'retaining the style of the Elizabethan translators', I have ventured to offer my own renderings and, where

---

[1] Translated in Watson's version, pp. 189 ff.

[2] Ibid., p. 102. Cf. p. 143: 'The Holy Spirit does not observe the strict rules of
grammar.'   [3] Ibid., p. 166.

[4] For example, ibid., pp. 74, 81, 85–87, &c.   [5] Ibid., p. 74.

[6] Ibid., p. 4. Why ever, for instance, leave out: 'Christ is the Son of God, which
of mere love gave himself for redemption'? See ibid., p. 178.

[7] Cf., for example, the gem on p. 500 of Watson's version: 'I was in the wild
wilderness, which being burnt up with the heat of the sun, *yieldeth an ouglesome
habitation* to the monks.' My italics.   [8] Ibid., p. 549.

[9] W.A. 40[1]. 78. 16, for example, reads: 'Nullum Deum scito extra istum hominem
Iesum Christum.' The E.T. has: 'Know thou *that there* is no other God *besides* this
man Christ Jesus' (Watson's edn., p. 43; italics mine). Yet there is no *esse* in the
Latin, and the natural significance of *extra* would be 'outside of'. Luther's meaning,
therefore, is strictly: 'Know no God outside of that man Jesus Christ.' That is to say,
the one true God can only be known in (or through) the manhood of Jesus.

the exact meaning seemed crucial, I have appended the Latin version in a footnote or in parentheses.

The merits and demerits of the *Commentary on Galatians* as a selected text must be carefully weighed. Problems of 'higher criticism' are dealt with by the editor of the Weimar edition in his introduction to the text and in various notes scattered throughout the text itself. An excellent editorial preface was also furnished by Watson to his revision of the Middleton translation.

The argument *against* using the *Commentary on Galatians* as a principal foundation for a discussion of Luther's theology is that in its present form it comes, not from his own pen, but from lecture-notes taken by his students. The claim of the earlier English translators that the Commentary was 'collected and gathered *word by word* out of his preaching' is (regrettably) inaccurate, even if we overlook the minor point that the exegesis was delivered in the classroom, not from the pulpit.[1] The Commentary was based upon notes taken by Luther's students during a course of forty-one lectures, which were delivered at Wittenberg from 3 July to 11 December 1531. Since Luther did not lecture from a full manuscript, but from marginal annotations ('glosses') in his own copy of the text and from more extended comments ('scholia') written into a notebook, he could not have given his pupils much in the way of assisting materials when they undertook to prepare their notes for the press. The preface and the commentary on Gal. v. 6 are the only parts which come directly from manuscripts of Luther's own.[2] How little care Luther took in planning the course or in preparing an outline of his lectures is apparent from the candid confession with which he began his lecture on 9 October: 'Ego oblitus sum.' He had quite forgotten where he had left off at the conclusion of the previous lecture.[3]

[1] Still, the English translators were not so grossly misleading as the publishers of the American printing of Watson's revision: 'This is the *complete* commentary', announces the blurb on the dust-cover, 'just as it came from Martin Luther's pen'. And again: '. . . Luther set it down in letters of flame and fearless devotion'.

[2] W.A. 40[1]. 33 ff. and 40[2]. 34 ff. The latter is from a sermon by Luther on *fides per charitatem efficax*.

[3] W.A. 40[1]. 530. 6. The Weimar editor offers this explanation: 'Er seit dem 26. September die Vorlesung hatte ruhen lassen.' In the meantime he had been preoccupied with his Michaelmas preaching and with his work on the prophets.

On the other hand, to consider now the case *for* using the *Commentary on Galatians*, Luther had a special affection for the Epistle itself and he also ranked his expositions of it above most of his other works.[1] Curiously (as it no doubt seems to us), it was the Psalms to which Luther returned most frequently for inspiration—the 'Bible in miniature', as he sometimes called them. It was in all likelihood one of the Psalms which he was expounding when he made his 'rediscovery of the Gospel'. Luther never lets us quite forget that he was once a 'Catholic'—and indeed a monk—whose daily meditations had for years been drawn from the Psalter. Yet it remains true that he confessed to a particular affection for St. Paul's letter to the Galatians: 'I am wedded to it; it is my Katie von Bora!' as he jocularly exclaimed.[2] And he lectured on the epistle more than once.[3]

But there is a far more important reason for taking the *Commentary on Galatians* as our main text: because of the content both of the Pauline epistle and of Luther's comments on it. For the theme of the epistle is what Luther again and again called 'the main point of Christian doctrine', namely, 'that we are justified by faith in Christ, without any works of the law'.[4] The *Commentary on Galatians* is probably the fullest of the works in which Luther puts forward his understanding of the Pauline vocabulary of salvation: 'faith', 'works', 'justification', and so on. And it is by no means accidental that in this same work the term *ratio* is employed well over two hundred times. For the proper context for Luther's conception of reason is precisely the theological controversy over faith and works. The *Commentary on Galatians*, then, is an appropriate text for three reasons: because Luther had a special affection for it, because it contains so rich a supply of references to 'reason', and because it sets the term within its proper context.

Of course, the problem of authenticity cannot be evaded. But it is not so alarming as one could imagine. Nothing is said

---

[1] W.A. 40¹. 2: editor's introduction.   [2] Ibid.

[3] The so-called 'Shorter Commentary' (to contrast it with the Commentary of 1535) was published in 1519 and a revised edn. appeared in 1523.

[4] The citation is from the *Open Letter on Translating*, P.E. v. 20. But of course Luther's writings are full of sayings which exalt the *articulus stantis et cadentis ecclesiae* above all others. In the present work see esp. W.A. 40¹. 33. 7: 'Nam in corde meo iste unus regnat articulus, scilicet Fides Christi, ex quo, per quem et in quem omnes meae diu noctuque fluunt et refluunt theologicae cogitationes.' Cf. also: 39. 10 and 24, &c.

in the *Commentary on Galatians* which could not be found else-where in Luther's writings, although in no other single writing is the whole matter put together so completely and so forcefully. Besides, those responsible for its production were reliable wit-nesses. The principal recorder was George Rörer, whose reputa-tion as an amanuensis ranks high. It was he who took the minutes at the meeting of Luther's commission for revising the Witten-berg Bible, and his notes on these occasions have stood the test of scholarly criticism. He had cultivated a private method of shorthand writing, which enabled him to take down notes at an extremely quick rate, so quick, in fact, that he frequently made slips in his spelling.[1] Occasionally he makes an error of a more material kind, although still, very palpably, a mere slip due to his eagerness to put everything down, missing nothing.[2] Rörer's manuscript does, in fact, read just like the report of a conscien-tious secretary. Fortunately, the manuscript has survived and is printed in the Weimar edition at the top of the page, with the Commentary of 1535 immediately underneath. It can, I believe, be assumed that we have in Rörer's manuscript something very close to Luther's own words. And our confidence is streng-thened when we recall that many of Luther's glosses must have been dictated (according to his usual custom) and that Rörer, in preparing his MS. for the press, had the assistance of others who had also heard the lectures. In particular, he received some assistance from Veit Dietrich, one of the most reliable reporters of Luther's *Table-Talk*, and still more from Caspar Cruciger, who evidently read Rörer's MS. carefully and made comments in the margin, which also are recorded in the 'critical apparatus' of the Weimar edition.[3] We can, then, understand how Luther was able to judge of the finished work: 'All the thoughts which I find expressed in this volume through the diligent labours of the brethren, I perceive to be my own.'[4]

The Commentary itself is, to be sure, considerably fuller

---

[1] 'Bei schwierigen Worten verschreibt sich Rörer oft,' as the Weimar editor comments on one obvious error (W.A. 40^1. 286. 9).

[2] For example, he writes (W.A. 40^1. 669. 6): 'Amissio felix, quando amitto legem et gratiam.' Clearly some such word as *retineo* has been left out before *gratiam*.

[3] In a letter to Bullinger (*Corpus Reformatorum*, x. 142) Bucer says that the Com-mentary was *exceptus per Caspar. Crucigerum*. But this is probably not quite accurate. See W.A. 40^1. 1–2.

[4] 'Sentio meas cogitationes esse omnes, quas in hoc scripto per fratres tanta diligentia signatas reperio' (W.A. 40^1. 33. 3).

than Rörer's MS., so that in following the Commentary rather than the MS. one increases the possibility of departing from Luther's actual words. Of course, in some respects the Commentary is an improvement, since Rörer's errors are corrected.[1] But the main motive for following the Commentary in preference to the MS. is that the Commentary (as we would only expect) makes smoother and more continuous reading. On the other hand, I have preferred the 1535 edition to the edition of 1538 (on which the English translation was based), because the revised version is almost certainly a step away from the Reformer's *ipsissima verba*.[2] So, then, my citations are mainly from the edition of 1535: not from Rörer's MS., because it is less connected and flowing, nor from the revision of 1538, because it is very probably farther from Luther's own words. Nevertheless, I have hesitated to make use of any passages from the Commentary which cannot be paralleled on Rörer's MS.[3] Further, I have not hesitated to use the expression 'Luther says so-and-so', in spite of the difficulties to which we have alluded.

It would, of course, be intolerably tedious to discuss in turn every reference Luther makes to *ratio* in the Commentary: there are, if my calculations are correct, about 230 references in the

[1] *Amitto legem et gratiam*, for instance, was changed to: *Lege amissa gratiam retinemus*. See p. 63, n. 2 above.

[2] The points at which the revision departed from the first printing are recorded in the footnotes of the Weimar edition, the symbols C, D, E being used to designate the three main printings of the revised version. It is clear that very few, if any, of the changes were made in the interests of more faithfully recovering Luther's original utterances. Some (perhaps most) are introduced for stylistic reasons; some (the *Überschriften*, for instance) for clarity's sake; and some to avoid giving offence to the Zwinglians. See, for example, W.A. 40[1]. 249. 10. The 1535 edn. has 'Papists, Zwinglians, Anabaptists'; the 1538 edn. has only 'Papists'. One or two other alterations are made for special reasons: for example, a passage in which Staupitz was apparently identified with Luther's position is carefully reworded in the new edition. W.A. 40[1]. 131. 23. The 1st edn. has Staupitz saying: *haec doctrina nostra*. The 2nd has: *doctrina quam praedicas*.

[3] As often as possible a double reference is given: e.g. 'W.A. 40[1]. 85. 6 and 21' would refer to Rörer's MS. (at the top part of the page in the Weimar edn.) and also to the Commentary underneath. 'Rörer's MS.' will henceforth be abbreviated to 'RM'. In the matter of orthography I have generally followed the Weimar edn.: hence I have written *charitas* for *caritas*. But the Latin is by no means consistent in matters of spelling or capitalization. In a single sentence the word for 'righteousness' may be found spelled in two different ways, e.g. W.A. 40[2]. 7. 16: '[Ratio] longe praefert iusticiam legis iustitiae fidei.' I have also adopted the Weimar editor's forms in citing Rörer's MS.: I have not reproduced Rörer's shorthand.

1535 edition and about 135 in Rörer's MS.[1] I have contented myself with classifying all the references, then speaking only about the more important ones in each class. As a general principle I have been shy of ambiguous uses, and have based no part of my argument upon them. Classification is close to falsification, but it is necessary if order and clarity are to be attained; and to be aware of the dangers is to be at least half-secure.

The Latin word *ratio* does, of course, have a great variety of meanings, and sometimes Luther's usage is not directly concerned with anything that we could translate by 'reason'. There are also a few 'border-line' uses as well: as, for instance, when *ratio* stands for an 'argument' brought forward to demonstrate a point, and not for the faculty of the human mind which produces or excogitates such arguments. These senses of the word should at least be mentioned, not only for the sake of completeness, but also to illustrate the flexibility of the Latin word: if anything, the associations of the Latin *ratio* are even wider than the English 'reason', and it instils a healthy cautiousness into us to be reminded of the fact. The charge of being 'irrationalist' is a pleasant and popular one to bring against all sorts of religious thinkers; but it might be used a little less frequently if only the critics realized how extraordinarily ambiguous the notion is.

We may set aside the occurrences of *ratio* in senses other than 'reason'.[2] But we cannot afford to overlook the sentences where

---

[1] The revised version of 1538 sometimes omits refs. which the earlier edn. contained, sometimes adds further refs. The critical apparatus to RM. also contains a few additional instances: it will be cited as 'CA.'. It is, of course, extremely easy to miss some of the references in a weighty work like this. The Latin text takes up almost nine hundred pages of closely printed type, much of it extremely small, in two quarto volumes. Even Luther was astonished at his own prolixity, as he concedes in the preface. But the exact number of the references to *ratio* is of no importance: it is sufficient simply to point out the remarkable liberality which which the word is used in a single work—and a work, at that, which deals with justification by faith—although, as we will see, some of the occurrences may be considered irrelevant for our purposes.

[2] There are four such uses in the *Commentary on Galatians*, all of which are found frequently in both Classical and Ecclesiastical Latin, so that it is not necessary to give references. (1) The expression *exigere rationem* ('to demand an account') appears three times, though never in Rörer's MS., and always to make the point that Christ does not demand of us an account of our past life. (2) *Rationem habere* ('to take account of' or 'to be concerned for') is a little more frequent. (3) Very often *ratio* occurs in some such ablative phrase as *qua ratione*, where we would

it stands for 'reason' in the sense of an 'argument', for here we
find evidence that Luther, if he was an irrationalist at all,
certainly was not the sort of irrationalist who simply repudiates
the demands of disciplined 'reasoning'. *Ratio* in the sense of
'explanation' or 'justification' is clearly within the range of
meanings which our own word 'reason' embraces: to 'give
reasons' is to offer an explanation, to state the grounds for
entertaining a certain belief or following a certain course of
action. In this sense 'reason' in the *Commentary on Galatians* sometimes approaches 'proof' or 'argument' (especially in relation
to belief), and sometimes 'cause' or 'motive' (especially in
relation to conduct).[1] The crucial thing is, however, not merely
to distinguish between the different kinds of 'reasons' which
Luther adduces, but to insist that he does argue his case like
any other well-trained thinker.[2] Here, for certain, is a use of
reason which he heartily approves—indeed, not so much
consciously approves as automatically accepts, takes for granted.
It would never have occurred to him that the use of disciplined
argument stood in need of any defence. (How else could one
defend disciplined thought, save by using it!) Occasionally, as
we have seen, he does commend rigorous training in the arts
of logic, grammar, and dialectic; but he presumes that the end of
such training is a self-evident good. Certainly, he was not an
irrationalist in the sense that some of his critics imply, as though
he spoke when, and how, animal passion guided. There *is* a

translate it as 'way' or 'manner'. (4) Similarly, we would translate *ratio* as 'way' or
'manner' when it is followed by a dependent genitive, as, for instance, in the
expression *ratio iustificandi*, i.e. the 'way in which we are justified'. In none of these
four uses are we presented with anything directly important for our main theme;
and yet it is clear that the last sense of *ratio* could often be given in English as
'rationale', thus both preserving the Latin root and approaching the meanings of
ratio which immediately concern us here.

[1] The critical apparatus to Rörer's MS. affords a good illustration of the difference between these two senses of 'reason': *firmissima ratio* (in W.A. 40[1]. 457. 6)
clearly means 'a very cogent proof', for the *ratio* is stated in the manner of formal
logic; but *ratio dubitandi* (589. 5) must mean 'cause for doubt'. Cf. also the critical
apparatus on 338. 11/12. *Ratio* is also used for 'argument' or 'proof': W.A. 40[1].
172. 25 (*rationem confutationis*), 180. 6 and 22 (*Hoc probabo et rationem reddam*), 193.
30, 318. 9 and 36, 424. 22, 509. 3 and 17, 520. 3 (pl.: *rationibus*); W.A. 40[2]. 153. 31.
And in the sense of 'cause' or 'reason why' or 'motive': W.A. 40[1]. 225. 23 (*ratio
quia*: virtually = 'because'), 281. 5, 449. 7 and 23, 589. 25, 602. 5 and 18, 615. 34
(RM. has only *quia*), 617. 34 (CDE), 641. 13; W.A. 40[2]. 59. 11.

[2] We could apply to Luther himself the words which he speaks of Paul: 'Involvit
suam rationem cum argumento; et confutatio [est].' (Ibid. 464. 9.)

place for reason in Luther's theology, if only as the tool of thought. On the other hand, we must be equally clear that reason is here being exercised upon revelation, not as its critic, but as its handmaid. The premisses for argument are drawn from the Scripture, and they remain unquestioned.

All the remaining senses which will be examined take *ratio* for a faculty of the human mind.[1] What we are now to consider are not so much basic differences of meaning as the little nuances within a single fundamental meaning which are indicative, less of the conventional significance of the word, than of the associations and attitudes which it calls forth in the one who utters it. The conventional significance is something given by common usage and the need for communication. Whilst, therefore, Luther and the 'sophists' (as he likes to call his Scholastic opponents) may be fully agreed on the kind of faculty human reason is, Luther's attitude towards it may be totally different because he associates the faculty with certain (as he considers them) illegitimate uses of it. To anticipate, reason is misused when it enters into an alliance with the law, believing that a just and holy God can only be approached by just and holy men and that obedience to the law is consequently an inescapable precondition to communion with God. Luther's tirades against reason in the *Commentary on Galatians* are mainly (though not, I think, exclusively) to be explained by this fact: that for him our capacity to make inferences is brought into disgrace by a particular false inference which we habitually make from the character of God and from the existence of His law. Reason is that faculty of the human mind which buttresses and perpetuates false religion, which is to say, legalistic religion; and it is only when Luther takes into his purview the religiously less harmful achievements of reason that his judgements become more complimentary. 'Reason and Law' is, accordingly, the theme of Chapter VI; 'Reason and Religion' the theme of Chapter VII. The next chapter (Chapter V) prepares the ground by showing how the attitude towards reason in the *Commentary*

---

[1] Cf. Lewis and Short, *Latin Dictionary*: '*ratio*', II. B. 2: 'That faculty of the mind which forms the basis of computation and calculation and hence of mental action in general, i.e., judgment, understanding, reason.' A good definition of *ratio* in this sense is cited from Cicero's *De Officiis*, I. 101.

on Galatians is related to our preliminary sketch in Chapter I: both how it confirms our previous findings and how it tends to focus attention upon the single issue of reason and the law, thus affording a convenient transition to the more direct and detailed treatment of this central issue in Chapters VI and VII.

V

THE LIMITS OF REASON

AT many points the *Commentary on Galatians* confirms the conclusions at which we arrived in the first chapter. Luther's attitude towards reason is seen to rest upon a fundamental dualism between the Kingdom of Christ (*regnum Christi*) and the Kingdom of the World (*regnum mundi*). Reason is properly exercised within the limits of the *regnum mundi*, and must not presume to trespass upon the *regnum Christi*. Nevertheless, it may become so illumined by faith as to be of some value even in 'spiritual affairs'. At certain points, however, the *Commentary on Galatians* does add to the earlier discussion, partly by clarification, partly by introducing fresh material. Further, the discussions of reason here seem to converge upon the single main question with which the following chapters in this section are concerned. The problem of religion and the law will, then, be approached by first indicating associations of reason in the *Commentary on Galatians* which are continuous with our earlier findings and showing how these associations become concentrated at a single point—the point, namely, in which they pass over into the specific area of religion and law. This area itself will then be discussed in greater detail.

The limits of reason

Many passages in the *Commentary on Galatians* make it clear that reason belongs to the Kingdom of the World. This is the import of such epithets as 'human', 'natural', and 'carnal' (used *passim* to qualify 'reason'). Not one of the terms is necessarily derogatory, though in practice Luther does tend to use them derogatively. He has fully grasped the significance of the Pauline term *sarx*.[1] The 'flesh' is, for him, anything untouched and unredeemed by the Spirit of God. It is, in an expression used by both Luther and Calvin, 'whatever is outside of Christ'.

---

[1] An excellent discussion of the Pauline term will be found in Rudolf Bultmann's *Theology of the New Testament*, I. 232 ff. (in the Eng. trans. by Kendrick Grobel).

Hence 'carnal' (or 'fleshly') is synonymous with 'human' and 'natural': that which is *merely* human. But it is not a sin to live in the world of the flesh: sin is rather carnal-mindedness, that is, the refusal to carry one's thoughts beyond the world of the flesh as well as to exercise them within it. We cannot help but live in the *regnum mundi*, but we have the possibility of living also in the *regnum Christi*—a possibility that is, however, only given from above, and can in no wise be realized by the natural powers, which are adequate solely to the world below. Man's flesh includes his reason and all his other 'powers'.[1] Amongst the 'powers' (*viribus*) of man Luther includes, besides reason: righteousness, wisdom, outward worship (*cultum*), piety or religiousness (*religionem*), intellect, and will.[2] Luther does sometimes appear to distinguish flesh and reason otherwise than by making reason a part of the flesh, but only, I think, to emphasize the cognitive and rational possibilities with which the flesh is endowed.[3] Man's natural capacities, taken inclusively, are what he normally designates by 'the flesh', and reason is the governing faculty which directs them and which may, therefore, be taken as a convenient shorthand term for them all. Hence Luther can speak about the 'works of natural reason', meaning thereby virtually 'what a man can do without grace, solely by means of his native capacities'.[4] To live according to reason (*secundum rationem*) is to live in human fashion (*humano more*).[5] To attain to the use of reason (*cum homo ad usum rationis pervenisset*) is to arrive at the age when one is able to exercise the faculty of judgement—the age of maturity until when, according to the fanatics, Baptism should be postponed.[6]

The flesh, it must be strongly emphasized, does not signify gross immorality, nor does Luther mean by 'concupiscence' (which is the sin of the flesh) merely abandonment to bodily

---

[1] 'Significat ergo caro totam naturam hominis cum ratione et omnibus viribus suis' (W.A. 40[1]. 244. 17; RM. has *sapientia* for *ratione*). *Caro* includes: '. . . cogitatio rationis, quae per legem vult iustificari'; Paul calls flesh 'quidquid optimum ac praestantissimum est in homine . . . scilicet summam sapientiam rationis et ipsam iustitiam legis' (W.A. 40[1]. 347. 9 and 26; RM. omits the second reference to *ratio*). For Luther's dualism in the present work see ibid. 46. 19 ff., 94. 14 ff.

[2] W.A. 40[1]. 244. 21 (RM. 244. 2).

[3] For example, W.A. 40[1]. 345. 33 (not in RM.): *Ratio et caro volunt cooperari.*

[4] W.A. 40[1]. 339. 28; RM. lacks *rationis*.

[5] W.A. 40[1]. 380. 2 and 15.

[6] Ibid. 381. 11 ff. and 26 ff.

lusts. Luther's understanding of concupiscence has been widely (not to say, wilfully) misinterpreted, and his frank acknowledgement that he was troubled by concupiscence in the monastery has been greeted as a confession of licentiousness. The meanings of both *caro* and *concupiscentia* ('flesh' and 'concupiscence') are perfectly clear in Luther's comments on Gal. v. 16. He does not take the terms in the narrow and specific sense which the Scholastics attached to them (or, at least, tended to attach to them). Nor, indeed, was he ever much troubled by concupiscence in *this* sense. Fundamentally concupiscence is 'self-love' or 'egocentricity', and the flesh is the 'whole man apart from Christ'. The sin of concupiscence is to be 'turned in upon oneself' (*incurvatus in se*): the concupiscent man is oriented towards the world, and at the centre of the world he puts his own self. The man of faith, on the other hand, lives his life towards the spiritual realm, and his centre is in Christ.[1]

Reason within its limits

The essentials of Luther's position on the scope of reason must now be quite clear. Nothing that belongs to the flesh could bring a man to God.[2] Reason is so tied down to its own proper sphere of activity that it has no perception in spiritual matters: the religious dimension lies beyond its reach. For perceiving the Kingdom of Christ one needs other eyes than reason affords, spiritual eyes.[3] Hence, for instance, reason fails to see the enormity of such sins as resentment against God.[4] The very concept of sin falls outside the province of reason, which is concerned only with the personal and social dimensions of immorality and injustice—with what Luther calls *crassa peccata*. Similarly, the fact that reason makes light of the Christian's freedom and

---

[1] See especially: W.A. 40². 83. 24 ff. (on Gal. v. 16): also W.A. 40¹. 244. 14 (RM. 243. 10) and W.A. 40². 91. 32. For discussions by the Luther-scholars see: A. S. Wood, 'The Theology of Luther's Lectures on Romans', *The Scottish Journal of Theology*, III (1950), 1–18 and 113–26; Watson, *Let God be God*, p. 30, nn. 41–42; Rupp, *The Righteousness of God*, pp. 24–25.

[2] 'Ideo maledictus est omnis legis operator et moralis Sanctus, qui per voluntatem et rationem humanam vult iustificari, quia incedit contra Deum in praesumptione iustitiae propriae' etc. (W.A. 40¹. 419. 13; some verbal differences in RM.).

[3] 'Tum poteritis aliis oculis inspicere Regnum Christi quam ratio, nempe spiritualibus' (W.A. 40². 108. 21). Cf. ibid. 177. 12: 'Non enim percipit [ratio] ea quae sunt Spiritus Dei' (an allusion to 1 Cor. ii. 14).

[4] '. . . impatientia, murmuratione, odio, blasphemia etc. contra Deum, quae peccata humanae rationi prorsus ignota sunt' (W.A. 40¹. 524. 23).

belittles his faith proves only that it lacks spiritual insight, that it belongs to the realm of the flesh.¹ And since reason belongs to the flesh, it cannot possibly be the instrument of translating man into the realm of the spirit.² 'That which is born of the flesh is flesh' (John iii. 6). Regeneration (or adoption) is the work of the Spirit, and it brings with it a 'new discernment' (*novum iudicium*) which is beyond the capacities of natural reason. It is, indeed, a 'new reason' (*nova ratio*), as we will see, which expresses itself through a quickened love for the Word and an eagerness to learn of Christ.³ The spiritual world, in short, is wholly incommensurate with the powers of natural reason.⁴

But this certainly does not imply that reason is incapable of performing the office for which it was designed.⁵ The Latin hexameter: 'Ultra posse viri non vult Deus ulla requiri',⁶ is perfectly true *in loco*, in its proper place. And it is in place only when said of political, domestic, and natural affairs. For these things rightfully belong within the *regnum rationis*. The Kingdom of Reason embraces such human activities as caring for a family, building a home, serving as a magistrate, and (as Rörer's MS. adds) looking after cows. All that can be demanded of me by God in such a sphere of activity is that I should 'do my best'. The important thing not to overlook is that this Kingdom has its boundaries; the error of the sophists is that they carry the saying 'to do one's best' (*facere quod in se est*) over into the *regnum spirituale*, in which a man is able to do nothing but sin. In outward affairs or in the affairs of the body man is master: 'He is hardly', as Luther drily remarks, 'the cow's servant.'

¹ Christian freedom *apparet rationi res parvi momenti esse* (W.A. 40¹. 688. 29; cf. 40². 1. 9 (RM.) and 6. 10); and the Christian's faith seems a *scintilla perexigua* (W.A. 40². 33. 22).
² 'Ista mutatio . . . non est opus humanae rationis aut virtutis, sed donum et effectus Spiritussancti' (W.A. 40¹. 572. 20; RM. 5).
³ 'Si aliquis sentit amorem erga verbum et libenter audit, loquitur, cogitat, dictat et scribit de Christo, is sciat hoc non esse opus humanae voluntatis aut rationis, sed donum spiritussancti' (W.A. 40¹. 574. 25; RM. 4). Note the inconsistency in spelling *spiritussancti* sometimes with a capital S, sometimes not, and often as two separate words.
⁴ *Talia non fiunt humanis viribus* (W.A. 40¹. 578. 34). The equivalent passage in RM. reads *ratione* for *humanis viribus* (578. 11). Cf. also: ibid. 596. 23.
⁵ For what follows see W.A. 40¹. 291. 29 ff. (RM. 9 ff.), the discussion which the 1538 edn. entitles: *Facere quod in se est*.
⁶ The German equivalent is: 'Gott fordert nicht von einem Man / Das er mehr thun sol denn er kan.' The English translation has: 'God will no more require of man / Than of himself perform he can.'

But in spiritual affairs he *is* a servant or slave, 'sold under sin'. 'For the Kingdom of Human Reason must be separated as far as possible from the Spiritual Kingdom.' The error of the School-men lies in their confusion of the two (*commiscuerunt politica cum ecclesiasticis*). Luther is even ready to grant that man's natural powers remain largely uncorrupted by the Fall. Again it is simply a matter of making careful distinctions: 'I make a dis-tinction between *naturalia* and *spiritualia*.' The *spiritualia* (or spiritual endowments) are certainly corrupt, so that no man loves God or keeps His Law; but the *naturalia* (natural endow-ments) are sound:

A man immersed in impiety and enslaved to the Devil neverthe-less has will, reason, freedom of choice, and the power to build a house, serve as a magistrate, navigate a ship, and perform other tasks (*officia*) over which man was given dominion (Gen. i). These things have not been taken from man; procreation, government, the management of household affairs, have not been done away.

And yet, since this is *all* that is left to man, since he cannot by his native capacities attain to righteousness before God, 'what is the point of boasting about the "rule of reason" (*de dictamine rationis*)?' *Coram Deo* reason is of no use to us.

So then, we grant that the saying is true [i.e., 'facere quod in se est'], but only in its own place, which is, in the Kingdom of the Body (*in regno corporali*). But if you drag it into the Kingdom of the Spirit (*in regnum spirituale*), before God, then we deny it completely.

There are some things, then, that reason can correctly determine without the illumination of faith. 'Unenlightened reason [so we may translate *ratio naturalis*], however blind it may be, is bound to agree that "promising" and "commanding" are two different things, as are "giving a gift" and "receiving one".' This is a straightforward question of grammar or logic (not to say just plain common sense), though it certainly is important for its theological consequences.[1] Indeed, Luther's charge against the papists is precisely that they are 'poor sorts of dialectician',[2] for they fail to observe distinctions: they mix things up. The list of things which 'even natural reason is bound to concede' as a matter of straightforward logic could be

[1] W.A. 40¹. 471. 13 and 30.   [2] Cf. ibid. 44. 21.

extended indefinitely.[1] And, of course, since good works are (as
Luther repeatedly affirms) done in this world, they too fall
within the scope of reason's judgement—at least, to some extent
(*aliquo modo*).[2] But even here reason is not wholly to be trusted,
both because it is corrupted and blinded *vitio diaboli* and also
because, when uninstructed by faith, it substitutes for love toward the neighbour 'childish ceremonies or monstrous works
which the justiciaries themselves think up'.[3] In many passages
Luther allows that man's reason is even able (again *aliquo modo*)
to attain to a certain sort of righteousness. The law is given him
to make the task easier.[4] The law is like the sun which lends its
brightness to the feeble torch of human reason. But what sort of
righteousness can reason, with the law's assistance, attain to?
The answer is: 'civil righteousness', not the kind which avails
a man before God. So Luther tries to hold two points together:
God approves the righteousness which reason can attain—
indeed, not merely approves (*approbat*), but demands (*requirit*)—
and yet this is not the kind of righteousness which is necessary
for justification. And if reason, even with the assistance of the
law, the best thing which this world possesses, is not able to
justify, what could reason do without the law?

So far, then, our earlier impressions are confirmed and at
some points (especially in the discussion of *facere quod in se est*)
amplified. The main charge against reason concerns its illegitimate incursion into the affairs of the spirit, and the error of
the Schoolmen is that they mix theology with philosophy. Yet
at one place[5] Luther accuses the Schoolmen, not so much of

[1] 'Cogitur autem ratio naturaliter assentiri et dicere, quod Christus non sit
meum opus' (W.A. 40¹. 458. 5 and 27). 'Ipsa ratio . . . cogitur fateri satius esse, ut
Petrus negligatur, quam ut divina Maiestas cedat aut fides periclitetur' (ibid. 212.
21). *Ratio fateri cogitur* that to avoid the law is not to be made just by it (ibid. 505.
6 and 23). 'Ipsa ratio fateri cogitur opinionem humanam non esse Deum' (ibid. 609.
11; cf. 609. 3 (CA)).

[2] 'Eam partem doctrinae [sc. de bonis moribus] aliquo modo intelligit et docet
etiam ratio'; but Luther quickly adds (lest we forget!): 'De doctrina fidei prorsus
vero nihil novit' (W.A. 40². 59. 7 and 23).

[3] Ibid. 66. 33 ff. (some variants in RM.); also 71. 16 and 32.

[4] See the whole passage in W.A. 40¹. 305. 7 ff. and 30 ff. The passage concerning
the 'addition' of the law is W.A. 40¹. 306. 17: 'Est quidem addita lex supra rationem,
ut illuminaret et adiuvaret hominem eique ostenderet, quid facere, quid omittere
debeat.'

[5] Ibid. 409. 5 ff. and 23 ff. The passage is titled (in the 1538 edn.): 'Responsio
ad argumenta quae adversarii opponunt contra doctrinam et iustitiam fidei.'

carrying philosophical categories into theology, but of turning philosophy upside down *before* using its characteristic terms in a theological context. For philosophy does, in one of its doctrines, afford at least an analogy for Luther's theological doctrines: it teaches that both in the natural and in the moral spheres 'being' (*esse*) precedes 'doing' (*operari*). In nature a tree *is* before it produces fruit; and in morals a 'good will' and a 'right reason' must precede good works. In a sense, we could even say of the philosophers that when speaking ethically they do justify the person before any works have been done. And yet as soon as the Schoolmen carry these terms over into theology, they invert the original order. 'Only there [in theology] do the stupid asses want to turn the thing around.' There alone they want to place 'works' before the good will! But, of course, Luther is not inferring that therefore we should break our previous rule and proceed to carry philosophical statements over into theology: at most we can see an analogy between 'A good will precedes good acts', on the one hand, and 'A man must be justified before he can perform good works', on the other. But a good will and a right reason, as philosophy understands them, will never procure justification. Nor does the philosopher or the legislator imagine that they will: for this reason they are more to be praised than the foolish monk. They seek only the public good.[1] Right reason is, to be sure, a kind of righteousness, but only the civil kind, not genuine righteousness: it belongs to the Earthly Kingdom. The error of the sophists is that they take it for Christian righteousness.[2]

The discussion turns around the theory, advocated in Occam's ethics, that a *recta ratio* must precede *bona opera*. For a recent exposition of the theory and of Occam's moral philosophy in general see Copleston's *History of Philosophy*, III. 105 ff. The sentence in W.A. 40¹. 402. 29 could almost have been written by Occam himself: '. . . opus morale externe factum si non fiat sincero corde, bona voluntate et recto dictamine rationis, esse simulatum opus.' Cf. ibid. 403. 1 and 15: Judas did the same things as the other apostles, but his deeds were evil because defective in *dictamen rationis*.

[1] 'Altius non assurgit Philosophus vel Legislator, non cogitat per rectam rationem etc. consequi remissionem peccatorum et vitam aeternam, ut Sophista aut Monachus. Ideo Gentilis Philosophus longe melior est tali Iusticiario; manet enim intra limites suos, habens tantum rationem honestatis et tranquillitatis publicae, non miscens humanis divina' (W.A. 40¹. 411. 15; RM. 2). A very important passage. It demonstrates that Aristotle himself was not usually the target of Luther's attacks on philosophy, but rather those who used him (or misused him) in theology.

[2] W.A. 40¹. 370. 23; also 498. 11: they wrongly conclude that the will and reason are good *erga legem Dei*.

Reason beyond its limits

But, of course, reason does *not* keep its bounds. And in this lies the key to at least part of Luther's invective against it. It is guilty of that *superbia* (arrogance), the essence of which is going beyond appointed limits. Reason constructs a 'theology of glory'; and the consequences of reason's overreaching its limits are two: incredulity and the attenuation of belief.

The arrogance of reason is made manifest in various ways. The light of reason, the freedom of the will, the integrity of man's natural capacities, and his good works are always the ground of the world's boasting: the world cannot understand the doctrine of justification by grace.[1] Reason would like to regard the law as something given for the exercise and display of its natural powers. 'So marvellously can Reason flatter herself.'[2] 'Believe in Christ' and 'Love thy neighbour as thyself' are not enough: reason is offended at such simplicity and wants to do some great thing.[3] And so it invents good works of its own, works not prescribed by the Law of God, and then imagines that it can justify itself before God by means of them.[4] Always to the forefront of Luther's mind, written there indelibly by years of bitter experience, were the works of the monks, to which he had learned to oppose the works 'of each man in his own calling'.[5] Especially he alludes to the harsh discipline of the Carthusians, who were to him the very paragons of reason's tragic misguidedness: 'True, they think about God, Christ, and religious matters; yet not from the Word of God, but from their own reason.'[6] Such labours cannot avail before God: they belong to the *regnum mundi*. 'Superspiritual' though the work's devotions may be, according to reason's judgement, yet according to Paul they are works of the flesh.[7] And the irony of the matter is that reason ends by being encumbered with what Luther con-

---

[1] W.A. 40^1. 74. 4 and 16; see also the 1538 edn.

[2] Ibid. 499. 18 ff. To the question: What, then, is the *proprium usum et officium* of the law? we will turn later.

[3] W.A. 40^2. 70. 27.

[4] Luther's favourite term for these self-imposed labours is 'will-works' (or 'elect-works')—'ea, quae ratio eligit sine mandato Dei' (ibid. 72. 11). See also ibid. 68. 12 ff.: they are *ex suis* [i.e. reason's and the flesh's] *cogitationibus*.

[5] Ibid. 72. 9.

[6] Ibid. 110. 31.

[7] 'Et tamen ista spiritualissima res [sc. monachi devotiones], ut ratio iudicat, est iuxta Paulum opus carnis' (ibid. 110. 21).

temptuously dismisses as silly superstitions. Reason's proud refusal to be bound by the Word leads only to idolatry.[1]

Reason does not only, when it transgresses its limits, invent will-works; it also pries into the majesty of the Hidden God.[2] Within the category of 'speculation' Luther certainly includes the invention of will-works; and it is, indeed, just this which he is mainly concerned to condemn in the passage under consideration, a fact of some importance, to which we will need to return shortly. To pry into the majesty of God is (at least partly) to endeavour to comprehend His will toward us by the judgement of reason,[3] that is, without having recourse to God's Word. The monk who pays his vows, the Turk with his 'Alcoran', the Jew with the Law of Moses—all are indulging in speculation in so far as each imagines that for the keeping of his respective rule he will be saved. To the same list Luther adds the 'fanatical spirits' of his own day, whose boast is in 'the spirit, visions, and what not' and who 'strut about amidst wonders that are beyond them'. Certainly, Luther does mean more than the invention of will-works by 'speculation', more than the endeavour to placate God by men's own self-imposed disciplines: he means also the attempt to perceive how God created and governs the world; to scrutinize the 'essence' (*naturam*) of God, instead of knowing His 'purpose' (*voluntatem*) as it is set before us in Christ. Hence, he who indulges in speculation runs the risk of being struck down by the naked majesty of the God who said: 'No man shall see me and live' (Exod. xxxiii. 20). In a striking phrase Luther warns that *speculatio* is 'more than the human body can bear, to say nothing of the mind'.[4] And he adds, significantly, 'I know from experience what I am saying.' His sense of God's awfulness sounds strangely in the ears of a modern Protestant, but there can be no doubt that in his monastery days the very thought of God's glory was to Luther something fearful and oppressive.[5] And yet the real danger of the *sensus*

---

[1] For example, ibid. 106. 28; 111. 7 (RM.): '. . . *ratio intellectus vexatur erroribus, superstitionibus*'; 111. 9 and 112. 11; 112. 17/18 (CDE).

[2] For what follows: W.A. 40[1]. 75. 27 ff. (RM. 9 ff.). In CDE the title is: 'Canon observandus. Abstinendum esse a speculatione maiestatis.'

[3] The expression *iudicio rationis* is only in CDE. But both the 1535 edn. and RM. have the term *speculatio*.

[4] W.A. 40[1]. 76. 12.

[5] 'Scrutator enim Maiestatis opprimitur a gloria. Ego expertus scio, quid dico' (ibid. 78. 18). 'Nam Deus in sua natura, ut est immensurabilis, incomprehensibilis

speculationis lies somewhere else, in its inability to calm the troubled conscience.[1] To seek God elsewhere than in Christ is to find a God whose glory is not His grace, a God who can only be approached in the terror of a burdened conscience. Speculation, if not synonymous with the invention of will-works, at least has this as an inevitable consequence. For the anxious sinner, not knowing God as He really is in Christ, resorts frantically to good works of his own invention in the forlorn effort to *make* God propitious. What may begin with the arrogance of superior wisdom and virtue may end with the torments of the afflicted conscience. 'Shutting out the Mediator Christ' cannot but lead to a fall like proud Lucifer's.

Si vis tutus esse—if you want to be *safe*, you must seek God in the manger. 'Begin where He began.' His descent was to prevent our ascent.[2] Only through this incarnate and human God is the way open to the heavens. As Christ himself said: 'I am the Way' (John xiv. 6). In him is the majesty of God 'sweetened and tempered to your capacity.'[3] He is the only ladder between heaven and earth: 'we must ascend by Jacob's ladder' (Gen. xxviii. 13; John i. 51). Outside the matter of justification it is all right to be a subtle dialectician; but here at least we must look only to the Man Jesus Christ.

One inevitable consequence of allowing reason to trespass in the province of faith is unbelief, scepticism. The *locus classicus* for Luther's feelings at this point is his commentary on Gal. iii. 6: 'Abraham believed God, and it was imputed to him for righteousness.'[4] Faith is an all-powerful thing because it gives God His glory. That is to say, it takes Him at His word, believes Him, reckons Him true to His promise, wise, just, merciful, omnipotent—in short, acknowledges in Him the source of all good. But what does the 'word of God' *say*? Sheer impossibilities,

et infinitus, ita intolerabilis est humanae naturae' (W.A. 40[1]. 77. 20). 'Nemo enim Deum novit' (W.A. 40[1]. 80. 14/16: CDE).
  [1] 'Nihil enim est periculosius, cum agendum est in agone contra legem, peccatum et mortem cum Deo, quam nos vagari nostris speculationibus in coelo et considerare Deum ipsum in sua incomprehensibili potentia, sapientia et maiestate . . .' (ibid. 77. 13).
  [2] 'Ipse descendit . . . ut per hoc ascensum in coelum et speculationem Maiestatis prohiberet' (ibid. 78. 10).
  [3] The trans. is literal: '. . . Maiestatem Dei dulcificatam et tuo captui attemperatam' (ibid. 79. 19; RM. 4).
  [4] W.A. 40[1]. 359. 17 ff., with the parallel passage in RM.

if you ask reason. For what could be more ridiculous than for God to tell Abraham that he would have a son from the sterile and ancient body of Sarah? And so it is with all the articles of faith: that Christ's Body and Blood are set before us in the Lord's Supper, that Baptism is the washing of regeneration, that the dead will rise at the last day, the Virgin Birth, the Crucifixion of God's own Son, his Resurrection and Ascension —all are absurd in the eyes of reason. 'Thus reason judges concerning all the articles of faith.'[1] Reason does not understand that the most perfect worship is to hear God's voice and believe. It strikes out on its own, does things of its own choosing, and imagines by this to please God. Faith and reason must always wrestle, as they did in Abraham. 'And so all the pious, entering with Abraham into the darkness of faith, put reason to death.'[2] This is the 'sacrifice of the godly', by which they slay God's mightiest enemy, the beast reason: in comparison with this noble work all the religions of the heathen and the merits of the monks are nothing.

It is not our purpose to champion utterances such as these, but only to interpret them, that is, to see what lies behind them. And it is not hard to understand what prompted Luther to make assertions of this kind, which are amongst the most outrageous of his invectives against reason. In the light of what we have observed already, it could hardly be argued that Luther's censure springs from an unqualified irrationalism. The source

---

[1] All the standard stumbling-blocks to reason are mentioned at various stages in the Commentary. The Incarnation: How could Christ have taken upon him human flesh? (W.A. 40¹. 452. 10). These things are *mysteria, aenigmata, vera Cabala* (452. 23). The Atonement: How can our sins be 'in him'? (445. 5 and 23). The Crucifixion: How could Christ be 'cursed of God'? (433. 1). Reason is also scandalized by the weakness of God's chosen vessels: 636. 12, 638. 14. And so forth. It is interesting to observe that RM. makes explicit reference to the Erasmians (W.A. 40¹. 361. 11): 'Sic Erasmiani metiuntur dei maiestatem secundum rationem.' But a note in the margin reads, 'I have left this out.' In the edition of 1535 'Erasmians' is simply changed to 'sophists and sectaries' (362. 14). In the revised edn. of 1538 the whole sentence is omitted. The reasons for the alterations are obvious enough: Luther's friends and even, generally, Luther himself did not go out of their way to give offence. Still it is a pity that the entire sentence was omitted in the latest version, for the phrase 'measuring the majesty of God by the canon of reason' is as fine a one as the *Spiritus sanctus non est Scepticus* which Luther threw at Erasmus in another place (*De Servo Arbitrio*: W.A. 18. 605. 32).

[2] 'Sic omnes pii, ingredientes cum Abraham tenebras fidei, mortificant rationem' (W.A. 40¹. 362. 23). The same sentiment is expressed several times in this passage, both in RM. and the Commentary.

of his vehemence is not contempt for reason, but allegiance to the Word. Here is an area where reason's competence runs out: we cannot measure the Word by the canon of reason. But, of course, the difficulty for this standpoint is that the miraculous does take place within the *regnum rationis*, even though its source may be 'from above'. It is precisely this fact which underlies the second consequence of what is, in Luther's view, reason's over-stepping its bounds. For even when reason is willing, in a measure, to bow to the Word, to accept the ridiculous, it will certainly try to make the absurd seem less so. It will ask: How could God's Word be true, and yet reason unoffended? Thus the champion of reason, if reluctant to take the path of scepticism, will try the way of attenuation. He trims down the unacceptable or explains it away, until the absurd makes sense. The retort invited by the 'rationalist's' case for accommodation is obvious: when the absurd ceases to be absurd, it ceases also to be Christian. It is a mark of the *pseudo-apostoli* that they teach 'human things, pleasing and plausible to reason'.[1] So, for example, the doctrine of original sin is qualified to make room for freewill and for human capacities to do good without the aid of grace. Of special interest in this connexion are Luther's comments on the Arians, his favourite example of the 'rationalisers'.[2] They were sharp fellows; but, when all is said and done, they had nothing to offer but 'specious opinions and such words as delight and please human reason'. Paul spoke otherwise: he attributes to Christ the works of God, therefore Christ is God *natura*, not *nominaliter*, by nature, not in name only. He is more than the most perfect of created things (*perfectissima creatura*). So, Luther glories in the paradox of the God-Man: any attempt to compromise with paganism in the interests of reason just does not interest him.

Yet we should not infer that the critical faculties are simply to be suspended in theological matters. Luther will not hesitate to indicate weaknesses even in the Apostle's arguments, though they are to be found in Holy Writ. When Paul (in Gal. iii. 15) uses an argument from analogy, reason could object: 'Surely, Paul, you are not going to apply human affairs to divine?'[3]

---

[1] W.A. 40^1. 124. 16.
[2] Ibid. 82. 14 ff. and RM. parallels. The 1538 heading is: *Christus natura Deus*.   [3] W.A. 40^1. 459. 29; cf. RM.

Surprisingly perhaps, Luther agrees: 'It is certainly quite true that arguments from human analogies are the weakest of all.' Paul's argument here, in fact, is only rhetorical, not dialectical: it seems rather weak (*infirmius*), when we consider the weighty matter under discussion. Clearly Luther feels some sympathy with reason's cavil; and after a short defence of some kinds of analogical argument, the most he can say for Paul's present argument is that it is 'strong enough' (*satis firmum*). Again, if Luther sometimes glories in the paradox of, say, a Holy Church composed of unholy members,[1] elsewhere, in a less belligerent mood, he is willing to appease reason and resolve the paradox by defining a 'Holy' Church as one that possesses the Word and Sacraments.[2]

Reason and regeneration

Reason, indeed, may be of service even in spiritual matters, provided it is kept subordinate to faith and is first illuminated by the Holy Spirit. In the discussion of *recta ratio*, to which reference has already been made,[3] Luther allows that the term 'right reason' should be retained in theology, but we must give it new content. 'In theology we have no right reason and good will save faith.' 'A right reason and a good will is a "faithful" reason and will.'[4] The governing principle of conduct in the believer is no longer natural reason, but reason enlightened by faith. Faith virtually takes the place of reason: right reason in spiritual matters *is* faith. But we may, if we will, continue to speak of reason. Nor, I think, is Luther emptying 'reason' of all its conventional significance. Reason is still reason, even in the domain of theology. But now it is illuminated by faith: it is 'right reason' in a theological sense. Rörer's MS. speaks of a *nova ratio*;[5] but a '*renewed*' reason' might convey Luther's

---

[1] 'Dicimus: "Credo Ecclesiam Sanctam." Si autem rationem et oculos tuos consulueris, diversum iudicabis' (W.A. 40¹. 444. 36 ff.; RM. 9 ff.).

[2] Ibid. 68. 7 ff. and 25 ff.

[3] Ibid. 410. 3 ff. and 15 ff.

[4] Ibid. 412. 23 (RM. 8); 417. 26 (RM. 6). Cf.: 415. 5 and 23: 'rectam rationem . . . id est, fidem in Christum'; 419. 5 and 19: 'sine recta ratione et bona voluntate Theologica, hoc est, sine cognitione Dei et fide'; 'rectam rationem . . . quae fides est' (457. 22); 'rectam rationem per fidem' (457. 7 and 26). The CA. to 412. 4/5 (RM.) has: ' "Facere" in theologia etiam requirit rectam rationem i.e. fidem in Christum.'

[5] Ibid. 412. 5.

meaning better than a '*new* reason'.[1] 'For reason must first be illuminated by faith, before it issues in works (*antequam operetur*).'[2]

Luther is certainly not suspicious of the intellectual element in faith. He is quite willing to speak of Christ's atoning work as apprehended by a 'reason which is illuminated by faith'.[3] He will even add: 'And that apprehension of Christ through faith is the speculative life, properly so called.'[4] This is in line with his repeated insistence that Christ is our true wisdom.[5] Faith is, indeed, for Luther a mode of cognition—though not only this, nor even primarily. This could be demonstrated from the contrast between faith and hope in the comments on Gal. v. 5.[6] The comparison is made in respect of subject, function (*officium*), object, order, and diversity of working. In the course of the comparison Luther affirms that faith is 'in the understanding' (*in intellectu*); that it is a kind of 'knowledge' (*notitia*); that its object is 'truth' (*veritatem*); that it is an 'instructor and judge' (*doctor et iudex*); and so on. Elsewhere, he calls faith 'right thinking about God' (*recte cogitare de Deo*). And reason, he says, is wrong thinking.[7]

There are, then, several considerations which tend to soften Luther's diatribes against reason. In particular, reason rules in the *regnum mundi*; and, even if it may never *rule* in the *regnum Christi* (otherwise the Kingdom would not be Christ's), yet it may *serve* there, once it has been redeemed by faith.[8] But this is not the most important conclusion to be drawn from the discussion so far. If we ask: What exactly does reason *do*, when it trespasses upon the domain of faith, when, that is, it wanders

---

[1] It is remarkable that Luther is able to speak of the 'old' and the 'new reason' in the same breath: *rectam rationem . . . incomprehensibilem rationi humanae* (W.A. 40[1]. 412. 18; RM.5). Cf. the 'new doing', which is also incomprehensible to reason (*incognita rationi*) in the old sense (411. 30).

[2] Ibid. 418. 30 (RM. 7).

[3] Ibid. 443. 13 and 444. 12. Cf.: *ratione seuintellectu illuminato fide* (447. 1 and 15); *alia ratio generatur, quae est fidei* (412. 20).

[4] Ibid. 447. 2 and 16.

[5] Ibid. 47. 19, 64. 18, &c.   [6] W.A. 40[2]. 25. 27 ff.

[7] W.A. 40[1]. 375. 12 and 376. 23.

[8] Even this 'reason illuminated by faith' or 'theological reason' is not the highest: it is only the highest for man *in via*. But it will be otherwise *in patria*: 'Ibi dum erit vera et perfecta noticia Dei, recta ratio et bona voluntas, non moralis aut Theologica, sed coelestis, divina et aeterna' (ibid. 429. 13; RM. 428. 8). Luther has in mind, of course, Paul's First Letter to the Corinthians, xiii. 12.

there uninvited and without faith to guide it? the chief and most characteristic answer of the Commentary is that it devises a host of religious exercises in the fond expectation of making itself approved by God. Even when Luther seems about to speak of a different sort of activity in which reason indulges, 'speculation', we discover that this is, after all, mainly another way of stating the same thing. To be sure, Luther does mean by reason other things than man's capacity for concocting practices unwarranted by the Word; yet to this point he returns again and again. Here is the focus of his interest in reason, and it is this which provides us with the key for understanding his violent censure.[1]

---

[1] A connexion between 'speculation' and 'works-righteousness' has been noted especially by those scholars who have stressed Luther's *theologia crucis*. See, for example, Paul Althaus, 'Die Bedeutung des Kreuzes im Denken Luthers', *Evangelium und Leben*, p. 54; Walter von Löwenich, *Luthers Theologia crucis*, p. 15. Brunner also notices the association of the *deus nudus* and works-righteousness, and concludes: 'Wie sie [die natürliche Gotteserkenntnis] die natürliche Erkenntnis der Vernunft ist, so ist sie auch die gesetzliche.' *Dogmatik* (Zürich, 1946), 1. 179. The natural knowledge of God, which is sought by the *theologia gloriae*, is not merely a product of reason, but also of legalism. This, clearly, brings us to the threshold of our next topic, 'Reason and Law'.

VI

REASON AND LAW

IT appears, then, that Luther does not wish to attack reason
per se, but only the misuse of it; and reason is being misused
when it is set up as the final and supreme judge in matters
of theology. Reason is indicted only when caught trespassing.
But a large part of the 'critique of reason' in the *Commentary on
Galatians* is directed against a quite specific blunder which reason
makes when it trespasses on the domain of faith. That is to say,
Luther is concerned with a particular error of reason, not merely
with the general error of making reason autonomous in an area
where, if allowed to enter at all, it should behave as faith's
handmaiden. To this particular error we must now turn. Our
theme has been narrowed down considerably. First, we saw how
reason is given due recognition by Luther as a divine endowment
with a proper sphere of use; next, we considered reason's
arrogant invasion of the domain of faith; now, we turn to just
one of the blunders which reason habitually makes when so
trespassing on faith's rightful estate. At this stage in the discussion *ratio* virtually denotes, not so much the general human
capacity for understanding and making inferences, but a
characteristic exercise of that capacity in the understanding of
a definite problem and in the drawing of a definite inference.
Ratio has become almost synonymous with a certain *opinio*,
and it is by no means accidental that the two terms are to be
found side by side in several passages.[1] Reason in general is
tarnished by one grave misunderstanding and one false inference
for which it is responsible.

Luther's critique at this point is easily misinterpreted, if we
fail to view it in the light of our previous discussion. No doubt,
the blame, should he be misinterpreted, would lie largely at his
own door. For he does not stop to tell us that of course his scorn
for reason is not for reason *sans réserve*, but only for reason when

[1] W.A. 40¹. 165. 6 and 23; 603. 27; 40². 7. 29. Perhaps there is some precedent
for this in the Classical authors, for they do sometimes use *ratio* for a 'view or
opinion resting upon reasonable grounds'. Lewis and Short, op. cit. II. B. 2. e.

it makes the error under consideration. Luther would not be
Luther if he spoke like that! The only way in which we can
avoid misinterpretation is by setting the isolated references
within the context of his total attitude, by comparing one facet
of his thought with another.

Reason's legalistic assumption

What, then, is this false opinion which Luther has in mind
when he castigates reason? It is the view that 'to live unto God
you must keep the law'; that 'the work of God in saving man
depends on personal worth'.[1] This being reason's *opinio*, it
cannot understand the true doctrine of faith in Christ.[2] Instead
of believing in him, as the Gospel demands, reason devises
works of its own and imagines that for the doing of them God,
who is merciful, will accept the doer. 'Das ist religio falsa', as
Luther puts it in that odd mixture of German and Latin, 'quae
concipi potest a ratione'.[3] And it is this same 'conception' of
reason's which puts Papist, Jew, and Mohammedan on an
equal footing, for it underlies the religion of them all.[4] Their
rites may differ in outward form, but the same *ratio*, the same
opinio, belongs to them all.[5] And here is the 'opinion' of reason:
'It wants to be justified by the law (*vult per legem iustificari*).'[6]
Reason 'will have nothing to do with God, unless it first be pure
and without sin'. 'Our flesh can see no other way of saving
itself from the sins in which it is immersed than by performing
works.'[7] The consequence is that reason has to pretend that the
burden of sin is lighter than it really is.[8] Here reason attenuates
the doctrines of Christianity, not on theoretical grounds (because
they are incredible), but on practical grounds (because they
seem to demand a higher standard than the flesh can attain to).
The whole world is affected by this opinion of reason, and

---

[1] 'Ratio . . . docet: Si vis vivere Deo, oportet te legem servare' (W.A. 40¹. 268.
13). 'Sententia . . . quod opus divinum pendeat ex dignitate personae' (36. 2).

[2] Ibid. 389. 21; 666. 28.

[3] 'That is the false religion which can be conceived by reason' (ibid. 603. 5 = 20).

[4] Ibid. 603. 6 and 21. Luther also considers that in this 'sententia quod opus
divinum pendeat ex dignitate personae' the Papists agree with the Schwärmer.
Ibid. 36. 1 ff.

[5] 'Eadem ratio, idem cor, eadem opinio et cogitatio est omnium.' (Ibid. 603. 27;
cf. RM. 8).

[6] Ibid. 347. 10 and 27.

[7] Ibid. 86. 18; 115. 21.   [8] Ibid. 86. 23 ff.

'especially those in the world who want to be best and holiest'.[1]
In short, reason 'far prefers the righteousness of the law to the
righteousness of faith'.[2] It is because of its legalistic assumptions
that reason must be 'shut out'; law and reason go out together.[3]

The extraordinary difficulty of shaking off what we may term
the 'legalistic assumption' (the assumption of natural reason that
salvation is by the works of the law) is a point to which Luther
returns again and again.[4] However well we may seem to have
learned the lesson of faith in Christ, yet when assailed by terrors
of conscience, or when faced with the threat of dying, it is our
own works which we begin to consider.[5]

Immediately, our past life comes to mind. Then in great mental
anguish the sinner groans, thinking to himself: 'Ah, how desperately
I have lived! If only I were allowed to live longer, then I would be
willing to amend my life.'[6]

So deeply is this error implanted in us—this 'unhappy *hexis*'
as Luther calls it—that reason cannot tear itself away from the
sight of 'active righteousness'.[7] The law may be the best thing
in the world (*summum omnium quae sunt in mundo*), but still it *is* 'in
the world' and cannot do anything in the kingdom of conscience
but destroy the sinner's assurance of pardon.[8] Justification by
faith is a 'slippery subject', not, of course, *per se*, but *quoad nos*.
In itself it is sure and certain; but we have difficulty in keeping
our grasp upon it, for we have against us a part of our very
selves, namely, reason and all reason's powers.[9] 'For that most
pernicious view of the law (*opinio de lege*), that it justifies, clings
most tenaciously to reason: all mankind are so entangled in it

---

[1] W.A. 40¹. 87. 7.

[2] W.A. 40². 7. 16.

[3] 'So kan lex nicht hin zu komen et ratio est conclusa.' W.A. 40¹. 471. 7 (RM.).

[4] Luther himself uses the expression *opinio legis* (e.g. in ibid. 345. 32), which
is quite close to 'legalistic assumption'. He also speaks of *opinio de lege* (504. 32).

[5] 'Ubi pavor mortis, ibi adhuc ratio, peccatum, lex' (ibid. 538. 1). 'Verba
facilia sunt, sed in agone . . .' (92. 10; RM. 2). Cf. also 'in agone conscientiae'
(141. 17); 'in agone mortis' (94. 11); 'in certamine mortis' (258. 17); 'in periculo
et pugna mortis' (87. 32); 'in hora mortis vel aliis agonibus conscientiae' (49. 33);
'sub horam tentationis' (205. 25); 'in tentatione' (207. 18); and so on. Luther offers
an *insigne exemplum* in 258. 22 ff. from the 'Lives of the Fathers'.

[6] W.A. 40¹. 42. 10 ff., from the *Argumentum Epistolae*.

[7] Ibid. *Iustitia activa* is the kind of righteousness that is produced (theoretically,
at least) by active *doing*. Luther opposes it to the *iustitia passiva* which we receive,
without 'doing' anything, from Christ.

[8] Ibid. 42. 22.   [9] Ibid. 129. 9 and 27.

that only with great difficulty are they able to get out.'[1] Even
Luther himself, on his own testimony, frequently went through
moments of temptation when he hankered after legal righteousness. Frankly he makes the confession: 'I would be glad to keep
both the righteousness of grace and that of works at the same
time.' This, in spite of the fact that he saw in the mixing of law
and Gospel, grace and works, the prime threat to the integrity
of the Christian Faith![2] For we are inclined to legalism by
nature, and our native inclination is confirmed by habit and
custom.[3]

It is clear, therefore, that many of Luther's derogatory
remarks against reason are made, not because of any under-
estimation of the values of careful thinking, but because reason
has entered into an alliance with the law. The danger to faith
lies neither in reason alone nor in the law alone, but in their
conspiracy together: *lex et ratio*, this is the combination which,
in Luther's view, bodes ill for faith. 'As soon as the law and
reason (*lex et ratio*) join together, immediately the purity of faith
(*virginitas fidei*) is violated. Nothing is more strongly opposed to
faith than the law and reason (*lex et ratio*).'[4] The association of
law and reason (we might almost write 'law-and-reason') is not
always represented as a 'ganging together': Luther speaks in
other characteristic ways also. The law is the *object* of reason, as
Christ is the object of faith. Reason *knows* nothing but the law.
Reason always relapses into *thinking* about the law. Sometimes
'law' and 'reason' simply appear side by side, often together
with 'works', in a list of those things which cannot procure justification.[5] One way or another Luther drives home his point:

---

[1] 'Ea enim perniciosa opinio de lege, quod iustificat, valde tenaciter adhaeret
rationi . . .' (W.A. 40². 7. 29).

[2] W.A. 40¹. 114. 5 and 22. Luther's comments on Gal. ii. 12 (concerning Peter's
withdrawing himself from the company of the Gentiles) are very apposite here.
Peter knew the article of justification better than we do, yet even he relapsed into
legalism.

[3] 'Consuetudo duplex natura' (ibid. 152. 7: RM.). 'Tanta vis autem est con-
suetudinis quae confirmat naturam, quae per sese inclinata est ad legem' (ibid. 152.
24: 1535).

[4] W.A. 40¹. 204. 11 ff. (RM. 1 ff.). The entire passage is very important for this
aspect of Luther's thought.

[5] 'Ratio humana obiectum habet legem. . . . Fides autem . . . nullum prorsus
aliud obiectum habet quam Iesum Christum' (W.A .40¹. 164. 21; RM. 6). 'Ratio
naturaliter habet cognitionem legis' (209. 22/23: CDE; see also 474. 22). 'Ratio
enim et natura humana non haeret Christo firmiter in amplexibus, sed subinde

law and reason are allies, working together. Consequently, reason is shocked and outraged when its ally is disparaged. Paul seems to invert the legalistic assumption, and consequently to belittle the law. For he says: 'I through the law am dead to the law, that I might live unto God' (Gal. ii. 19). 'This is a kind of rhetorical inversion', comments Luther. The pseudo-apostles say: 'Unless you have lived to the law, you have not lived to God.' Paul retorts: 'Unless you have died to the law, you will not live to God.'[1] Reason is astounded by such disparagement of the law, and moved to anger.[2] It considers Paul's description of the law—'the ministration of death', 'the letter that killeth' &c.—nothing short of blasphemous.[3] And the grounds for its fury are ultimately reason's pride in its own achievement, wrought through the law.[4]

Reason's false inference

But why should the association of law and reason be thought so 'natural'? Why, indeed, is there supposed to be something inherently 'reasonable' in legalism? The answer is, I think, that the legalist's case rests squarely upon two plausible inferences which reason is led to make. First, reason argues that, since God is just and has given men a rule for righteousness in the law, then nothing but the keeping of this rule can be of any avail before Him. God commands, *therefore* only he who obeys will be saved. Second, reason argues that if obedience to the law does not obtain salvation, if on the contrary salvation is given irrespectively of good works, then the law is nothing and men may as well do evil. 'By the works of the law shall no flesh be justified'; *therefore* the law is useless. With the first inference reason buttresses the case *for* the legalists, often indeed by arguing from Scripture itself; with the second inference reason seeks to refute the case *against* the legalists, by reducing the rival view to absurdity. I propose to leave the first inference for the next chapter, where it can profitably be set within the context of a somewhat more synoptic survey of Luther's understanding of true and false religion.

relabitur ad cogitationes de lege' (W.A. 40¹. 214. 21). For 'lists' of those things which cannot justify, including reason and the law, see, e.g. ibid. 379. 1, 4, and 18.
 [1] Ibid. 267. 11 (RM.).
 [2] See esp. ibid. 266. 8 and 26, 270. 4 and 17, 271. 33, 275. 17.
 [3] Ibid. 559. 17.   [4] Ibid. 366. 1 ff. and 16 ff.

The second false inference is described repeatedly. What it is that offends reason in Luther's understanding of works and the law is admirably set out in the comments on Gal. iii. 2 (concerning the 'hearing of faith'). In fine, provocative, sententious style Luther asserts: 'Hearing, not doing, makes a Christian.' And he gives an illustration: 'Mary sits, she does nothing.'[1] In the exegesis of Gal. iii. 19 ('Wherefore then serveth the law?') the objection of reason is taken up in some detail. The question: 'What, then, is the point of the law, if it does not justify?' is certainly no easy one. The Jews who toiled under the yoke of the law for so many years were very naturally outraged to find it all (so Paul alleged) in vain. And so also did the Papists complain in Luther's own day:

Of what profit has it been that we have lived twenty, thirty, forty years in a monastery, have taken the vow of chastity, poverty, and obedience, recited the canonical hours and masses, punished our bodies with fasting, prayers (*orationibus*), and chastisements, etc., if a husband, wife, prince, governor, teacher, scholar, if a hireling or a servant carrying sacks, if a maidservant sweeping the house are not only our equals, but even better and more deserving?[2]

Reason, then, hearing Paul's denial that the purpose of the law is for justification, infers that therefore the law is nothing. 'This is the way it judges: Paul does away with the law, because he says that we may not be justified by it.'[3] Reason's inference is, indeed, 'Let us live as the Gentiles which have not the law'— precisely what was said in objection to Paul's standpoint even in his own day. In other passages Luther states reason's inference more succinctly: 'For reason, on hearing that it is by grace and the promise that righteousness or blesssedness is attained, immediately infers: therefore the law is no use (*nihil prodest*).'[4] But, Luther insists, reason's arguments prove only that it has never understood the purpose for which the law really was given.[5] We must not follow the judgement of reason, else it will tell us, because it does not know the true office of the law, that

[1] Ibid. 344. 10 = 345. 14; 343. 4. The illustration alludes to Luke x. 38 ff.
[2] See the entire passage on *Quid igitur lex?* in W.A. 40¹. 473. 7 ff. and 24 ff.
[3] Ibid. 474. 25.
[4] Ibid. 527. 31; cf. RM. 530. 10.
[5] *Non intelligit officium et finem legis* (ibid. 474. 22/24: CDE). What this 'office' is, will be discussed in the next chapter.

God is angry with transgressors. And so reason must be slain not now for its scepticism, but for its legalism. Every Christian is a high priest, for he sacrifices his own reason. And this is the sacrifice which gives God His glory.[1] But we must be quite clear *why* God is glorified through reason's sacrifice: not because it means the suspension of human rationality in general, the crucifixion of the intellect, but because it is the removal of a particular false understanding about God which makes of Him a harsh Judge, whereas in truth He is merciful and has sent His Son to be our Saviour. The charge is, indeed, brought quite explicitly against reason, that it turns Christ into a Law-giver or (what is tantamount to the same thing) an Example: that is to say, reason imagines that Christ's 'office' is to show us what *we* must do to be saved, whereas the Gospel tells us that *Christ* has done all that needs to be done. 'Reason makes Christ a lawgiver.'[2] Hence reason is incorrect thinking about God, just as faith is correct thinking, and the grounds for Luther's condemnation are reason's fundamental misunderstanding of God.[3] But when we have said this, we must immediately add that Luther means to condemn only 'carnal reason'—reason unenlightened by faith—and that the essence of carnal reason's wrong thinking lies in its incurable legalism.

Reason and the miracle of forgiveness

What reason cannot grasp is, in the final analysis, the sheer miracle of forgiveness. Reason would like acceptance by God to be strictly on the basis of a *quid pro quo*, for it cannot understand how so inestimable a treasure should be given for nothing. As Luther puts it in a simple, but eloquent passage:

The human heart does not understand, nor does it believe, that so great a treasure as the Holy Spirit is given simply for the hearing of faith, but it argues like this: 'It is a weighty matter (*magna res*)— forgiveness of sins, deliverance from sin and death, the giving of the Holy Spirit, of righteousness and eternal life; therefore you must offer something of weight, if you would obtain those unutterable gifts.' This opinion (*opinionem*) the Devil approves and fosters in the heart. And so when reason hears: 'You can do nothing to obtain the

---

[1] W.A. 40¹. 369. 20/21 (CDE); 369. 6 and 370. 12.
[2] Ibid. 562. 5 (RM.; cf. CA.). Also: 434. 5, 533. 15 ff. (= RM. 1 ff.), 563. 15, 563. 22.
[3] Ibid. 376. 6 ff. and 23 ff.

remission of sins, but ought only to hear the Word of God', it immediately cries out: 'No! you make the forgiveness of sins too mean and contemptible.' So, it is the very magnitude of the gift which prevents our accepting it; and because so great a treasure is offered for nothing, it is despised.[1]

If, therefore, we are ever to come to a knowledge of God's grace, it will be by revelation from the Word: 'This is a kind of doctrine which is divinely given (*divinitus datum*), not discovered (*repertum*) by any freewill, reason, or wisdom.'[2] Free forgiveness is not something which the human reason could 'excogitate' for itself, because reason is shot through with legalistic presuppositions. It cannot be learned by study; it is revealed by God Himself.[3] It is shown me by the Gospel, not by human reason.[4] It is a kind of doctrine that cannot be learned or taught by man, but only by God in the 'external Word' (*per Deum externo verbo*): then the Spirit reveals it within (*intus*).[5] Christian righteousness is an 'unspeakable gift which surpasses reason'.[6]

Here we are in a completely different world, outside of reason (*in alio prorsus mundo extra rationem*), where there is no arguing about what we ought to do, or by what kind of works we should earn (*mereamur*) grace and the forgiveness of sins. Here we are in divine theology, where we hear this Gospel, that Christ died for us, and that believing this we are accounted righteous, though sins nevertheless remain in us—and big ones at that.[7]

'By my reason I cannot grasp that I am received into grace because of Christ: but I hear this announced through the Gospel, and I grasp it by faith.'[8] The mercy of God is beyond words: our minds are too small to understand it, leave alone telling it in words.[9]

---

[1] Ibid. 343. 22. Cf. 444. 23: 'Difficile est rationi, ista tam inaestimabilia bona credere.' 455. 19: 'Quinetiam ipsa magnitudo divinae misericordiae . . . incredulitatem parit.'

[2] Ibid. 73. 16; cf. 73. 6 (RM.).

[3] 'Non discitur aut acquiritur ullo studio, diligentia aut sapientia hominum, aut lege etiam divina, sed per Deum ipsum . . . revelatur' (ibid. 141. 19/142. 16: CDE).

[4] Ibid. 141. 23.

[5] Ibid. 142. 1 (RM.). Cf. W.A. 40². 31. 30.

[6] W.A. 40¹. 370. 24.   [7] Ibid. 371. 21 (RM. 4).

[8] Ibid., 377. 4 and 17.

[9] '. . . non potest angusta cordis humani comprehendere, multo minus eloqui' (ibid. 455. 15 ff.; RM. 1 ff.). Cf.: 'Ideo Scriptura sancta loquitur de aliis rebus

Little comment is necessary on the catena of passages which can be put together from the Commentary. They prove quite conclusively that in Luther's mind, when he so summarily dismissed the powers of human reason, was an overwhelming sense of awe before the mystery of free forgiveness. The real object of Luther's assault is, then, legalism. Reason receives a share of the criticism when it allies itself to the law, for to establish the law is to abolish the Gospel.[1] To say that *reason* cannot understand the 'magnitude' of forgiveness and freedom from sin, is tantamount to saying that the *legalists* (the *iusticiarii*) cannot understand.[2] And the suggestion that legalism is somehow reasonable, does not make it normative, something we ought to accept. Indeed, it is a bewitchment, a prodigious illusion of the Devil by which he has driven nearly all mankind insane.[3]

To conclude this chapter, two questions will be asked and briefly answered. If this is the heart of Luther's assault on *ratio* in the *Commentary on Galatians*, (1) Can the same teaching be found elsewhere in Luther's writings? and (2) How far is it an aspect of his thought which the Luther-scholars—and, indeed, Protestant theologians generally—have emphasized?

The answer to the first question is that there are many passages scattered throughout Luther's writings where the association of reason and the law is clearly set forth, yet nowhere, I believe, at such length as in the *Commentary on Galatians*. Indeed, the legalistic assumption is mentioned in connexion with reason, with philosophy, and with Aristotle.

Reason or Nature (Luther has been using the words interchangeably) goes insane in spiritual matters: it builds on sand, uses cobwebs for clothing, sand for making bread, and so on. For, if you ask her what it is that you must do to be saved, she will reply:

Ah! You must build churches, cast bells, institute masses, hold vigils; make chalices, monstrances, images, ornaments; burn candles, pray so much, keep the fast of St. Catherine, become a priest or a

quam Politicus, Philosophicus aut Mosaicus liber, nempe de inenarrabilibus ac plane divinis donis quae omnem humanum et Angelicum captum et simpliciter omnia superant' (455. 27).

[1] W.A. 40¹. 207. 16.   [2] W.A. 40². 6. 10 and 18.
[3] W.A. 40¹. 322. 1 ff. and 13 ff.; cf. 327. 3 ff. and 18 ff. Also: 326. 14.

monk; run off to Rome and St. James; wear hairshirts, whip yourself; and so on.

These are the good works with which Reason paves the road to heaven! And if you ask her how she knows all this, all she can reply is: 'That's the way it seems to her (*es dunkt sie so recht seyn*).'[1] It is this arrogant attempt of man to prescribe for himself the conditions of his salvation that lies at the heart of the legalistic assumption. Prophets, wise men, scribes—none of God's messengers can persuade obstinate reason to abandon its self-appointed modes of worship. Reason prefers to cling to its own chosen works, and when God's messengers call its worship 'idolatry', they are put to death, exiled, or persecuted.[2] If Eve may stand as the type of reason's disobedience, and Nicodemus of reason's blindness, then Cain is the type of reason's legalism and foolish persistence in devising works which the Word does not demand.[3] The struggle of Cain and Abel reflects the ageless conflict between reason's self-appointed worship and the divinely-appointed worship of faith.

The whole dispute lies in this, that the false saints quarrelled with the true saints over the service of God (*gottisdienst*) and good works. The former said: 'This is the service of God.' The latter said: 'No, it is idolatry and unbelief.' So it has been from the beginning, and so it will be until the end.[4]

The importance of this summing-up of 'the whole dispute' could hardly be overestimated, for it shows quite clearly what Luther had often in mind when he spoke of the conflict of faith and reason: reason is not identified with scepticism, but with what John Oman liked to call the religion of 'ceremonial-legalism.'[5] Hence, the Papists had reason on their side, not because they

---

[1] W.A. 10¹, ¹. 532. 2 ff. and 532. 8 (postil for Epiphany, on Isa. lx. 1–6). Luther goes on, it may be said in passing, to state what is often regarded as the distinctive principle of Calvin's conception of authority in contradistinction to the German Reformer's: 'Was nit gott gepotten hatt, das soll man meyden auffs aller vleyssigst' (534.4).

[2] Ibid. 271. 4 ff. (St. Stephen's Day, on Matt. xxiii. 34–39).

[3] W.A. 42. 117. 15 ff. and esp. 118. 41; 10¹, ². 298. 5 ff.; 10¹, ¹. 325. 21 ff. Abel typifies 'faithful works', Cain typifies 'will-works'. The basis for the distinction lies in Luther's exegesis of Gen. iv. 4: 'The Lord had respect unto Abel and his offering.' That is to say, God accepted the person first, then the works: Abel was 'justified' before his 'works' could be acceptable to God.

[4] W.A. 10¹, ¹. 274. 5.

[5] *The Natural and the Supernatural* (Cambridge, 1931), esp. pp. 429 ff.

championed the rational discipline of Scholastic philosophy, but because they fostered the kind of religion which expects God to favour works that He has never required. Reason knows that we should be pious towards God, but when called upon to tell us *how*, it 'fools around with works' (*narret mit den werken*)— fasting, praying, building churches, ringing bells, burning incense, intoning, singing, wearing cowls, shaving heads, burning candles, and unending silly works. The Roman mass itself is, according to Luther, an invention of reason.[1]

Many of the specific points raised in the *Commentary on Galatians*, as well as the general association of reason and law, could be paralleled elsewhere in Luther's works. Reason only knows God as a terrible, angry Judge. It is quite the opposite of grace since its behaviour is always calculative: it is kind only to the rich and the powerful, to guests and friends. Even when reason grasps that God is merciful, it cannot believe that God will be merciful *to it*: as Luther often says, man finds it hard to use the personal pronoun, to say that God loves *me*.[2] The failure of reason is summed up in the *Disputation concerning Justification*:[3]

> This is the way reason argues: 'If you are justified, you cannot be a sinner.' But the argument is not in the least valid. For reason neither knows nor understands the greatness of divine mercy, nor how great and effectual is faith. And so men cease not from burying the Word of God with human inventions.

It is in the contemplation of future judgement that reason's legalism is most clearly exposed: grace must 'take us out of ourselves', for reason cannot instruct us.[4] Reason cannot go beyond the external piety of works: the more clever it is, the more it depends upon its works. In times of temptation man cannot but grope around for works, which he enumerates in vain, only sinking deeper into despair. Indeed, even believers must daily contend against this error of reason. 'Thus we must work ourselves out of ourselves and rise above reason.' Reason is no guide in the Kingdom of Christ simply because His is the Kingdom of Grace, not of works (*das reich der gnaden*).[5]

[1] W.A. 10¹· ¹. 205. 4; 10¹· ². 407. 8.
[2] W.A. 17¹. 430. 38; 10¹· ². 180. 17; 19. 206. 15.
[3] W.A. 39¹. 97. 6. Cf. American edn. xxxiv. 166.
[4] W.A. 10¹·¹. 41. 13 ff.; esp. 42. 20, 43. 1.
[5] W.A. 29. 571. 25 ff.; 572. 20; 570. 24.

There can, then, be no doubt that in other writings, too, Luther's understanding of reason is set within the context of the conflict between law and grace. The same holds for his understanding of philosophy in general and Aristotelian philosophy in particular: they also are sometimes repudiated because they buttress the legalistic assumption of the natural man. 'That is the opinion of the Pope *and of all the philosophers*: "If I am godly, then I will have a gracious God."' The legalistic assumption could not more explicitly be stated. And in another passage, where Luther is talking of philosophy's endless speculations about God, the soul, and life eternal, he adds: 'Then, even when the Word is proffered, we again seek God with devotions and superstitions.'[1] Further, even in the *Disputation on the Sentence*, '*The Word was made flesh*', as Karl Heim points out,[2] Luther asserts that philosophy understands only the law: the justification of the sinner through grace remains incomprehensible to philosophy.

Turning to Aristotle, if we ask why exactly Luther assailed the Greek philosopher in, say, the *Disputation against Scholastic Theology*,[3] the answer is not at all hard to determine. The main concern of the theses is to defend Augustine's views on the bondage of the will against the Pelagian tendencies of Scotus and of the Nominalists, Occam, 'the Cardinal' (D'Ailly), and 'Gabriel' (Biel). Luther attacks the characteristic phrases of the later Schoolmen: 'to love God above all things', 'to do what in one lies', and so on. For the same erroneous assumption underlies the use of them all, namely, that it is possible for man to prepare himself for grace. But, in fact, there can be no preparation for grace on man's side: the only preparation is on God's side, and it consists in the decree of election (theses 29–30). The root error of Nominalism is that it gives man something to boast of: man does not want God to be God, he himself wants to be God. For nature necessarily 'glories and takes pride in every work which is apparently and outwardly good' (theses 17 and 37). Only after such assertions as these does Luther introduce Aristotle, and, when he finally does introduce him,

---

[1] 'Illa cogitatio papae et omnium philosophorum: Bin ich fromm, so hab ich einen gnedigen Got' (TR. 1, no. 447). The italics are mine. The other citation is from TR. 5, no. 6064.

[2] Op. cit., p. 16.

[3] W.A. 1. 224 ff. Trans. in American edn., vol. xxxi.

it is specifically to object to the doctrine that we may become righteous by doing righteous deeds (thesis 40). Then comes the famous remark: 'Almost the whole of Aristotle's *Ethics* is the worst enemy of grace' (thesis 41).[1] It is, in short, the doctrine of *habitus* (*hexis*) which is the focal point of Luther's assault on Aristotle, for, as used by the Nominalists, it was diametrically opposed to Luther's own fundamental doctrine that a man is justified by faith without works, that he must first be righteous before he can do any righteous deeds.[2] Of course, Luther knew perfectly well that Aristotle himself was not propounding a rival soteriology to St. Paul's; hence the repeated assertion that the Schoolmen misunderstood Aristotle, applying to theology propositions which belonged originally only to philosophy. Only in the light of these considerations can we see the significance of theses 43–44 in the present disputation: 'It is an error to say that no man can become a theologian without Aristotle. . . . Indeed, a man can *only* become a theologian without Aristotle.' For the crux of Luther's opposition to the Schoolmen is that they force Aristotle into the service of their own legalistic presuppositions.[3]

Our second question—concerning the extent to which Luther's understanding of reason and law has been emphasized by the Luther-scholars—can be more briefly dismissed. The subject nowhere (I believe) receives extended treatment, but the essentials of Luther's position have been pointed out incidentally by several writers. The general setting for Luther's

---

[1] W.A. 1. 226. 10. Cf. the *Address to the German Nobility*, W.A. 6. 458 14.

[2] Cf. W.A. 10[1, 1]. 327. 6: Reason protests, 'Denn also hatt Aristoteles geleret: wer viel gutts thutt, der wirt dadurch gutt'—and this devilish doctrine holds sway over all the high schools. W.A. 1. 84. 19: 'Non qui iusta operatur iustus est, ut Aristoteles ait, neque operando iusta et dicimur iusti sed credendo et sperando in Deum.' W.A. 5. 33. 8: '[Habitum] recentiores Theologi ex Aristotele invexerunt ad subvertendam intelligentiam scripturae.'

[3] It has frequently been pointed out that Aristotle's teaching on moral virtue is paradoxical, even if it does not actually argue in a circle. For, whilst Aristotle certainly says *ta dikaia prattontes dikaioi ginometha* (*Eth. Nic.* II. 1), he also perceived that no act was genuinely 'just' unless it came from a just disposition. Hence, Luther makes two qualifications in rejecting Aristotle's ethics. First, he insists that the doctrine of *hexis*, properly understood, has nothing to do with justification. Second, he was fond of pointing to the other element in Aristotle's moral philosophy, which appeared in Scholasticism as the doctrine that *recta ratio et bona voluntas* must precede genuinely good works. For this second qualification, see (in addition to passages already cited) W.A. 42. 608. 41.

quarrel with reason has, according to E. M. Carlson,[1] been shown by the Swedish scholars to be primarily soteriological: 'There is general agreement among Swedish students that Luther's rejection of reason applies primarily, if not exclusively, to the matter of justification.' P. S. Watson leans heavily on the Swedish Luther-interpreters, and his discussion of reason (under the heading: 'The False Religion of the Natural Man') is very largely an analysis of relevant passages in the *Commentary on Galatians*.[2] If any adverse criticism is justifiable in considering Watson's valuable discussion, it would perhaps be that he stresses too one-sidedly a single aspect of Luther's teaching on reason. For, if Luther's thinking on the place of reason does tend to be concentrated on the question of legalism, it does not seem possible to reduce *all* his relevant utterances to a single pattern. The beginning of any attempt to solve the problem of Luther's polemic against reason must be made elsewhere, namely, in a consideration of his basic dualism: the question of reason and law is one specific issue—probably the most important one— within this wider framework.

The German Luther-scholars have also drawn attention to the distinctive associations of reason in Luther's writings. Hence, in an extremely discerning interpretation of Luther's attitude towards reason, Karl Holl wrote:

> The God who answered to 'reason' could never be anything but the God of works-righteousness (*der Gott der Werkgerechtigkeit*). For 'reason' was bound to cling to the thesis that God wishes a man well who strives to lead a blameless life. A God who concerned Himself with *sinners* was, on this proposition, something incomprehensible.

Following A. V. Müller, Holl rightly insists that it is this aspect of Luther's thought which makes his understanding of the 'unreasonableness' of Christian doctrine utterly different from anything that Occam had to say on the subject. Luther's opposition to reason is as much directed against Scotus and Occam as any others of the Schoolmen.[3] The heart of Luther's assault on reason lies in his conviction that justification is 'anything but something rational, a logical conclusion that man

---

[1] *The Reinterpretation of Luther*, p. 127.
[2] *Let God be God!*, pp. 85 ff.
[3] *Gesammelte Aufsätze*, I. 37.

could infer from the fact of the moral law'. Justification is *wider
alle Vernunft*—against all reason, against even morality and
conscience. 'A doctrine like that of the Gospel, that God wants
to concern Himself with the *sinner*, must seem' to reason 'a
subversion of all morality'.[1]

Many other witnesses could, no doubt, be called to testify
to the peculiarities of Luther's attitude towards reason. Bengt
Hägglund shows that 'reason', in Luther, stands for the 'attitude
of the natural man', not simply for a certain faculty of the mind.
'To reason belongs a definite knowledge of the law and, with it,
the opinion that by fulfilling the law man is justified.'[2] And
Roland Bainton writes that 'Luther, as no one before him in
more than a thousand years, sensed the import of the miracle
of divine forgiveness. It is a miracle because there is no reason
for it according to man's standards.' And this, according to
Bainton, is why Luther 'so decried reason'.[3] Such an 'evangelical
irrationalism', as J. S. Whale calls it,[4] is not to be understood as
a condemnation of reason generally: it is merely the forgiven
sinner's way of expressing his astonishment at the grace of God.
Forgiveness, Brunner likes to say, can never be taken for granted.
It always comes as a surprise. And the sceptic who says, 'Dieu
pardonnera: c'est son métier', has not the least notion of what
forgiveness means.[5] The 'miracle of divine forgiveness'—this,
then, is the conviction which lies at the heart of Luther's case
against reason, and it is a conviction which is inseparable from
the Protestant Faith. Let P. T. Forsyth be our last witness:
'There is nothing which is such a surprise, such a permanent
surprise, and such a growing surprise to reason as grace.'[6]
Luther's own feelings could hardly have been expressed more
perfectly: the words might almost be his.[7]

---

[1] *Gesammelte Aufsätze*, 1. 77.
[2] *Theologie und Philosophie bei Luther*, p. 84.
[3] *The Reformation of the Sixteenth Century*, pp. 34–35.
[4] *The Protestant Tradition*, p. 71.
[5] See, for example, Brunner's *The Scandal of Christianity* (London: S.C.M. Press Ltd., 1951), pp. 16–17 and 80–81.
[6] *The Principle of Authority* (London: Hodder and Stoughton, n.d.), p. 455.
[7] It is surprising that Lohse's *Ratio und Fides* does not give more attention to reason's resistance against the evangelical doctrine of free forgiveness, since this is in many ways the most interesting feature of Luther's standpoint. Possibly this is because Lohse allows his interpretation to be determined very largely by the 'Young Luther' (cf. his remarks on p. 20), whereas we ourselves have used mainly

The problem to which we must now turn is: How does this special sense of 'reason' fit into Luther's understanding of true and false religion, particularly his understanding of the place and function of the 'law' in God's plan of salvation? For, if reason's misinterpretation of law lies at the heart of false religion, how can we assign a proper place to law in the divine economy? Can we, indeed, evade the charge of antinomianism?

the writings of the 'Mature Luther'. To be sure, he does have a brief section on *Ratio und Gesetz* (pp. 82–86), in which reason's abuse of the law is mentioned; but he certainly gives no special prominence to this area of the problem or to its implications. If Lohse's interpretation has a focal point, it is perhaps his repeated insistence that *ratio*, according to Luther, is corrupted by the perverted will of fallen man— by *Eigenwille* or *Ichwille*—and must therefore (as Paul suggests in 2 Cor. x. 5) be brought into captivity to the obedience of Christ. See, for instance, Lohse's summing-up on pp. 53–54. Clearly, this brings his interpretation closer to our own than might at first appear, since Lohse also perceives that reason, for Luther, is not just a synonym for 'rationality', but rather denotes a definite attitude of the natural man. Stürmer, on the other hand, does emphasize very strongly the connexion between reason and works-righteousness, and, conversely, between *Gottesgerechtigkeit* and *Gottesweisheit*—indeed, this is precisely the thesis of his book. But (quite apart from some questionable points of detailed interpretation), Stürmer fails to stress the fact that, at the crucial point, the condemnation of worldly reason is not parallel, but subordinate, to the condemnation of works-righteousness: indeed, the two are virtually identical, so that (*pace* Stürmer's remarks on pp. 96–97) reason and moralism really are just *one* enemy of the Church. Stürmer is perhaps mislead by his laudable aim to show that Luther can answer the fundamental question of an age which no longer asks, 'How can I get a gracious God?' (see his Foreword). But this tempts him into an un-Lutheran elevation of epistemology to the side of soteriology. He even entertains the possibility of a second *articulus stantis et cadentis ecclesiae* (p. 96).

VII

REASON AND RELIGION

THE advice of the English translators of the Commentary was that we should 'reade it wholy together, and not by peeces and parts here and there'.[1] The present chapter is an attempt to view the Commentary 'wholy together', as they would have wished. In this manner, some of the loose threads inevitably left by piecemeal investigation may be drawn together. In particular an overall survey of Luther's teaching on true and false religion should enable us to perceive how, according to him, the legalistic assumption arises, and wherein lies its superficial plausibility to the judgement of natural reason. We must, in other words, take up the first of reason's two false inferences. We will see that it is an inference made from the 'general knowledge of God', which is available to man through his experience of the natural order, apart from the revelation in Christ. From this knowledge he constructs a false picture of the Deity and a false manner of worshipping. The true office of God's Law is to shatter this false religion, not to buttress it; thereby making room for faith, and through faith, true Christian righteousness. Once again we will see that what Luther decries is not reason *per se*, but the abuse of it—not our capacity to make logical inferences, but certain particular false inferences which we habitually make.

Reason: the origin of false religion

Reason, according to Luther, is a most excellent thing, save when it is in the devil's pay: and reason is very clearly in the devil's pay when, contemplating God's general revelation, it concludes that God is of such a character as to be approachable only by one who has performed certain requisite 'works' and 'ceremonies'.[2] This conclusion is the first of the 'two inferences' stated above, and to it we must now give our attention.

[1] In Watson's edn., p. 11.
[2] The *locus classicus* for Luther's teaching on this theme is to be found in his comments on Gal. iv. 8 f.

The content of the 'false religion' which man constructs through this abuse of reason corresponds exactly with the content of the revelation. By means of God's 'general revelation' (which Luther carefully distinguishes from the 'special revelation' in Christ) man is made aware of God as Creator and Judge.[1] Nor is he mistaken in this awareness: for God is, as we would say, both 'omnipotent' and 'just'. But this knowledge, accurate though it is as far as it goes, is not sufficient to prevent man from misrepresenting the character of God: it is like the limited knowledge which we have of some 'nodding acquaintance'[2] and which by no means guarantees that we shall be free from error in the impression which we inevitably form about him. Man, knowing that God is a just God who punishes sinners, assumes that only the righteous man—that is, the man who keeps the law—can draw nigh to Him. More particularly, reason argues that since God is omnipotent, it will be useful to keep Him in its debt; and because God is just, the only means of keeping Him in debt will be by the performance of 'good works'. In other words, religion becomes both eudaemonistic and legalistic. The determining categories in such a religion will be 'merit', 'reward', and 'law'. And so even the Deity becomes a means to an end, an instrument for the gratification of human desires. 'The burden of Luther's complaint against *ratio*, then, is that it subserves the egocentricity of the natural man.'[3] But in so subordinating his idea of God to his own needs and desires, man finds himself worshipping a fictitious God who exists only in the worshipper's wishful imagination. For the true God is far different.[4]

---

[1] 'Duplex est cognitio Dei, Generalis et propria. Generalem habent omnes homines, scilicet, quod Deus sit, quod creaverit coelum et terram, quod sit iustus, quod puniat impios etc.' (W.A. 40[1]. 607. 28). In this chapter the references to W.A. 40[1]–40[2] are all to the edition of 1535, save where expressly otherwise stated: refs. to the RM. parallels are not given, since in no case are the differences more than verbal.

[2] The comparison is Luther's own: he contrasts knowing a man *facie* ('by sight') and knowing him *vere*, comparing general knowledge of God to the former and special to the latter. Ibid. 607. 33. Fundamentally, the contrast is between knowing God's *esse* (that He exists), but not His *velle* (what is His will). Luther's point is that we do not really know a person unless we know his 'will toward us' (his *voluntas*). The general revelation of God does not tell us: 'quid Deus de nobis cogitet, quid dare et facere velit'.

[3] P. S. Watson, *Let God Be God!*, p. 88. The whole discussion in chap. iii is an excellent summary of Luther's viewpoint, albeit dressed up in modern jargon.

[4] The exposition which I have presented is a good deal more explicit than

Luther admits the plausibility of this false religion; indeed, one cannot help feeling that the very frequency with which reason is allowed to state its case is an indication of the force which Luther found in reason's arguments. There is something very natural about the legalistic approach to God: it seems so obvious that, if there be a Righteous God at all, righteousness must be a prerequisite of man's communion with Him. And Luther fully recognized this 'naturalness'. Indeed, he saw that Scripture itself seems often to be on the side of reason and law. Consequently, man's reason is able to cite the Old Testament in support of its legalistic assumption. 'For it is written: "Do this, and thou shalt live." '[1] Further, he certainly felt the deepest horror towards antinomianism, and legalism thrives on its criticism of antinomianism.[2]

Nevertheless, he is uncompromising in his criticisms. In the first place, full and perfect knowledge of God is available only in Christ, and the error of reason is that it by-passes the perfect revelation, building only upon a revelation which is (though true) very imperfect.[3] Often Luther speaks as if there were no general revelation at all.[4] But this certainly is not his

Luther is in any one passage. But he affirms *passim*: (1) that idolatry only arises because there exists a general revelation; (2) that the essence of idolatry is a kind of conspiracy between law and reason, reason interpreting revelation legalistically. 'Nam hinc, quod homines tenuerunt hanc Maiorem: Deus est, nata est omnis idololatria, quae sine cognitione divinitatis ignota fuisset in mundo. Quia vero homines hanc naturalem cognitionem de Deo habebant, conceperunt extra et contra verbum vanas et impias de Deo cogitationes, quas amplexi sunt tanquam ipsam veritatem illisque Deum finxerunt aliter quam natura est. Ut Monachus fingit deum talem, qui remittat peccata . . . propter observationem Regulae suae.' This is perhaps the clearest outline, at least in the *Com. on Gal.* (W.A. 40¹. 608. 25). Cf. Vilmos Vajta, *Luther on Worship*, ch. 1; G. W. Forell, *Faith Active in Love*, pp. 67 f. and 114 ff.; Lohse, op. cit., pp. 59 ff.

¹ W.A. 40¹. 268. 13. Hence Reason's inference seems quite inescapable, so that careful instruction is needed to refute it: 'Ut cum audit [sc. the seeker after godliness] bona opera esse facienda, Christum esse imitandum, possit recte iudicare, et dicere: Bene, libenter ista faciam. Quid amplius?—Tunc salvus eris! Non.' Ibid. 263. 27. (RM. is more sententious: 'Oportet hoc facere!—Bene.—Et tum salvus eris!—Non.') The inference is also stated in the negative form: 'Non servasti praecepta, ergo Deus est offensus et irascitur tibi; Estque haec consequentia inseparabilis: Peccavi, ergo moriar . . . Tu peccasti, ergo Deus irascitur tibi . . .' (260. 17). Cf. also: 'Hoc si feceris, mereberis' (264. 6).

² Ibid. 344. 23.

³ Luther would, I think, find it hard to defend himself against the charge of unwittingly criticizing the general revelation itself: for it is clear that he blames reason for what is really a weakness in the revelation.

⁴ For example, W.A. 40¹. 602. 18.

only line of thought: elsewhere, he approaches the idea of a 'sacramental universe', so firm is his insistence that *all creation* is the medium of God's self-disclosure.[1] What Luther is always careful to maintain is that all knowledge of God is revealed knowledge; and this leads us on to his second criticism of reason and reason's misunderstanding of God.

For, in the second place, he insists that reason inverts the true direction of religion, that is to say, reason thinks of man's approach to God rather than of God's approach to man. This is the crux of Luther's diatribes against the 'ladders' of Scholastic theology.[2]

In the third place, reason's legalistic religion is based upon a *false* inference. It is clear—through special, no less than through general, revelation—that God's character is such that He requires His children to perform 'good works', but reason quite wrongly infers that works are therefore required *for salvation itself*. Works certainly ought to be performed, and that 'ought' is an obligation grounded in the character of God. But still, our acceptance with God does not depend upon our ability to satisfy Him with good works: on the contrary, our ability to perform good works depends upon our first being accepted by God, for He is the source of all goodness.[3]

In the fourth place, and this is the heart of Luther's criticism, reason's attitude is essentially arrogance. This single charge sums up the whole of Luther's indictment. The highest and noblest thing of which man is capable is to give God glory: 'It is not reason that does this, but faith.'[4] The grounds on which Luther makes this assertion we have already seen: reason is man's Tower of Babel by which he seeks to force an entry into heaven.

[1] For Luther's doctrine of the *larvae Dei*, see P. S. Watson, *Let God Be God!*, pp. 76 ff.
[2] Cf. Nygren, *Agape and Eros*, pp. 621 ff. The 'three ladders' are 'rationalism', 'mysticism', and 'legalism': all of them have this in common, that they are essentially a striving to reach God 'from beneath'.
[3] See, for example, W.A. 40^1. 263. 13 ff., where Luther criticizes the false inference of reason. He concludes: 'Concedo omnia bona esse facienda, mala ferenda, sanguinem esse fundendum, si res ita postulet, propter Christum; sed per haec non iustificor nec salutem consequor.' Cf. also the repeated affirmation that character makes conduct, just as the tree produces fruit: 'Fides primum personam facit quae postea facit opera.' Ibid. 402. 13 ff.
[4] Ibid. 360. 24.

Works: *the expression of false religion*

The false religion of the natural man arises, then, from the abuse of reason. We must now go on to consider the way in which it expresses itself, namely, in 'good works'.

Luther's attitude towards 'works' and 'ceremonies' is very clear-cut, and there is no difficulty whatever in understanding his oft-repeated standpoint in the *Commentary on Galatians*. That Luther's teaching on works *has* often been misunderstood—and even grossly misrepresented—is regrettably true. But it is also true that there can be no other reason for such misunderstanding than sheer ignorance of what Luther actually says.

Paul's own terse affirmation, 'By the works of the law there shall no flesh be justified',[1] sums up Luther's uncompromising standpoint. Again and again he takes his stand by Paul's side, constantly reaffirming the impossibility of salvation by works: for it cannot be 'beaten into men's heads sufficiently'.[2] It is faith *alone* that justifies,[3] although the faith which justifies does not *abide* alone.

One of Luther's longest excursuses admirably illustrates his attitude, namely, his discussion of the message contained in the Acts of the Apostles.[4] His choice of a text is, perhaps, somewhat curious, since Acts is by no means consistently 'Pauline' in its theology. It is especially curious that Luther should take Cornelius for an example, since Acts explicitly says that Cornelius had been noticed by God because of his 'prayers' and 'alms'.[5] Nevertheless, whether exegetically sound or not, Luther's comments finely illustrate his own position: Cornelius and his friends *do* nothing, save listen to Peter. Therefore, the Holy Ghost is received by the hearing of faith, and not by the doing of the law. 'Ipsi sedentes nihil agunt': they sit by and do nothing—what more perfect illustration could Luther have

---

[1] Gal. ii. 16 (Rome. iii. 20).

[2] W.A. 40¹. 266. 24: a favourite expression (I have given the rendering of the 'Middleton' Eng. trans., revised by P. S. Watson, p. 157.)

[3] For the controversy which has—quite unnecessarily, so far as linguistics are concerned—long been raging over Luther's *sola fide*, see Flew and Davies, *Catholicity of Protestantism*, pp. 70–71.

[4] W.A. 40¹. 331–40.

[5] Ibid. 337. 23 ff., shows that Luther is aware of the difficulty. (The reference in Acts is x. 4: 'Thy prayers and thine alms are come up for a memorial before God' —A.V.).

found of the contrast between faith and works? And so, he argues, it is with the rest of the Acts: the Holy Ghost—and, therefore, salvation—is given by the hearing of faith.[1]

An objection which has constantly been alleged against Luther's attitude to 'good works' (and still is, even in our own day) is stated and rebutted in the comments on Galatians iii. 10. The objectors point out that there are numerous passages in Scripture where God is represented as accepting worshippers on the grounds of some work performed or some ceremony enacted. Luther's reply is rather sophistic, and he was evidently uneasy about it.[2] On the basis of Hebrews xi he argues that no work is acceptable to God unless prompted by faith.[3] Thus, for example, Abel was accepted by reason of his offering, but his offering was made acceptable by his faith. The 'doing' which God approves is 'faithful doing', and rewards are offered only to a 'faith which works'.[4] The relation between faith and works is, in this context, so intimate that Luther speaks of a 'composite, concrete, or incarnate faith'.[5] The last is a particularly interesting adjective: Luther can even say that faith is the divinity of works, being spread throughout the works as the divinity throughout the humanity of Christ.[6] Hence he concludes that Scripture sometimes can attribute to works what strictly belongs only to faith, or, better, to 'working faith'.[7]

Again we may well doubt whether Luther succeeds in his attempt to meet objectors on exegetical grounds. But, in the attempt, he certainly makes his own position clear: no man can be justified by works, even though we admit that the only kind of faith which justifies is the faith which produces works. All works, without any distinction, are of no avail, because all spring from a fundamentally false understanding of God and of

---

[1] 'Totus namque ille liber nihil aliud agit, quam quod decet ex lege non dari spiritum sanctum sed ex auditu Evangelii' (W.A. 40[1]. 331. 21).

[2] W.A. 40[1]. 419–20 (CDE). He is even driven, in the last resort, to take refuge in his 'Christocentric' conception of Biblical authority: 'Tu urges servum, hoc est, scripturam, et eam non totam. . . . Ego urgeo dominum, qui rex est Scripturae.'

[3] 'Habes itaque Canonem ex cap. 11 ad Ebrae. . . .' (Ibid. 414. 10: CDE).

[4] Ibid. 415. 21, 25. Luther describes his juggling with words as a *nova et theologica grammatica* (ibid. 418. 24).

[5] Ibid. 415. 16.

[6] Ibid. 417. 15.

[7] Ibid. 418. 32: 'Quidquid fidei tribuitur, postea etiam operibus tribuatur, sed propter solam fidem.'

religion. Luther finds it strange that the different orders of monks are unable to agree amongst themselves, for really they are all as much alike as one egg is like another![1] They are all guilty of the same fatal error of assuming that God is to be placated by human works: 'If I do thus, I will have a merciful God.'[2]

Luther criticizes on many grounds this fatal error which underlies all works-religions. No less than ten distinct charges are brought against it in the *Commentary on Galatians* alone. (1) The assumption that God can be placated by human works can only be made because man underestimates the price of redemption: the *Cross* was God's price, not any works of man.[3] (2) Obedience to the Law, rightly understood, is impossible, for it requires an 'inwardness' which Law itself cannot produce.[4] (3) Man's will is not free to perform the good works which it sets before itself.[5] (4) Good works and ceremonies are only done 'in the body', and do not affect the condition of the 'spirit'.[6] (5) Similarly, they are only done 'in this world', not 'in the kingdom of Christ'.[7] (6) The attempt to win salvation by obedience to the law is to misunderstand the Law's proper function.[8] (7) Works-religion tyrannizes the conscience, leading to perpetual fear of falling short of the required standard.[9] (8) Works-religion panders to man's cardinal sin, his pride in his own achievement and his desire to be self-sufficient.[10] (9) It is not works which make a man accepted by God, but being accepted by God that makes a man perform good works.[11] (10) The desire to win salvation by works robs God of His glory, because it is His gracious prerogative to give salvation freely to the undeserving.[12]

Again we must say that the sum of Luther's objections lies in

---

[1] W.A. 40[1]. 604. 20. RM. has: 'Ovum non tam simile ovo ut Tartar, Turca, et Papa: Sic vivam, ergo miseretur Deus; sic non vixi, ergo non etc.'

[2] Ibid. 603. 10 (RM.). The edn. of 1535 reads: 'Si hoc vel illud fecero, habebo Deum propitium, si non, habebo iratum' (603. 29).

[3] Ibid. 295. 20 ff. Luther is fond of emphasizing the difference between God's standard and man's. Cf. the story of the dying eremite in ibid. 258. 29: 'In mentem ei venit Deum longe aliter iudicare quam homines.'

[4] Ibid. 221. 13, 403. 11, 407. 26, 518. 27 ff.

[5] Ibid. 293. 24.

[6] Ibid. 270. 29.

[7] Ibid. 95. 12.

[8] Ibid. 73. 21.

[9] Ibid. 353. 35.

[10] Ibid. 325. 33 ff.

[11] Ibid. 287. 21.

[12] Ibid. 442. 22.

the charge of pride or arrogance. Like Paul, Luther contrasts faith with that 'boasting' which is invariably an accompaniment of all attempts to earn salvation by good works. Reason's religion of works is symptomatic of that fundamental self-love which leads a man into the blasphemy of seeking his own even in God and of imagining that any merely human goodness can be perfect enough to put God in his debt.

Law: the error of false religion

We have seen that false religion arises through reason's legalistic misunderstanding of general revelation. We have also seen that one of Luther's criticisms of false religion is that it fails to grasp the true meaning of the law. How, then, does Luther think of the law, and what significance has the law for the interpretation of faith and reason?

Luther uses names to describe the law that are no less shocking than his description of reason, and he claims Pauline precedent for doing so.[1] His vehemence is partly, no doubt, a reflection of bitter experience, partly an indication that Luther saw in legalism his subtlest enemy. But what exactly does Luther mean by 'the law'? Like Paul, he oscillates between 'Law' in the strictly Jewish sense (the Law of Moses) and 'law' generally as a method of self-salvation. Occasionally the distinction can be indicated by using a capital 'L' where the Old Testament Law is intended; but it is not always possible to be sure which meaning Luther has in mind, and often, no doubt, no distinction is required. The law, in fact, is given in three stages. First, there is the 'law of nature', which is possessed by all men, Jew and Gentile alike. Second, God gave the 'Law of Moses' to the Jewish nation, as an act of special revelation. Third, Christ himself reveals the law. It is in Christ that the demands of God are most fully manifested, so that it is quite true to regard him as a lawgiver. What is not true is to make him a lawgiver and nothing else, and this is (as we have seen) one of reason's worst misunderstandings. For, if it is the office of Christ to reveal the law, yet it is not his 'chief and proper office'. Further, Luther firmly rejects the suggestion that Paul's opposition to the law is limited to the ceremonial laws of Judaism: even when he speaks

[1] Ibid. 553. 28.

of 'Law' (in the strictly Jewish sense), he means to include the Moral Law given in the Ten Commandments.[1]

The case of the legalists is admittedly strong. Nevertheless, in the face of perennial objections, Luther will not move from his position that, as far as salvation or justification is concerned, obedience to the law could avail nothing. For the *primary* function of the law was, not to assist, but to crush the attempt of man to win salvation by his own achievement.

The law has, in fact, a double purpose, civil and theological.[2] Civil laws—which, Luther insists, are ordained of God—are intended to restrain sin: so far from making a man righteous, they prove that he is *not* righteous, just as the chains which restrain a bear or a lion do not make it tame, but rather display its savagery.[3]

The second—that is, the 'proper' or 'theological'—use of the law is to show a man the enormity of his sin by setting before him an unattainable standard.[4] Hence, the real end of the law is, not the achievement of salvation, but the condemnation of sin: for the law brings sin to light, accuses and terrifies the conscience, driving man to desperation.[5] It does nothing else but destroy.[6] And if this is true of God's law alone, how much more true when there are added the laws and traditions devised by the reason of men![7]

Luther has a remarkable store of illustrations by which he

---

[1] See the discussion in P. S. Watson, *Let God Be God!*, pp. 105 ff. On the question of 'ceremonial' and 'moral' Law see: W.A. 40[1]. 218. 24, 219. 34, 302. 18 ff. It is interesting to observe that the Roman Catholics of today still make use of the evasion which Luther is parrying. Cf., for example, Garrigou-Lagrange, *Grace: A Commentary on the Summa Theologica*, p. 338 n.; for the inadequacy of this kind of argument see Bultmann, op. cit. 1. 260 ff.

[2] 'Hic sciendum est duplicem esse legis usum. Alter civilis est. . . . Alter legis usus est theologicus seu spiritualis.' W.A. 40[1]. 479. 17, 480. 32.

[3] 'Deus ordinavit civiles, imo omnes leges ad cohercendas transgressiones. Ergo omnis lex lata est ad impedienda peccata. Ergo lex, cum cohercet peccata, iustificat? Nihil minus. Quod enim non occido . . . non volens aut virtutis amore facio, sed gladium et carnificem metuo' (1535: the 1538 edn. substitutes *carcerem, gladium* for *gladium et carnificem*). Ibid. 479. 17 ff. Cf. also 480. 15 (for the idea that all the various media of restraint are ordained by God); and 480. 23 (for the value and necessity of civil restraint).

[4] Ibid. pp. 481–2 (*passim*).

[5] Ibid. 73. 21/74. 12 (CDE): 'Non remittitur [sc. *peccatum*] propter impletionem legis, quia nemo legi satisfacit, sed lex potius ostendit peccatum, accusat et praeterrefacit conscientiam, iram Dei annuntiat et in desperationem adigit.'

[6] Ibid. 263. 14.

[7] Ibid. 391. 30.

endeavours to elucidate the import of the law. The law is a 'Hercules' sent by God to destroy the savage monster of human pride; it is the 'hammer' of God, shattering all human righteousness; it is the 'thunder' and 'lightning' of God's wrath against the obstinate; it is a dazzling light that reveals God's judgement upon the works of men; and so on.[1] The figure of which Luther is particularly fond is that of the giving of the Decalogue at Sinai: for the 'terrible show and majesty' which accompanied the giving of the law at the very first were, he suggests, a kind of 'representation' of the law's proper use. The proper office of the law is to lead us out of our tents—that is, out of the false ease and security in which we dwell—and to set us before the scrutiny of God, until we cry out in dread, 'We will die, we will die: let not the Lord speak unto us.'[2]

Another illustration given by Luther stresses the positive— albeit indirect—value of the law, which is perhaps too much in the background in the illustrations already referred to. Luther finds a parable of the law in the Old Testament story of Elijah's watch upon Mount Horeb.[3] The wind, the earthquake, and the fire symbolize the law; and Elijah covers his face. Yet after the tempest came the gentle wind and whisper of God: 'The tempest of fire, of wind, and the shaking of the earth *had* to go first (*oportebat . . . praecedere*), before the Lord Himself followed in the whispering of a gentle breeze.'

The law *must* precede the Gospel, else would no man believe the Gospel. The law is given to humble man's pride, to make him receptive. The one thing which stands between God and man is man's arrogant assumption that he can *win* salvation. Hence Luther is fond of repeating the dictum of St. Bernard: 'The greatest temptation is to have no temptation.'[4] Man lives 'secure' in the 'false opinion of righteousness', until the law comes with its message of condemnation.[5] Nevertheless, we must not lose sight of the fact that God's apparent cruelty is His way of being kind. For a man can only be brought to Christ after the law has done its work: therefore, the law, though not a direct

---

[1] Ibid. 481. 18/25 (CDE); 482. 15; 482–4 (*passim*); 485. 28.
[2] Ibid. 259. 18. Cf. 483. 20.
[3] Ibid. 483. 16.
[4] Quoted Rupp, *The Righteousness of God*, p. 115. Cf. Whale, op. cit., p. 40; Pauck, *Heritage of the Reformation*, pp. 21–22.
[5] Amongst other refs. see: W.A. 40¹. 44. 12, 14; 45. 14; 257. 19; 488. 12.

cause of salvation, indirectly 'ministers to' salvation (*servit ad iustificationem*).[1] In the law God does a work 'foreign to His very nature' (an *opus alienum*), and He does it only that He may at length bring in His 'proper work' (*opus proprium*).[2] Of course, the law does not always succeed in attaining its true end: sometimes it leaves a man in despair, and sometimes it only drives him to resentment, and in neither condition can he receive the Gospel.[3] But sometimes it does achieve its intended purpose, and leaves the sinner emptied of all his arrogance, 'humbled'. And this humility is, at least in part, the meaning of faith. For faith is justified, not by its own righteousness, but by a righteousness which it receives as a gift from God. At this point, then, faith does indeed appear in Luther's thinking as the direct antithesis of reason. But this is not strictly either 'fideism' or 'irrationalism'. Luther is rather using the terms *fides* and *ratio* (eccentrically perhaps) as the names for two very different types of religiousness.

From an examination of the two categories of 'reason' and 'works', we have established that the essence of reason's false religion of works is 'pride', 'arrogance', 'egotism'. This egotistic religion expresses itself in legalism. But we have seen that it is the very same law which egotism employs to lift itself to heaven and which ultimately shatters egotism. In other words, works-religions are all, in the end, self-destroying: by an unforeseen reversal the worshipper finds that the law begins to break down the very self-confidence which he had built upon the law. And so the sinner is left humbled, despairing, emptied of his self-sufficiency.

But it is precisely out of this hopelessness that faith is born. For before a man can begin to 'have nothing but Christ in his mouth', he must learn to stop saying, 'I, I, I....'[4] God's 'strange work' is designed to show a man what he really is: it gives a

---

[1] 'Officium et usus eius non est solum ostendere peccatum ac iram Dei, sed etiam compellere ad Christum. . . . Quare si contritus es malleo isto, ne perverse utaris ista contritione, ut oneres te pluribus legibus...'. W.A. 40¹. 490. 15 ff. Cf. also 556. 25.

[2] See refs. in Rupp, *The Righteousness of God*, p. 219. For the idea of an *opus alienum Dei* cf. Watson, *Let God Be God!*, pp. 124, 158–60. Christ's work as legislator is also described as his *opus alienum*.

[3] W.A. 40¹. 487. 17, 24–25. See esp. the contrast in 86. 9 ff. and 86. 29 ff. between those who find it hard to believe because they are *too* anxious about their sins and those who find believing hard because they are not anxious *enough*.

[4] Ibid. 82. 31, 600. 13, 603. 14.

man a true self-understanding (*aperit homini cognitionem sui*).[1]
And when the sinner sees himself for what he really is, when he
sees himself *coram Deo*, then all his boasting will cease, and he
will be ready to hear the gentle word of the Gospel.

Faith, then, in the experience of the justified sinner, is born
out of humility. I think we may go a step farther and maintain
that the concept of faith was born out of the concept of humility
in the actual development of Luther's thought. As early as the
Lectures on the Psalms of 1513–15 there appears in Luther's
theology an antithesis between *superbia* and *humilitas*. It is
exactly this antithesis that epitomises the entire conflict between
religions of works and the religion of faith. For it is the nature of
superbia to seek to justify and excuse itself, whereas *humilitas* is
'self-accusation' (*accusatio sui*) which looks for justification, not
in itself, but in a gracious God.[2]

In the *Lectures on Romans* (1515–16) the transition from *humilitas* to *fides* can be observed.[3] As Rupp has said:

> Humility is finally replaced by faith, not in the sense that the word
> drops out of Luther's vocabulary, or ceases to have meaning for him
> as a Christian virtue, but that the conception of a man's passive
> waiting upon God is taken up into the word 'Faith', as the means
> whereby man abandons his own self-righteousness and apprehends
> the righteousness of God.[4]

Luther can still speak of 'imputation by humility',[5] no less readily
than he speaks of 'justification by faith'. Nevertheless, the term
'faith' can clearly be seen, first accompanying, then superseding,
the older term. Thus we find the two terms lying side by side in
various combinations—'humility *and* faith', 'humble faith', the
'humility *of* faith'.[6] And the same emphasis on humility as the
heart of faith underlies the doctrine of salvation in the *Commentary on Galatians*, written some twenty years later in the period
of Luther's full maturity:

> God is the God of the lowly (*Deus humilium*), the pitiable, the

[1] Ibid. 487. 32.
[2] See Mackinnon, op. cit. 1. 163. Also Rupp, *The Righteousness of God*, pp. 147–50.
Both Mackinnon and Rupp quote the saying: 'Nemo per fidem iustificatur nisi
prius per humilitatem sese iniustum confiteatur.'
[3] Again see Mackinnon, op cit., pp. 194–200; and Rupp, *The Righteousness of
God*, pp. 167–8. Also Wood, op. cit., pp. 12–13.
[4] *The Righteousness of God*, pp. 149–50.
[5] Mackinnon, op. cit., pp. 189 ff. [6] W.A. 56. 218. 13, 276. 32, 282. 12.

afflicted, the oppressed, the despairing—of those who have been
reduced to absolutely nothing. It is God's nature to exalt the lowly,
to feed the hungry, to give light to the blind, to comfort the pitiable
and the afflicted, to justify sinners, to raise the dead, to save the
damned and despairing. . . . In that very moment when conscience
has been terrified by the law, the law gives place to the teaching of
the Gospel and of grace which raises a man up again and brings
him comfort, saying: 'Christ came not into the world to crush the
trembling reed, or to quench the smouldering flax, but to proclaim
the Gospel to the poor, to heal the contrite in heart, to preach
deliverance to those in bondage. . . .'[1]

It is this 'humble faith' that receives righteousness from God.
In the introductory 'Argument' to the Commentary Luther
describes Paul's purpose as the drawing of distinctions between
Christian righteousness and all other kinds of righteousness:
'For righteousness is manifold (*multiplex*).'[2] He proceeds to
name four kinds of righteousness: civil, ceremonial, legal, and
Christian. It is the last that Luther calls the 'righteousness of
faith' (*iustitia fidei*), and he goes on to define it in some detail.
Primarily, it is a 'passive' righteousness; 'For in it we do no
works, offer nothing to God, but only receive and experience
another's working in us, that is, God's.'

This, then, is the whole theme of Galatians, according to
Luther: that we are saved by 'passive righteousness'. It is
'passive' because we receive it 'from outside': as Luther says
in his Preface, we are saved *per alienum auxilium*.[3] This 'righteousness from outside' he identifies with the righteousness of Christ.[4]
It is also one with the righteousness of God, since Luther always identifies the work of Christ with God's own work.[5]

It is not always easy to be quite sure what the term 'righteousness' (*iustitia*) suggests for Luther: he clearly alternates
between an ethical and a forensic connotation (as, indeed,
St. Paul himself did). Sometimes *iustitia* is an ethical quality (as,
presumably, the *iustitia Christi*); sometimes it seems to be the
verdict of God, accepting us, putting us in the right—and so
may be used in apposition with 'faith, grace, and the forgiveness
of sins'.[6]

But the fundamental and underlying thought is always trans-

[1] W.A. 40[1]. 488. 15 ff. and 25 ff.   [2] Ibid. 40. 19.
[3] 'By the help of another' (ibid. 33. 18).   [4] Ibid. 43. 15.
[5] Ibid. 81. 16.   [6] Ibid. 40. 17.

parently clear: salvation is a work of *God*, not of the sinner who is saved. This is brought out even more forcefully in the much earlier *Lectures on Romans*, delivered when Luther's theology was still in the making. In the very beginning[1] Luther states Paul's purpose in the familiar words of Jeremiah (i. 10), namely, to '"pull down, pluck up, and destroy" all wisdom and righteousness of the flesh'. God's intention is to save us, not by our own righteousness (*domesticam iustitiam*), but a righteousness 'from without' (*extraneam iustitiam*), 'from beyond' (*aliunde*), 'from heaven' (*de coelo*).[2]

In this fashion Luther not only ensured peace of mind to the anxious soul, but also ensured that all the credit for man's salvation should be God's, and God's alone. Salvation is a divine work, wrought by 'the one and only Majesty' (*unius et solius Maiestatis*). Therefore the glory must be His alone.[3] The sin of the legalists is precisely that they do not give to God the glory of His divinity: they attribute salvation to their own works, making themselves as Gods[4] and spurning the Death of Christ.[5] And the fierce attack of Luther upon reason is explained chiefly by the fact that reason, as he understands it, identifies itself with the blasphemous error of the 'work-mongers'.[6]

[1] 'Summarium huius epistolae est destruere et evellere et disperdere omnem sapientiam et iustitiam carnis . . .' (W.A. 56. 157. 2: scholia; cf. the glosses, ibid. 3. 6).

[2] Ibid. 158. 10: 'Deus enim nos non per domesticam, sed per extraneam iustitiam et sapientiam vult salvare, non que veniat et nascatur ex nobis, sed que aliunde veniat in nos, non que in terra nostra oritur, sed que de celo venit. Igitur omnino externa et aliena iustitia oportet erudiri. Quare primum oportet propriam et domesticam evelli.'

[3] W.A. 40¹. 81. 16 ff. With these sentiments cf. Calvin: *Inst.* III. xiii and xv.

[4] W.A. 40¹. 253. 19 and 265. 13. Also: ibid. 406. 19.   [5] Ibid. 83. 29.

[6] In relation to Luther's understanding of law, this chapter has touched on two controversial issues which cannot be allowed to detain us. (1) First, there is the very difficult problem of 'natural law' in Luther. On this there is a good survey of the older literature by J. T. McNeill, 'Natural Law in the Thought of Luther', *Church History*, vol. x (1941). At the centre of more recent discussions on all aspects of law in Luther's theology stands the learned monograph of J. Heckel, *Lex charitatis*. (2) The question whether Luther taught a 'third use' of the law (besides the civil and theological uses), is still debated. Some of the more important literature is given by Cranz, op. cit., p. 103, n. 102. In general, it can be said that both these controversial issues must be related to the doctrine of the 'two kingdoms'. As Cranz rightly argues, Heckel's work is marred by an incorrect understanding of Luther's mature doctrine on the two kingdoms (ibid., p. 180). Again, if one follows Wingren's interpretation of the two kingdoms, then it is hard to avoid his conclusion that there is no place for a 'third use' in Luther's theology (op. cit., p. 63, n. 20).

VIII

LUTHER AGAINST SCHOLASTICISM

IT will now be necessary to modify somewhat our conclusions to Part I. There it was conceded that Luther was, in many respects, an Occamite, so that his assault on reason's capabilities in the domain of theological assertions may well have been suggested to him by his training in the *via moderna*. But to infer from this that therefore there is *no more* in Luther's assault than there was in Occam's would be a grave misunderstanding. The truth of the matter is that Luther's own distinctive contribution to the Nominalists' 'critique of reason' finally made the Nominalists themselves the chief objects of his attack. The purpose of this chapter, accordingly, is to demonstrate that what may have been, at the outset, a distrust born from Nominalist teaching became, in the end, a distrust of reason precisely in the teachings of the Nominalists themselves. But it will also be shown how the habits of thought which Luther detected chiefly in the Nominalists he detected in Thomas Aquinas, too; indeed, in Luther's judgement, it was St. Thomas himself who, by the introduction of Aristotelian ethical and metaphysical categories into theology, laid the foundations for the peculiar way in which the later Schoolmen allowed legalism to corrupt the Gospel of Christ.

The White Devil

Luther's crucial question can be asked in the form: *Whom does God accept, believing sinners or sanctified saints?* Does God receive the sinner whilst still a sinner, or does He first make the sinner a saint? Luther's answer is unequivocal: 'God wants sinners only. . . . God has nothing to do with holy men: a "holy man" is a fiction.' Anders Nygren sums up the Reformer's standpoint in a single telling phrase: 'Fellowship with God on the basis of sin.' The phrase is startling, no doubt, and one can understand why the authors of *Catholicity* would raise their eyebrows.[1] But it is not perhaps more startling than Paul's 'Him that justifieth the ungodly' (Rom. iv. 5) or Jesus' 'not the righteous but sinners' (Mark ii. 17). Indeed, it contains within itself the whole meaning of justification 'by faith alone'—and even, we may say, of the Gospel, as Luther understood it. Here is his 'simple Gospel', in a form which all can understand, yet which none could dare to have expected: God takes us exactly as we are. This is precisely what constitutes the Gospel 'good news', that which makes it what it is. By 'justification' Luther does not mean that God takes us 'just as if we were . . .' (this being the *traditional* Protestant view); nor that God takes us 'just as we will become' (which is the view of much of our *modern* Protestantism). He means that God takes us 'just as we are'. In a striking passage from the *Commentary on Galatians* Luther recalls a confession of his vicar-general:[2]

I remember that Staupitz used to say: 'I have vowed to God more than a thousand times that I would be better (*me fore probiorem*); but I never kept my vow. Hereafter I will make no such vow, for I know for certain that I would not keep it.'

And this, in Luther's eyes, is the 'holy desperation' (the *sancta desperatio*) out of which faith is born.

Man's constant peril is that as soon as his thoughts turn to God, he may try to make himself righteous. A very laudable desire, it may seem. Yet it is the voice, not of God, but of the Devil, that says: First, you must be holy. Luther can even say, in his comments on Psalm li:[3]

It is an infernal thing not to be willing to run to God unless first I feel myself pure from sins. . . . Should I not rather say: 'Have mercy upon me'? For if I were godly, then I would have no need of mercy [the *Miserere*]. . . . A most lively sighing goes on throughout the whole length of life: 'I would so like to be godly (*from*).' To overcome this natural desire (*naturam*) is a theological virtue.

[1] The citations from Luther are in W.A. 40². 327. 5, 347. 9 (*Enarratio in Ps. li*). For Nygren's provocative summing-up of Luther's standpoint (based, in part, on Luther's exposition of Ps. li), see *Agape and Eros*, p. 684. The contributors to *Catholicity* (E. S. Abbott, *et al.*) singled out Nygren's assertion for special reprobation (p. 25).
[2] W.A. 40². 92. 24.
[3] Ibid. 333. 1, 3; 339. 9. *Miserere*, of course, can be translated as 'the *Miserere*', i.e. Psalm li.

Luther does not stop even at such daring outbursts as these, so
passionate is he in his campaign against the one thing which
infallibly keeps a man from God, that is, self-righteousness
(*praesumptio, superbia, fiducia operum, opinio iustitiae*, or call it what
you will).

Frequently he makes the same point by affirming that we have
to be sinners—real sinners—if we want to be saved by Christ.
Hence the famous counsel to Melanchthon: 'Sin boldly . . .'.
The phrase in Gal. i. 4, 'Who gave himself for our sins', provides
Luther with an excellent text by which to hammer home this
lesson:

> Christ was given, not for feigned or fictitious sins, but for real ones;
> not for little sins, but for huge ones; not for this sin or that sin, but
> for all sins. . . . Unless you are found in the number of those who say:
> 'For our sins' (*nostris*, sc. *peccatis*) . . . there is no salvation for you.

Here is heaven's thunder against all 'righteousnesses': the
sinner has hope precisely because of his sin. If the Devil accuse
our conscience, we can slay him with his own sword: 'In that
you say I am a sinner, you arm me against yourself, enabling
me to cut your throat with your own sword and to trample you
under foot.' Luther could not more explicitly have affirmed the
principle: 'Just as I am . . .'[1]

Luther's constant struggle was, in fact, against what he liked
to call the 'White Devil' or 'Holy Satan'.[2] For this White Devil
drives men to spiritual sins which try to sell themselves as
righteousness.[3] There is much wisdom in the old proverb:
'Mischief always begins in the name of God.'[4] The White Devil's
technique is exemplified not only in the reasoning of the sophists,
but also in the specious claims of the spiritualists, who agree
with Luther, yet 'go beyond him'[5]—just as the Galatian pseudo-
apostles said, 'Paul made a good beginning', then utterly ruined
his labours in the pretence of improving them. When the Devil

[1] W.A. 40¹. 87. 25 and 89. 25.
[2] See esp. ibid. 88. 1 and 13 (*heiliger Teufel*; *Sancte Satan*); 88. 26 (callidus: 'cunning', because he appears in disguise; cf. 108. 27); 95. 9 (*der weise* [=*weisse*] *Teuffel*); 96. 10, 108. 20, 109. 29 (*candidus diabolus*); 108. 6 (*albus*).
[3] 'Candidus diabolus, qui impellit homines ad spiritualia peccata, quae sese venditant pro iustitia' (Ibid. 96. 10/11, CDE).
[4] 'Inn Gottes namen hebt sich als ungluck an' (ibid. 109. 31).
[5] Ibid. 109–10.

cannot destroy by 'breaking down', he achieves his aim by
'building up'. 'Sic perdit meliorando.'¹ The truth is, however
paradoxical, that the world is at its worst when it is best,² for
then its trust is in its own virtue, not in Christ. The Church may
be 'holy', and yet all is lost when it forgets to say, 'Father,
forgive . . .'.³ Even Luther himself had once tried to make himself a saint: 'Outwardly I was not as other men.' Yet beneath
the cloak of self-made righteousness he fostered a corroding
scepticism; nor did he perceive that such saints are very precious
to Satan.⁴

The 'White Devil' is clearly a virtual personification of
reason's legalistic assumption. Here again Luther is speaking
of a religious viewpoint corrupted by what is fundamentally an
ethical viewpoint. The error of the Scholastics is that they
'mixed things up'. Works have nothing to do with justification,
which is obtained by faith alone.⁵ Works must not be confused
with faith, nor law with grace.⁶ These things must all be kept
clearly distinct. Granted this distinction, works are to be en-
joined.⁷ Indeed, even 'ceremonies' and 'traditions' should be
observed, if only their performance is not mixed up with justi-
fication.⁸ Luther vows that he is ready even to kiss the Pope's
feet, provided the Pope will grant that God justifies sinners
gratuitously through Christ.⁹ Moreover, he has some exceed-
ingly harsh words for the antinomians who, ironically, thought
they had Luther on their side: they are swine, and Luther
wishes them still subject to the tyranny of the Pope.¹⁰

There are, in fact, a whole series of 'pairs' or 'doublets'

¹ 'Thus he destroys by making better' (ibid. 110. 7: RM.). Cf. 110. 1 (RM):
'Diaboli natura: quando non potest perdere homines nocendo et insectando, facit
meliorando.' Also: 118. 8 ff. and 24 ff.
² *Mundus tunc omnium pessimus, quando optimus* (ibid. 95. 6 and 28).
³ Ibid. 132. 2.
⁴ Ibid. 137. 3, 14, 19. 'Sub ista sanctitate et fiducia mei alebam perpetuam diffi-
dentiam' (137. 22). 'Eiusmodi sanctos diligit Satan, ac pro suavissimis deliciis
habet' (137. 25). 'Quo sanctiores fuimus, hoc magis excaecati eramus et purius
diabolum adorabamus' (138. 26). In this chapter I have not usually given refs. to
the parallels in RM.   ⁵ Ibid. 239. 18 ff.
⁶ Ibid. 263. 24: 'Non confundimus legem et gratiam, fidem et opera, sed ea
longissime separamus.'
⁷ Ibid. 156. 11 ff. and 35 ff. '. . . sed suo tempore et loco, quando scilicet quaestio
est de operibus extra hunc capitalem articulum' (240. 17).
⁸ Ibid. 166. 33; 169. 18.   ⁹ Ibid. 177. 22, 181. 11.
¹⁰ Ibid. 475. 29; W.A. 40². 60. 35.

scattered throughout Luther's writings, and Luther insists that, in each doublet, the two members be kept distinct. Thus we find 'grace and law'; 'faith and works'; 'spiritual righteousness and civil righteousness'; 'gift and example'; 'theology and philosophy'; 'spirit and body'; and so forth.[1] All, in the last analysis, say the same thing: works have nothing to do with conscience or with justification, and the Pope's error is his failure to observe the distinctions.[2] The entire purpose of Luther's *Commentary on Galatians* could be summed up in a single phrase: 'to prevent the confusion of faith and morals' (*ne confundantur mores et fides*).[3] Luther's idea of a good theologian is one who can rightly distinguish Gospel and Law, for this theme contains the whole of Christian Doctrine in summary form.[4] Yet Luther insists again and again: both are necessary, Gospel and Law, faith and ethics.[5] Indeed, it is very largely for this reason that Luther's critics have been able to accuse him of inconsistency. One minute he preaches good works: the next minute he utterly condemns them. The same, Luther tells us, happened to Paul. If the critics only stopped to ask *how* the law was to be observed, their charge of inconsistency could never have been made.[6] Under this 'how' Luther is prepared to make large concessions. Besides insisting that good works must be done *after* faith, he will even allow that the Jew and the Pope should keep their ceremonies, provided they do not expect to earn salvation by means of them. 'When in Rome, do as Rome does.'[7] But *in loco iustificationis*—when the subject under discussion is justification— Luther remains firm: here the White Devil must be kept out

---

[1] W.A. 40¹. 209. 25 (Gospel and Law); 240. 29 (Christ and Law); 252. 29 (Justification and Law); 259. 30 (Gospel and Law); 557. 14 (Promise and Law); 558. 24 (Justification and Law); 239. 18 (Faith and Works); 208. 14, 392. 20, 393. 14, 394. 29 (Theological and Civil Righteousness); 389. 16; 40². 42. 19 (Gift and Example); 40¹. 402. 24, 407. 30 (Theology and Philosophy); 270. 29, 279. 33, 392. 29; 40². 62. 13 (Conscience and Flesh, &c.).

[2] W.A. 40¹. 209. 12. Cf. ibid. 131. 19/142. 16 (CDE).

[3] Ibid. 45. 25; cf. RM. 51. 12.

[4] 'Esse Theologum' is 'discernere Evangelium a lege' (ibid. 207. 17). 'Locus de discrimine legis et Evangelii . . . continet summam totius Christianae doctrinae' (209. 16).

[5] Ibid. 45. 26: 'Est utraque necessaria [i.e. both *mores* and *fides*], sed quaelibet intra suos fines contineri debet.'

[6] Ibid. 125. 8 (RM.).

[7] Ibid. 146. 21: *Cum fueris Romae, romano vivito more* (Luther here makes explicit allusion to 1 Cor. ix. 19 ff.). For the Pope's mistake (making ceremonies requisite to salvation): ibid. 162. 19.

at all costs, and there is no room for reason's legalistic assumption.

It can hardly escape our notice that behind Luther's views on righteousness, as on reason, lies the doctrine of the two kingdoms. All the 'doublets' we have listed come back, in the last analysis, to this crucial doctrine. In his mature theology (and most clearly perhaps in the very *Commentary on Galatians* with which we are especially concerned) Luther is thinking of the two kingdoms as two dimensions of existence. At one and the same time, the Christian faces towards God in the Heavenly Kingdom, and towards his neighbour in the Earthly Kingdom. He lives in relation to God, and he lives in society with his fellows. To the Heavenly Kingdom belong grace, faith, and spiritual righteousness; to the Earthly Kingdom, law, works, and civil righteousness. That is to say, before God moral attainment, being always tainted with the disease of self-will, counts for nothing. Here a man is justified only by the righteousness of Christ, appropriated through faith, and the works of the law have no place. In the Earthly Kingdom, on the other hand, as we face our neighbour, we do stand under the imperative of the law. For our faith does not benefit our neighbour; he needs our works of love. Indeed, Luther is quite willing to assert that, before our fellow men, we should seek to be justified by our *works*, though he admits that this is not altogether possible, so that forgiveness must be sought even in the Earthly Kingdom. We must say to our brother, as we say to God, 'Forgive us our trespasses.' Towards our fellows, therefore, we do live by a mixture of grace and works, by a combination of the works of love, on the one hand, and, on the other hand, a humility which is not ashamed to ask for pardon.[1] And it quite clearly follows from this that in the Earthly Kingdom there is the possibility of improvement, daily growth in the righteousness of love; whereas in the Heavenly Kingdom the Christian is already *wholly* righteous, because the righteousness of faith is the perfect righteousness of Christ. Justification before God is instantaneous and complete; and, if we are to

---

[1] Luther's finest presentation of these ideas is perhaps in his *Sermon on the Sum of the Christian Life*, preached in 1532 (W.A. 36. 352–75; trans. in A.E., vol. LI,). The sermon is a beautiful summary of 'evangelical theology', based on 1 Tim. i. 5–7. The two sorts of justification are also described in the *Commentary on Galatians* of 1519 (W.A. 2. 489. 21 ff.); in the *Disputation Concerning Justification* of 1536 (W.A. 39[1]. 82–86); &c.

distinguish clearly between Luther's position and that of the Schoolmen, this 'all at once' (*ganz auff eyn mal*) is perhaps as important as the 'faith alone' (*sola fide*).[1]

Having clarified Luther's own position, as far as our immediate theme required,[2] we can now turn to the Scholastics, both Thomists and Occamites, and see why he was led to make the charge of legalism against them. How far, in Luther's judgement, did reason's legalistic outlook corrupt the Schoolmen's understanding of justification? How, in other words, did it come about that the two kingdoms were confused?

Legalism in the Nominalists

Luther's critique of Scholastic theology was, of course, directed mainly against the Nominalists, and the charge of legalism is more understandable when made against them than against St. Thomas. Indeed, the present-day Thomist would, in part, approve of Luther's judgements on the adherents of the *via moderna*; and there are some students of Reformation history who represent the conflict of Protestantism with the Church of Rome as largely a misunderstanding, since to join controversy with the Nominalists is to champion the Catholic Faith more than to undermine it.[3] It will perhaps be best, therefore, to

---

[1] W.A. 10[1, 1]. 343. 24 ff. Cf. ibid. 107. 12, 108. 1, 112. 10. In some of his *Disputations*, especially those directed against the Antinomians, Luther brings out very clearly his contrast between the Christian's total righteousness before God and his progressive righteousness before men (e.g. W.A. 39[1]. 383. 3 ff., 431. 8 ff., 434. 1 ff., and 491. 23 ff.). It is also in the *Disputations* that he develops his idea of the Christian as already living in heaven, 'surrounded by the heaven of mercy' (39[1]. 521. 6). Of course, the Christian, as he stands before God, is righteous only 'in Christ'; in himself he remains a sinner. Hence the paradox, *simul iustus et peccator* (W.A. 39[1]. 523. 19, 564. 3, &c.).

[2] The literature on this theme is, of course, extensive, but the various ramifications of Luther's teaching on justification by faith are not germane to our present concerns. In a more comprehensive examination of Luther's views on Christian righteousness it would be necessary, for instance, to show that the distinction between the two kingdoms is by no means a complete separation, as though religion and ethics were totally divorced. Luther's standpoint amounts to saying that, whilst our behaviour in the Earthly Kingdom cannot give us righteousness *coram Deo*, nevertheless receiving righteousness in the Heavenly Kingdom must inevitably issue in good works towards our neighbour. See, for example, the *Theses Concerning Faith and Law* of 1535 (W.A. 39[1]. 44–53). In English, the best discussion on this area of Luther's thought is the work of Cranz, already referred to. Also valuable is Uuras Saarnivaara, *Luther Discovers the Gospel*, a careful analysis of Luther's views on righteousness at various stages of his development.

[3] Thus Karl Adam, for example, has argued that Luther remained close to the

invert chronology and to speak of Luther in relation to Thomism
only after we have discovered the reasons for his revolt against
the Nominalist theology in which he was trained. For whilst
the case against the 'decadent' theology of the later Schoolmen
is plain, it is not so evident why Luther considered that Thomas
Aquinas hastened the decline.

Luther's criticism is, then, mainly directed against the *via
moderna* of Occam, D'Ailly, and Biel, whose scheme of salvation
he outlines scarcely less often than his own.[1] The main point of
this scheme is the use made of the distinction between *meritum
de congruo* and *meritum de condigno*. Thomas himself had, of
course, employed the same distinction. But (generally, at least) he
had applied both terms to one and the same effect of 'cooperative grace': it was not in the external act itself that the distinction lay, but in the standpoint from which it was viewed, that is,
whether as an act of the Holy Spirit (in which case the merit
was *de condigno*) or of man (in which case it was only *de congruo*).[2]
The Nominalists, on the other hand, regarded *meritum de congruo*
as attainable before, and apart from, the gift of grace. For, in
spite of his sin, man's will was free and he could, of his own
natural powers (*ex puris naturalibus*), perform works worthy of
some merit.[3] Indeed, according to some, it was possible without

'traditional Catholic doctrine of grace', as found in Thomas Aquinas and others,
and that his battle was really with the 'Ockhamist perversion of the Catholic
doctrine'. *One and Holy* (trans. by Cecily Hastings, New York: Sheed and Ward,
1951), pp. 37 and 60. A similar view is presented in Louis Bouyer's *The Spirit and
Forms of Protestantism* (trans. by A. V. Littledale, Westminster, Maryland: The
Newman Press, 1956). It is interesting that both these authors nevertheless regard
Occam's doctrine of *acceptatio* as exercising a positive influence on the Reformer's
theological development.

[1] In the comments on a single verse, Gal. ii. 16, Luther outlines the Nominalist
scheme of salvation no less than three times (W.A. 40[1]. 220. 4 ff., 225. 26 ff., and
230 f.).

[2] *Sum. Theol.* ii. 1, q. 114, art. 3. The terms are sometimes inelegantly anglicized
as 'congruous merit' and 'condign merit'; but I have preferred to retain the Latin
forms. The distinction is between approximate merit and strict merit: the former
it is 'fitting' (*de congruo*) that God reward in His mercy; the latter is 'fully deserving'
(*condignum*) of the reward which God apportions in His justice.

[3] We will take our descriptions of the Nominalist scheme of salvation mainly
from Luther himself, since it is his understanding of it that concerns us. Since he
was trained in the Nominalist school, his statements are, in any case, well informed.
In dealing with St. Thomas, on the other hand, whom Luther seems not to have
studied so carefully, we are sometimes obliged to piece together the argument for
ourselves. It is certainly the Nominalists he has chiefly in mind when he writes of
the *sophistae*, and he occasionally refers to the earlier Schoolmen as 'better'. But he

the aid of grace to love God and one's neighbour above all things, so fulfilling the law and the commandments. But, on the whole, the Nominalists were ready to concede that this love was not *strictly* meritorious: something more was needed, and that something is grace.[1] Hence, whilst they certainly taught the possibility of earning merit *of a kind* even before grace had been received, they nevertheless insisted that merit *in the strict sense* required the assistance of grace. Here lay the foundations for the peculiarly Nominalist manner of distinguishing *merita de congruo* and *merita de condigno*.

We can now state the Nominalist scheme very briefly. First, acting upon his own native powers a man may perform acts worthy of merit *de congruo*. Now, strictly speaking, God is not obliged to reward such imperfect merit: God is not thereby made a debtor (*Deus non est debitor*). Still, provided only that a man has done his best (*quod in se est*), it is at least fitting (*decet*) that God, being both just and good, should crown human endeavour with divine grace. Thereupon, the second stage in man's attainment of eternal life begins: equipped with the in-pouring of divine charity, he is enabled to perform works meritorious in the strictest sense, that is, *de condigno*. God now becomes, quite precisely, a debtor, and He is obliged (*cogitur*) to grant eternal life as a well-earned reward.[2]

From all this it appears that Luther's criticism of the *via*

does not always make nice distinctions. A careful statement of Nominalist soteriology by a modern scholar will be found in Seeberg's *History of Doctrines*, Eng. trans. II. 201–2. For the Nominalist use of the expression *ex puris naturalibus*, see W.A. 40¹. 291. 16, &c.

[1] They justified their position by distinguishing between two ways in which the law may be performed: first, according to the substance of the deed (*secundum substantiam facti*), and, second, according to the intention of the Lawgiver (*secundum intentionem praecipientis*). Only in the former manner can the law be fulfilled without the assistance of divine grace. The latter way is further defined as doing the law 'in love' (*in charitate*)—and, of course, this love must itself be qualified as, not the love which man possesses by nature, but rather that which God Himself confers. Ibid. 227. 21 ff.

[2] I have taken this summary from Luther's comments on Gal. ii. 16 (ibid. 220. 4 ff.; cf. 225. 26 ff.). The Latin reads: 'Dicunt enim: Opus bonum ante gratiam valere ad impetrandam gratiam de congruo. Impetrata iam vero gratia sequens opus mereri vitam aeternam de condigno. . . . In primo quidem Deus non est debitor, sed quia est bonus et iustus, decet eum, ut approbet tale opus . . . et reddat pro tali officio gratiam. Post gratiam autem iam factus est debitor et iure cogitur dare vitam aeternam, quia iam non solum est opus liberi arbitrii, factum secundum substantiam, sed etiam factum in gratia gratificante, hoc est in dilectione.'

moderna was such that Thomas Aquinas himself would hardly have disapproved, since the scheme of salvation in Nominalism puts good works *before* the approach of divine grace, and, indeed, the works are the condition of God's gracious approach. Luther was convinced that in making his objections he had the New Testament on his side. Quite apart from isolated texts (including our Lord's saying concerning the 'tree and the fruit', which Luther is so fond of citing), it could surely be argued that the entire New Testament ethic is undermined by the kind of soteriology against which Luther is arguing. For the New Testament puts forward as its chief ethical motivation the fact that God has already accepted us whilst still sinners. Even in the Old Testament right conduct arises out of the fact of redemption: the preface to the Tables of the Law founds the ethical sanction upon Israel's deliverance from the 'house of bondage'. Throughout the Bible the ethical appeal is made to the 'mercies of God' in the acts by which He brought about salvation. Luther's problem was, in fact, precisely the same as St. Paul's: how to break the chains of a hard legalism which held down the 'theological ethic' of the most distinctive Biblical tradition, whilst carefully guarding against all appearance of anti-nomianism. Both found the solution in a faith which justifies apart from works, but which nevertheless, by reason of its very nature, produces works (we might almost say) 'automatically'.

Legalism in St. Thomas

If it is true, as we have claimed, that a Thomist would not need to quarrel with Luther's fundamental objection to the Nominalist views on salvation, we must surely raise the question: Why, then, did Luther so consistently find in Thomas himself the fountainhead of Scholastic legalism? In Thomas's doctrine of justification we are left in no doubt at all that the initiative lies with God, whose approach to the sinner is wholly unmerited. No 'good works' (that is, no meritorious works) precede the gift of grace. Thomas would be quite able to give a 'Catholic' interpretation to the two Scripture passages quoted above (Rom. iv. 5 and Mark ii. 17): for him, as for Luther, the wonder of grace is precisely that it is extended to sinners, the sick and not the whole, so that the phrase 'justification of the ungodly' presents no difficulties to him.¹ If we consider what it is that justification achieves, then, according to Thomas, we are bound to say that it is an even greater work of God than the Creation itself.² Indeed, Thomas would not perhaps disapprove even of the claim that God 'takes us as we are', if that is meant to exclude the possibility of man's preparing himself for grace by his natural powers.

In general, the Thomistic theology will not allow that man can do anything whatever apart from the providential assistance of God (the divine *auxilium*, which is certainly gracious, being an expression of God's love for his creatures).³ But there are two special reasons why grace is necessary for justification and eternal life: first, because eternal life is a 'good which exceeds what is commensurate with created nature'; second, because of the 'impediment of sin'.⁴ The gap between man's supernatural goal, on the one hand, and his fallen natural powers, on the other, cannot be bridged save from God's side by a grace which both 'elevates' and 'heals'. To ask whether this grace can be merited, is to deny its graciousness: even the receiving of it is something divinely given. No man can turn to God unless God turns him to Himself.⁵ Moreover, after turn-

---

¹ The phrase is used (*passim*) in *Sum. Theol.* II. 1, q. 113. All subsequent refs. to Thomas are to the *Treatise on Grace* (Prima Secundae of the *Sum. Theol.*), unless otherwise stated. There is a translation in vol. XI of the *Library of Christian Classics*.

² Q. 113, art. 9; with ref. to the remark of Augustine: 'Maius opus est ut ex impio iustus fiat, quam creare caelum et terram. Caelum enim et terra transibit, praedestinatorum autem salus et iustificatio permanebit.' Nevertheless, justification is not strictly miraculous (q. 113, art. 10).

³ Q. 109, *passim*. The very fact that God gives all creatures their natural being is a token of his love (q. 110, art. 1). Certainly God owes His creatures nothing (q. 111, art. 1).

⁴ Q. 109, art. 5; q. 114, art. 2. Only God can 'deify' human nature (q. 112, art. 1). It is a consequence of this twofold need for grace that Adam, according to Thomas, needed grace even before the Fall to raise him to his supernatural good; after the Fall he needed grace for both reasons, to raise him above created nature and to heal sinful nature.

⁵ The 'proofs' are Jer. xxxi. 18, Lam. v. 21, John vi. 44, John xv. 5, &c. In Thomas's technical jargon: that the *gratiae habitualis donum* is received by the human will, is itself due to the *auxilium gratuitum Dei*, i.e. the reception of 'habitual' grace is an effect of 'actual' grace (q. 109, art. 6). True, Thomas speaks of a 'disposition' for grace in q. 112, art. 2. But (1) this refers only to grace as *habituale donum*; (2) the disposition is said to be the effect of grace as *auxilium Dei*; (3) it is expressly denied that such disposition is meritorious; and (4) God is not bound to grant the *donum* even to those whom He predisposes (cf. q. 112, art. 3). Similarly, q. 113, arts. 3–5, speak of a double movement of the freewill as 'required' for justification. But this does not mean that such a movement must precede justification; rather that

ing to God and receiving the gift of grace (as *gratia habitualis*), man still needs the constant assistance of grace (the *auxilium gratiae*), nor will he be able to dispense with it even in the state of glory.[1]

If, however, the Thomistic starting-point is, not merits *de congruo*, but grace, this does not mean that the notion of merit is excluded. There is, to be sure, no possibility of man's claiming the grace of justification by doing the best that native powers allow. Grace anticipates merit. But, nevertheless, merits must follow grace. Thomas's scheme clearly cannot be considered 'legalistic' in the sense that *grace* can be earned, but it is legalistic in the sense that *salvation* is earned. He never imagines that grace is granted in recognition of 'natural' works, but he does claim that grace is given to make possible 'supernatural' works. Grace is not the prize for merit, but the principle of merit. And eternal life is still a matter of reward.[2] For a full understanding of the Thomistic doctrine of justification by grace we must stress, not only that grace (or, at least, 'first grace') cannot be merited by works, but also that grace is subordinated to meritorious works as means to end. And we do, after all, end up with a different view of salvation than Luther's. Perhaps the crucial difference lies in the fact that justification for Thomas is not yet salvation: it is only the beginning of the road, nor is it the guarantee of finally arriving.[3] For Luther, on the other hand, justification and salvation are virtually synonymous.[4] Heaven

justification by grace includes it, or brings it about. The argument of q. 113, arts. 7-8, is that all the other requirements are subsequent to the infusion of grace (though not in a chronological sense).

[1] Q. 109, art. 9. This point is important, since the notion of *habitus* is alleged by some Protestant critics of Thomism to imply some sort of autonomy of the Christian over against God, a power to perform deeds of love without further intervention by God. In fact, 'habitual grace' signifies a 'disposition maintained in us by God to act no more but under the impulse of actual grace'. So Louis Bouyer, op. cit., p. 208.

[2] Q. 109, art. 5. This view of salvation is, of course, basically Augustinian. Cf. the citations from Augustine in q. 111, art. 2, and q. 114, art. 8. As one commentator on St. Thomas puts it, we can merit the end of our supernatural life, but not its beginning, 'any more than a man can give birth to himself'. Walter Farrell, *A Companion to the Summa*, II. 431.

[3] This 'not yet' is brought out especially clearly in Thomas's discussions on 'perseverance' (q. 109, art. 10; q. 114, art. 9). Cf. also the succinct statement in q. 114, art. 8: eternal life is the final term of a movement of grace (*terminus motus gratiae*), and progress in this movement is *secundum augmentum charitatis*.

[4] A point well made by A. C. McGiffert, *Protestant Thought Before Kant*, pp. 24-26; *A History of Christian Thought*, II. 283.

is here; the pilgrim has arrived and lives already in the sphere of grace. There is no necessity for the Christian to establish *another* relation with God, on the basis of merits. We might almost say that for Luther eschatology is 'realized'. The Christian has been translated already into the Kingdom of Christ (*eyn mal*, once and for all), and his standing there is entirely a matter of faith, not of merits (*sola fide*).[1]

Admittedly, it was not so much against the doctrines of Thomas Aquinas, but rather against Nominalism, that Luther developed his own understanding of justification. But three comments must now be made on our comparison of Luther and Thomas. First, Luther eventually came to recognize that he had departed, not merely from the 'modernist' doctrine of salvation, but from the position of St. Augustine as well. Hence from being Augustine's advocate against the semi-Pelagianism of the Nominalists he finally (and with evident reluctance) became the critic of Augustinianism itself.[2] It is as we see Luther struggling to distinguish his own view of justification from Augustine's that his differences from Thomas also become most apparent; for the Augustinian principle, that all our merits are gifts of God, is the cornerstone of Thomas's doctrine of salvation.

Second, in so far as Luther directly assails Thomas himself, his critique generally comes to a focus in his rejection of the formula, *fides charitate formata* ('faith formed by love').[3] It has been alleged that Luther's 'polemic against *fides caritate formata*

---

[1] True, Thomas seems in one place to say of justification precisely what Luther says, that it is 'instantaneous' (q. 113, art. 7). And no one would deny that he has a certain sense of present possession. Nevertheless, justification remains only part one of salvation, and the possession of *eternal life* lies beyond (*in patria*, not *in via*).

[2] For further discussion (with ample references both to the primary and to the secondary sources) see the studies by Cranz and Saarnivaara, noted above. The present writer should perhaps say that he finds it impossible to agree entirely with these two authors concerning the chronology of Luther's theological development, but their analysis of the main stages in his intellectual pilgrimage seems to be substantially correct.

[3] For Thomas's own position see q. 113, arts. 4 and 5; q. 114, arts. 4 and 5. Faith is more fully discussed as one of the 'theological virtues' in Secunda Secundae, qq. 1-7; see especially q. 4, arts. 3 and 4. The Thomistic formula, *fides charitate formata*, was but the translation into Aristotelian terminology of a conception already widely accepted by Scholastic thought. The virtue, or value, of faith resides (so it was believed) in the love by which it is perfected. In Aristotelian language: Love is the 'form' which gives specific character to Christian faith. Without love it is *fides informis*, that is 'matter' without its specific 'form.'

. . . proves only that he never understood St. Thomas'.[1] But the truth rather is that he understood the implications of Thomas's doctrine well enough to divine that just here is disclosed the fundamental presupposition of Scholastic soteriology, namely, that 'virtue' (in one form or another) is absolutely necessary for acceptance with God: justification is through faith—yes, but faith is a virtue, and its justifying power is in the love which 'informs' it. Luther perceived this consequence clearly; hence the demand that his opponents should call a spade a spade and confess that, for them, justification is by love, and not by faith.[2] If the sophists appeal to Gal. v. 6, the answer is that Paul speaks of a faith which 'works' through love, not which 'justifies' through love.[3] Moreover, Luther will have nothing to do with a faith which is, apart from love, 'un-formed': for in this very passage from St. Paul faith is spoken of as active (in Luther's language, *efficax*). He is willing to concede that there *is* a kind of faith which is too feeble a thing to be the means of justification, namely, 'historic' or 'acquired' faith (mere assent to the Gospel-story). And it is interesting that Thomas's *fides charitate formata* and Luther's *fides salvifica* (true, 'saving' faith) own a common criterion, that is, the production of good works. For Luther's 'true and lively faith' is known to be true only through the good works which it prompts (*urget*). A genuine faith proves itself in works of love—and yet it is not for this reason that it justifies. Thus, Luther concludes, Paul's intention in this passage is to shut out both the *operarii* (who think to earn salvation by their works) and also, no less, the *ignavi* (who imagine that it is

---

[1] John Burnaby, *Amor Dei*, p. 277. Burnaby's point is that charity is not a 'work', but something which 'the love of God "creates and infuses"'. But surely the important point is that, according to the Thomists, love is a *virtue*, and none the less virtuous for being conferred by God.

[2] 'Cur non potius appellant scapham scapham?' W.A. 40¹. 255. 30. See also Luther's comments on Gal. v. 6 (W.A. 40². 34. 10 ff.). 'Adeo in totum transferunt iustificationem a fide et soli tribuunt . . . charitati' (34. 16). The use of the *soli* amounts to an accusation that the sophists have a doctrine of *sola charitate*.

[3] Ibid. 35. 21. Cf.: 'At quis est tam rudis Grammaticus, qui non ex vocabulorum virtute intelligat aliud esse Iustificari, aliud Operari? Clara enim et aperta sunt verba Pauli: "Fides per charitatem OPERATUR"' (ibid. 35. 26). The capitalization is in the Weimar edn. Tertullian apparently took Paul's *energoumene* in the passive sense, so that the phrase could be taken to mean that faith is 'perfected by love' (*per dilectionem perfici*). Luther's interpretation translates *energoumene* as the middle voice: faith is 'active through love'. Either interpretation is grammatically possible, but Paul's general usage seems to favour the middle voice. So, at least, Lightfoot in his *Commentary* on this verse.

enough to believe and 'work nothing'). Paul's meaning, in fact,
is this: 'It is true that faith alone justifies, without works. But
I am speaking of a true faith which, once it has procured
justification (*postquam iustificaverit*), does not stand idle, but is
active (*operosa*) through love.'[1]

In any inquiry concerning the Thomistic doctrine of justification, the notions of 'grace' and 'merit' are even more in
need of definition than the notion of 'faith'. Indeed, Luther's
entire critique of Scholastic theology turns around the meaning
of these two terms. His claim is—and this is our third comment
(3)—that Thomas was largely to blame for the distinctive
Scholastic content given to 'grace' and 'merit' in medieval
theology: and in his view this meant that the strictly religious
viewpoint of the apostle Paul had been sacrificed to the ethical
and metaphysical categories of Aristotle. To a fuller explanation
of this decisive point we must now turn.

Grace and merit

Luther's repeated comments on these two terms show quite
clearly that he considered the former to have been totally misunderstood by the Scholastics, the latter to have no business
in theology at all. A large part of Luther's hostility towards
Aristotelianism is to be explained by his conviction that it was
the 'pagan philosopher' who was responsible for the corruption
of the one term and the introduction of the other. More
precisely, his anger was directed against Thomas Aquinas, for
it was all his doing that Aristotle ever came to conquer the
schools.[2]

---

[1] W.A. 40². 37. 23. Louis Bouyer is right, in one sense, when he argues that the
Protestant *sola fide* is intended to exclude works done after justification as well as
before, and that this explains the assault on the Scholastic *fides charitate formata* (op.
cit., pp. 139–40). But whilst Bouyer perceives that works are excluded 'for salvation', he does not do justice to Luther's strenuous insistence that works are demanded
as service towards the neighbour. It is perhaps significant that *charitas* apparently
suggests to Luther's opponents primarily 'love for God', whereas Luther himself
generally has in mind 'love for neighbour' (which he describes as coming from God
rather than directed to Him).

[2] Thomas was the culprit who brought Aristotelian philosophy into the Schools:
'vel primus vel maximus fuit autor invehendae in orbem Christianum philosophiae
solus' (W.A. 7. 737. 16); 'autor est regnantis Aristotelis' (8. 127. 20). To Luther
the name of Thomas is virtually synonymous with Aristotle: 'Aristotelicissimus ac
plane Aristoteles ipse' (7. 737. 17); 'ex Thoma seu ex Aristotele' (4. 537. 12);

Luther's objection to the Scholastic understanding of grace is essentially the same as the objection which he brings against the Scholastic understanding of righteousness: the sophists imagine that righteousness is a 'quality', which can properly be said to be both 'infused' and 'diffused'.[1] Indeed, in actual practice the Scholastic terms *iustitia*, *gratia* (i.e. *gratia gratum faciens*), and *charitas* (or *dilectio*) tend to be used almost synonymously.[2] They all refer to that which God pours into the soul in order to make it righteous and therefore worthy of salvation. In his work *Against Latomus* (1521) Luther states his objection bluntly: 'Grace must be properly understood as the "favour of God", not as a "quality of soul"'[3] (a point reminiscent of Melanchthon's celebrated dictum, 'Grace is not medicine, but good will').

A careful examination of St. Thomas's treatise on grace makes clear the manner in which 'Catholic' theology at its best conceives of grace; equally clear, I think, the reasons why Luther (rightly or wrongly) regarded the conception with suspicion. This is no place for a detailed analysis, but some of the main points may be mentioned. (1) Grace is not thought of as for-

'Thomistica, hoc est Aristotelica' (6. 508. 12). It is his fault that Aristotle has been elevated into the place of Christ ('quantum ad autoritatem et fidem pertinet'), that the Sun (Christ) has been darkened, that moral virtues have been put in the place of faith and endless opinions in the place of truth (7. 737. 23). With malicious wit Luther describes the method of Thomas: 'This is the order in which Thomas argues. First, he takes sentences (or opinions: *sententias*) out of Paul, Peter, John, Isaiah, &c. Then he concludes: But Aristotle says so-and-so. And he proceeds to interpret Scripture in the light of Aristotle.' W.A. TR. 1. 118. 1; cf. ibid. 5. 686. 15.

[1] W.A. 40¹. 370. 4 and 22. Cf. Rom. v. 5, where Paul speaks of God's love as 'poured out (*ekkechutai*) in our hearts'. Grammatically, no doubt, the genitive in the phrase *he agape tou theou* could be taken objectively, i.e. to give the sense: 'Love *for* God is shed abroad in our hearts by the Holy Spirit.' Once again (as with Gal. v. 6) grammar alone is unable to decide an issue of some theological importance. And yet here, too, Paul's general usage does seem to count against the Augustinian interpretation. See, for example, Nygren's discussion of this verse in his *Commentary on Romans*.

[2] W.A. 40¹. 225. 31.

[3] W.A. 8. 106. 10. Luther regularly interprets *gratia* as 'favour' (W.A. 11. 302. 5, 40². 421. 5 and 21; W.A. DB. 7. 9. 10), as 'forgiveness' (W.A. 40¹. 73. 1 and 72. 29, 74. 3 and 14; 46. 658. 5), or as the gracious presence of God Himself (7. 571. 5). In his *Loci Communes* (1521) Melanchthon follows Luther, arguing that the Gk. *charis* stands for the Heb. *ḥēn* and should therefore be translated by the Latin *favor* rather than *gratia*. Hence grace is 'nothing but the benevolence of God towards us, or the will of God which has had pity on us'. It designates, not a *qualitas*, but a *voluntas*. 'In short, grace is nothing but the forgiveness or remission of sin.' *Melanchthons Werke in Auswahl* (Hans Engelland, Gütersloh, 1952), II. 1, 85 ff. (There is a translation of the 1521 *Loci* by Charles Leander Hill.)

giving, but as regenerating, so that justification, the 'first effect'
of grace, is inevitably said to be a '*making* righteous'.¹ To be sure,
Thomas answers the question: 'Is justification the forgiveness
of sins?' in the affirmative. But it is apparent that, for him,
justification really means much more than the 'non-imputation'
of sins. The fundamental premiss for Thomas's standpoint is
that being 'justified' implies a 'transmutation', an actual change
from a state of injustice to a state of justice ('transmutationem
quandam de statu iniustitiae ad statum iustitiae'). The grounds
for this definition are partly etymological: justification, taken
in the passive sense (on the analogy of 'calefaction'), means a
'movement towards justice'.² But it is not merely etymology that
determines his understanding of justification by grace: it is his
whole outlook and manner of thinking. The 'Catholic' mind
appears unwilling to think of anything rendering a man acceptable to God other than actual moral attainment. 'If it were not
so,' writes a modern Catholic theologian, 'it would follow that
. . . God would love sinners as His friends and His children.'³
This is not a point for beginning the argument: it is final. The
possibility that perhaps God *does*, as a matter of fact, love

¹ Q. 113, art. 1. In this same article Thomas speaks of justification as being *per
remissionem*, 'through forgiveness'. It is clear, I think, that even the notion of forgiveness means something different for him than for Luther: it is not simply the
'non-imputation' of sins, but an actual 'blotting out', a cleansing through grace.
Hence (in q. 113, art. 6) he speaks of forgiveness as the 'end' for which the infusion
of grace is given. The sanctifying character of grace is also manifest in q. 110,
art. 3 (grace, though not itself a virtue, is the fountainhead of all the virtues);
in q. 110, art. 4 (it is the 'principle of meritorious works'); and in q. 114, art. 4
(meritorious works proceed from grace). Similarly, God's love (*dilectio*) is said to be,
not mere acceptance (an act of the divine will), but something creative which
actually transforms its recipient (q. 110, art. 1; q. 113, art. 2). This is the difference
between man's love, which *finds* something pleasing in its object, and God's love,
which *causes* its object to be pleasing—an idea which Luther himself echoes in the
Heidelberg Disputation of 1518. Cf. also Thomas's reply to the second 'objection' in
q. 114, art. 5: 'It must be said that God gives grace only to the worthy—not,
however, because they were worthy beforehand, but because He Himself makes
them worthy through grace.'
² 'Respondeo. Dicendum quod iustificatio passiva accepta importat motum ad
iustitiam; sicut et calefactio motum ad calorem.' Of course, both *accepta* and
importat could be taken literally; then the meaning would be, 'Passively received,
justification introduces a movement . . . .' But this seems a little clumsy, and, in
any case, gives the same sense.
³ 'S'il en était autrement, il s'ensuivrait que l'homme serait en même temps juste
et injuste, que Dieu aimerait les pécheurs comme ses amis et ses enfants, et que
ceux-ci, tout en restant dans l'état de péché, seraient dignes de recevoir la vie
éternelle.' Garrigou-Lagrange, *La Synthèse thomiste*, p. 490.

sinners as His children is not even entertained. The argument is a *reductio ad absurdum*.

Secondly (2), the whole discussion is set within the framework of Aristotelian kinetics. For example, the 'necessity for grace' is defended largely by insisting on the need for a first mover (to initiate motion) and a form (by which any created thing acts). So then, grace is needed for 'knowing anything', 'doing any good', and so on.[1]

Thirdly (3), no doubt because metaphysical categories are, in part, determinative of the discussion, grace is spoken of as a substance, not as a relation. It 'denotes something in the soul';[2] it is an actual gift (*donum gratis datum*), a supernatural something (*quiddam supernaturale*), something which can properly be said to be 'poured into the soul' (*infunditur animae*). In general, it appears that grace, for Thomas, is a supernatural power, and especially a sanctifying power. To be sure, like Luther, he says that *gratia* may also mean 'benevolence',[3] but little use is made of this interpretation (save, perhaps, in so far as the sanctifying power is thought of as grounded in God's mercy). Certainly, 'benevolence' could seldom be used as an accurate translation of *gratia* in the *Treatise on Grace*.

Turning now to the concept of merit, we may again illustrate the argument by referring to St. Thomas. Merit is the 'second effect' of grace: more precisely, it is the effect of 'cooperative

---

[1] Q. 109, arts. 1 ff. Similarly, the enumeration of things required for justification is finally (in q. 113, art. 6) related to the general principles of Aristotelian kinetics: when one thing is moved by another, we need a *motio moventis*, a *motus mobilis*, and the *consummatio motus*; that is, in respect of the doctrine of justification, we need an infusion of grace, a movement of the freewill, and the remission of guilt. So, then, both the *auxilium Dei* and the *habituale donum* are related by Thomas to his Aristotelian categories. (Perhaps it should be mentioned that sometimes, especially in q. 109, Thomas seems to make a distinction between *gratia* and *auxilium*. But the distinction is not rigidly maintained. In q. 109, art. 6, God's aid is termed *auxilium gratuitum*; in art. 9 Thomas speaks of *auxilium gratiae*; and in q. 111, art. 2, it is explicitly said that grace is to be understood in a twofold manner, i.e. of the *divinum auxilium* and the *donum habituale*.)

[2] *Ponat aliquid in anima* (q. 110, art. 1). *Ponat* could be translated literally, 'places' or 'deposits'. Understood as *auxilium*, rather than *habituale donum*, grace is not a 'quality', but a 'movement' (q. 110, art. 2). It hardly needs to be pointed out that Thomas' conception of infused grace is of one piece with his sacramental theology. Even though the sacraments are not dealt with in the *Treatise on Grace*, one can readily perceive that here, too, grace is sacramental.

[3] Q. 110, arts. 1 and 2. As 'benevolence', *gratia* is what the modern Catholic refers to as 'uncreated grace'. Garrigou-Lagrange, *Grace*, p. 3.

grace', as justification was the effect of 'operative grace'. The
scheme alone is significant, since it clearly shows that justification
is not enough, not even when interpreted as itself a 'making'
righteous. It is merely the first step towards ultimate salvation,
and eternal life is only to be obtained by the justified man who
goes on, in the power of habitual grace, to perform meritorious
works. And Thomas leaves us in no doubt whatever as to the
meaning that he attaches to the term 'merit': it is the price paid
for work done.[1] There are, perhaps, two main reasons why he
arrives at this position. First, and obviously, there was his desire
to preserve human freedom and responsibility, no easy aim to
achieve within an Augustinian framework.[2] Second, and
possibly even more important, was his desire to preserve the
justice of God—and, therefore, the integrity of the moral order.
Salvation is given according to God's just judgement (*secundum
iudicium iustitiae*); and from this it follows of necessity that salvation is given as a reward, indeed a reward *ex condigno*.[3]

By various qualifications, Thomas seeks to protect his conclusions against just the kind of criticisms which Luther was
later to bring against the idea of merit. True, says Thomas,
man can merit the increase of grace;[4] but, of course, he cannot
merit the *first* grace,[5] nor can he merit restitution after a lapse.[6]
And, anyway, the merit entailed is never *strictly* deserving of
eternal life (at least, not when we look at it from man's standpoint).[7] And so on. But Thomas clearly refuses to say of *all*
grace what he certainly says of *first* grace, that it cannot be
merited. More correctly, he does say, 'All merit is incompatible
with grace (*omne meritum repugnat gratiae*)',[8] and yet appears to

---

[1] Q. 114, art. 1.
[2] See especially q. 113, arts. 3, 4, 5.
[3] Q. 114, art. 3.   [4] Ibid., art. 8.
[5] Ibid., art. 5.   [6] Ibid., art. 7.
[7] Ibid., art. 1; cf. art. 3. Because of the great inequality between man and God,
man can never claim anything from God in strict justice, save what God Himself
determines to give. God is bound by His own 'ordination', not by the meritorious
work considered as an achievement of man's freewill. Interestingly enough, Calvin
approaches very closely to this view when he endeavours to deal, from a 'Protestant'
standpoint, with the Biblical statements concerning rewards (*Inst.* III. xviii. 7).
Cf. also Luther in the *Bondage of the Will* (W.A. 18. 693. 19). The common source
for this view is, as Calvin makes clear, Augustine. In commenting on Thomas's
doctrine of the *divina ordinatio*, Garrigou-Lagrange concedes that 'this is the element
of truth contained in the error of the Protestants, of Baius, and of the Jansenists'.
Grace, p. 365.   [8] Q. 114, art. 5.

forget about it. Of course, the Augustinian doctrine that all our merits are gifts of grace really does exculpate Thomas from the charge of 'Pelagianism' (a fact which some Protestant polemicists have persistently ignored). But Luther found it irrelevant to ask *how* a man *can* acquire merit (be it by his own native efforts or by an infusion of divine grace). He considered grace and merit to be mutually exclusive; and on this view the mere claim *that* men *must* acquire merit, or else remain unsaved, has already translated them out of the realm of grace (if by 'grace' we mean God's unmerited favour) into the realm of legal requirements, grace being preserved only in name.[1]

Present-day Thomists will insist (and rightly) that such notions as that of 'merit' cannot fairly be understood in the deviations of Nominalism, much less in the popular piety of the fifteenth and sixteenth centuries. But we may not overlook the fact that Luther, in his own opinion, was not merely attacking either corruptions or vulgarizations of Scholasticism: he was taking his stand against a theology which is rooted in Thomism itself. In Thomas's *Treatise on Grace* we are confronted with a doctrine of salvation which is legalistic without being Pelagian, or even semi-Pelagian. For although salvation is given as a *quid pro quo*, a price paid for work done, the merit which acquires it is a divine gift. The scheme is not Pelagian, but Augustinian.[2] The modern advocate of St. Thomas will have no difficulty in pointing out that this synthesis of grace and merit, divine condescension and human effort, makes much better sense of many Biblical utterances concerning 'reward' (and perhaps also

---

[1] Luther states categorically in the *Bondage of the Will* that there is no such thing as merit (*nullum esse meritum prorsus*: W.A. 18. 769. 33). He does, however, speak occasionally of the 'merits of Christ' (e.g. in 8. 599. 20). For, as Luther says explicitly in one place, the merits of Christ are identical with grace (2. 427. 23). To say that we live by Christ's merits meant, for Luther, that for us ourselves to acquire merit is neither possible nor necessary. Cf. Calvin, *Inst.* II. xvii.

[2] Regin Prenter has brought out this point with great clarity, arguing that it was from Augustine, not Pelagius, that the distinctive combination of Old Testament legalistic piety and Hellenic idealism passed into the mainstream of medieval thought. Grace, on the Augustinian-Scholastic view, is understood as supernatural power enabling man, by the acquisition of virtue, to attain to God as his Highest Good. *Spiritus Creator*, pp. 19–27. The closeness of this evaluation of Scholasticism to the thesis maintained by Nygren in part two of his *Agape and Eros*, is quite apparent. Wilhelm Link adopts a somewhat different perspective in his discussion of Luther's attitude towards Scholasticism, pointing to 'conditionalism' as the major object of Luther's criticism—that is, the Thomistic subjection of salvation to certain conditions which man must fulfil. *Das Ringen Luthers*, pp. 191 ff.

'law') than was possible on Luther's presuppositions.[1] Never-theless, Luther's claim, right or wrong, was that Scholastic theology was, not a judicious synthesis, but an erroneous mix-ture, for it places salvation at the end of a long process of human endeavour. The legalistic assumption of reason had corrupted the Gospel. In seeking what lay behind this charge we have found that there is, at the very least, an identification of the ethical and religious viewpoints at each step of the way in Thomas's views on justification and eternal life: he sets the whole discussion of grace within what is strictly a treatise on ethics;[2] he insists that salvation must be a reward accorded to merit; he views faith as 'unformed' without the virtue of charity; and he regards justification itself as a real improvement in the moral and religious personality. The whole plan of salvation is thus under the sign of the law. Eternal life and moral attain-ment are inextricably bound up together in Thomas, as in the Nominalists. That is to say, from Luther's point of view, the two kingdoms are confused. The increase in righteousness, which is certainly possible in the Earthly Kingdom, is transferred to the Heavenly Kingdom, where it becomes the basis of man's stand-ing before God. To sum up, against Thomas's attempt to wed grace and merit, faith and works, stands Luther's *sola gratia*, *sola fide*; and against Thomas's view of salvation as a gradual process leading to eternal life stands Luther's *eyn mal*—full 'righteousness' (*coram Deo*) here and now. And the diagnosis of Thomas's error is that he tried to synthesize the Christian Faith with Aristotelian philosophy. Adolf Harnack was exactly ex-pressing Luther's critique of Scholasticism when he argued, in his great *History of Dogma*,[3] that by the side of religion the Schoolmen introduced physics and morality, until grace became the medicine of immortality and justification a matter of being made virtuous. That is the kernel of Luther's revolt against

---

[1] Cf. Karl Adam, op. cit., p. 46. For Thomas's view see, for example, q. 109, art. 5. Luther wrestles with the problem at length in his *Bondage of the Will*. Perhaps the most forthright comment Luther ever made on law is in the opening paragraph of his *Treatise on the New Testament*, where it is claimed that God gave the people of Israel laws 'solely that human nature should learn how utterly useless many laws are to make people pious' (W.A. 6. 353. 12).

[2] That is, part two of the *Summa Theologiae*.

[3] vi. 281. See W.A. 7. 737. 26 and 39[1]. 229. 22, where Harnack's judgement is closely paralleled. '. . . pro fide inductis moralibus virtutibus.' 'Cum vocabula physica in theologiam translata sunt, facta est inde scholastica quaedam theologia.'

Scholasticism, and it is clearly bound up with his diatribes against 'reason' and 'philosophy'.[1]

To conclude both the present chapter and Part II as well, it only remains to underscore the fact that it is misleading to speak of the 'problem of faith and reason' in relation to Luther's theology, since, inevitably, we read into this expression the presuppositions of our own present-day understanding of the problem. Of course, we have seen that Luther does bring faith and reason into explicit relation with one another; and the way in which he speaks of this relation does lend a certain speciousness to the case of the critics who place him in the succession of Christian irrationalists which goes back at least to Tertullian. But, if our argument so far has been correct, what is wrong with the critics' case is simply that for Luther the problem of faith and reason is not so much an epistemological question (as they clearly suppose): it is a soteriological question. His 'critique of reason' is theological through and through. 'Faith' and 'reason' stand, so we have maintained, for two different types of religiousness, two different ways of salvation; and 'rationality' (if we dare use so vague a term) is not more characteristic of the one type than the other.

For this cause our problem is better stated as the 'problem of *grace* and reason' in the theology of Luther; and this is the way in which our enquiry was delineated in the preface (as well as the title) to the present essay. As with all Luther's teachings, we find ourselves understanding the meaning of his utterances on

[1] It is not part of our present purpose to evaluate Luther's critique of Scholasticism, much less to champion it. But two comments may perhaps be permitted in passing. (1) To interpret grace as forgiveness or 'unmerited favour' need not exclude a view of grace as 'sanctifying power', since it surely has to be granted that forgiveness does not leave a man's actual condition unchanged. Grace, as the Protestant understands it, is *nothing but* undeserved pardon, but surely no Protestant has ever denied that pardon renews and transforms the sinner. Cf. W.A. 2. 71. 31 ff., 10[1, 1]. 114. 20 ff.; also 39[1]. 48. 14, where justification is termed a 'rebirth'. (2) If salvation is divided into 'justification' *and* 'sanctification' (as became the rule in Protestant Orthodoxy), then the gap between 'Protestant' and 'Catholic' soteriologies is greatly narrowed, for on either view it is taken as axiomatic that without actual or personal holiness salvation is incomplete. Luther's critique of Scholasticism has plausibility only if we are willing to accept his identifying justification with salvation, and to find (as he did) another basis for ethics than as the means to life eternal. In Luther's theology the Christian has been freed *from* the necessity to merit salvation and thus freed *for* the opportunity to serve his neighbour (without an eye to self-salvation or self-sanctification).

reason only when we have sought to relate the notion of reason to the central themes of his theological thinking. Reason is seen by Luther as a threat to the cardinal doctrine of *sola gratia*, and we can make the main thrust of his argument more apparent by insisting that the antithesis of '*faith* and reason' will never be grasped, in its significance for Luther, unless it is interpreted by the antithesis of '*grace* and reason'.

We have found, in fact, many problems (even within the limitations imposed by our topic) converging upon a single point. Why did Luther direct all his very considerable powers of invective against 'reason'? Why did he attack the concept of 'law' not a whit less vehemently? How are we to explain his scorn for St. Thomas and his rejection of Aristotle? Why did he turn with such unmitigated fury upon the very way of life which he had earlier embraced as the only infallible means to salvation? Why was the one who occupied the throne of St. Peter and who had once seemed to Luther the very vicar of Christ upon earth, later identified by him with the Antichrist, and his See with Babylon, Mother of Harlots? The answer is simple: reason, law, Schoolmen, monks, and the Pope himself were all, to Luther, the many forms under which the White Devil manifests his presence in the world, and he considered it his mission to defend the Theology of Grace against the subtle wiles of this arch-enemy of a merciful God. Strangely, perhaps, we therefore arrive at the conclusion that the two standard objections alluded to in our preface are, in fact, reactions against one and the same feature of Luther's thought. He belabours reason and law from precisely the same motive. Were his critics a little more discerning, they might accuse him of being an irrationalist precisely *because* he was an antinomian. Yet, if they were *very* discerning, they should see that fundamentally he was neither, for neither term is applicable without so much qualification that it is more likely to mislead than to illuminate. Should we call anyone an irrationalist who allows that reason has its place, though it also has its limits? And should we call anyone an antinomian who is as insistent as Luther on the need for good works, albeit *in suo loco*? Well, possibly Luther's critics would still choose to call him both, since he certainly considers some of his beliefs to be contrary to reason, and he does not regard virtue as a prerequisite to salvation. But the critic who so chooses must be careful not to do less justice to the subtlety of Luther's thought than he deserves. If the interpretation of Luther's teachings which has been put forward here is correct, then it is quite certain that many of his critics have missed his point entirely. For Luther is not simply 'against' law and reason; he is against an unwarranted transferring of them from their proper place, which is (with qualifications) the Earthly Kingdom, to the Heavenly Kingdom, where they generally lead only to the agonies of a tormented conscience. It is precisely the work of the Devil to 'mix the Kingdoms' in this way.[1] When Luther said that Reason was the 'devil's Whore', he meant that Reason may be prostituted for the ends of evil. He meant, in fact, just what he said: he was not merely throwing out senseless abuse. Reason is the Devil's Whore: more precisely, Reason is the White Devil's Whore.

[1] In general, it may be said that the law is the way in which God governs the Earthly Kingdom; Gospel, the way in which He governs the Heavenly Kingdom. The work of the Devil—who is not, of course, sovereign over the Earthly Kingdom any more than over the Heavenly—consists in trying to confuse the divine order either by introducing law into the Heavenly Realm or (though this does not concern us here) by introducing the Gospel into the Kingdom of the World. But qualifications are obviously needed, since the divine order sometimes requires God Himself to force law into the Heavenly Kingdom, this 'strange work' being the spiritual or theological use of the law. (The matter is discussed, with ample documentation, in Wingren, op. cit., esp. pp. 107 ff.) Similarly, as we have seen, reason may be admitted into the spiritual Kingdom of Christ, though only when regenerated.

PART III

REASON AND SCHOLARSHIP

IX

REASON AND THE TASK OF THE SCHOLAR

THE main part of our inquiry is now completed. An explanation has been offered of Luther's intention when he assailed reason as the 'Devil's Whore', and it was suggested in the conclusion to the previous section that Luther's meaning might better be conveyed by speaking of the 'White Devil's Whore', for he saw reason chiefly as the champion of legalism or moralism. But it was shown in our introduction that the formal charge of irrationalism, commonly levelled against Luther, is often accompanied in the prosecutor's mind by an elaborate picture of Luther as a gross philistine, uncultured, indifferent to the demands of logical thought and the discipline of painstaking study. After all, did not Luther give himself away when he exclaimed: 'I am a peasant's son'?[1]

Denifle's picture of Luther as an 'ossified Occamite' was accordingly set beside yet another portrait, which showed him as, in general, a 'crass ignoramus'. This was, indeed, the original feature of Denifle's work. Luther's moral degeneracy, his gluttony, drunkenness, and bawdiness, were well known to the Catholic writers of the sixteenth century. 'Only the crass ignoramus is a new discovery made by Denifle.'[2] To be sure, Denifle's case has not been confirmed by careful inquiry since his devastating polemic. O. G. Schmidt demonstrated that Luther,

---

[1] TR. 1. 421. 4; cf. 5. 558. 13.
[2] Boehmer, *Luther in Light of Recent Research*, pp. 177–8.

however slight his knowledge of Greek authors, knew the Romans well. W. Koehler established Luther's knowledge of history in general, and of church history in particular. Luther was widely read in the Fathers and Schoolmen, in the Mystics and the Humanists. Heinrich Boehmer gives such reading-lists as no historical theologian need be ashamed of: Luther knew them all, some he had by heart.[1]

But the portrait of Luther as a crass ignoramus needs to be corrected, not merely in a piecemeal fashion, by trying to go over some of the details afresh; it also calls for an entirely new beginning, for another portrait which begins from a different (and truer) conception of the man and his place in the history of the sixteenth century. Boehmer writes: 'As far as critical acumen is concerned he was at least the equal of the renowned Erasmus.' And again: 'Even regarded purely as an intellectual character he was a phenomenon without equal.'[2] Why is it that Boehmer arrives at such a radically different Luther from Denifle's? Partly, no doubt, the answer is that Boehmer starts out with a more sympathetic disposition. But partly also the answer lies in the fact that Boehmer has not looked in the same places as Denifle did, at least, has not looked there *only*. He has also seen Luther at work in the area of Humanist learning. 'Upon close scrutiny the crass ignoramus, therefore, reveals himself as a very sound and respectable scholar.'[3] Denifle is mesmerized by the Luther who assailed Scholasticism, and he does not notice the Luther who borrowed all the tools of Humanism and laboured with them incessantly until even his body could stand no more—all for the sake of illuminating the Sacred Book, making it available to the 'boorish Saxons'. In other words, it is not enough to see Luther's 'assault on reason' against the background of his Scholastic education: one must also see it in the wider context of the Renaissance and the 'revival of learning'. For the revolt against Scholasticism was by no means peculiar to Luther: it was part and parcel of the Humanist programme. In short, Luther must be compared, not only with Occam, but also with Erasmus.

Any conception of 'reason' which fails to include the skills of

---

[1] Ibid., pp. 178 ff. Many of Boehmer's remarks can now be checked from the Weimar edn. index-vol., which contains refs. to Luther's comments on books he had read.   [2] Op. cit., pp. 182 and 183.   [3] Ibid., p. 181.

the scholar can hardly be taken seriously. Rationality is not the private property of the philosopher. Charles Beard has a judicious comment which may fittingly be cited at this point:

> I use the word reason here, in its largest sense, as denoting the faculties of the human mind in their collective application to all problems of science and life, and without wishing to imply that methods of inquiry are absolutely the same in all branches of knowledge.[1]

Luther himself considered that the work of the scholar was an exercise of *Vernunft*; and we must not overlook this judgement, however strange the connexion of 'reason' and 'scholarship' may sound to our own ears. Certainly, Luther always insisted that something else was needed first: like Paul, he first received illumination, then study also entered in (*deinde accessit studium*).[2] First comes the reception of grace solely by God's gift. Reflection *upon* revelation is legitimate, but you cannot substitute reflection *instead* of revelation. Both sides of Luther's position must be stressed: neither illumination nor scholarship is sufficient alone.

'I know perfectly well', Luther writes, '. . . how much skill, industry, reason, understanding are required in a good translator.' And yet, almost immediately, he adds: the whole matter is 'beyond all the world's wisdom and reason'.[3] This is not to be thought of as an inconsistency in Luther's position. It is no accident that the qualifying epithet 'worldly' is added in the second statement. The solution to the apparent contradiction lies, in fact, in another passage which we have already had occasion to mention:[4] we have to make a distinction between the abuse of a thing and the thing itself, so that reason, when illuminated by the Holy Spirit, does help in understanding Scripture. Reason, like the tongue, can be used to praise God or to blaspheme. Reason may be used to serve faith, and without faith it is useless. 'When illuminated, reason takes all its thoughts from the Word.' Clearly by reason here Luther means simply the organs of human thought, the faculty by which man organizes, and makes inferences from, what is given. The 'illumina-

---

[1] Op. cit., p. 147. [2] W.A. 40[1]. 145. 20.
[3] 'Ich weiß wol . . . was fur kunst, fleiß, vernunfft, verstandt zum gutten dolmetscher gehöret.' '. . . uber aller welt weißheit und vernunfft'. From the *Open Letter on Translating* of 1530 (W.A. 30[2]. 633. 29, 636. 8). [4] TR. 1, no. 439.

tion' of reason virtually consists in humble acceptance of a new set of premises, namely, those provided by the 'Word'. What reason may not do is to sit in judgement upon the Word. This is not strictly a limitation upon reason as a purely mental faculty, but a refusal to allow reason to bring to faith premises derived from a sphere outside of faith. And this is really what Luther means by 'natural' reason—or, indeed, reason 'possessed by the Devil'. This is apparent from another passage in the *Table-Talk*:[1] 'If anyone summons reason to the council, assent to our articles of faith is impossible. . . . We will abide by these articles even against reason.' So far as the premises are subject to rational testing, it must be the test of experience: 'I do not so much believe as know from experience.' And this, of course, means chiefly Luther's own 'evangelical experience'—a point to which we must shortly return.

From such passages as these it soon becomes apparent that our task will not be complete until account has been taken of this 'scholarly reason', which Luther, although with some qualifications, evidently approves. Once again our problem is complicated by the extreme flexibility of the word *ratio*. A similar flexibility appears also in the English 'reason'; and yet we often overlook it in our discussions of 'faith and reason', treating the problem as if it were a straightforward question of religion, on the one side, and philosophy, on the other. What we find in the intellectual development of Luther is a man trained originally in the philosophy of the Nominalist School-men, but turning more and more to the Biblical Humanists as his 'new theology' was hammered out. In the present chapter, then, it will be shown very briefly how much Luther's work owed to the Biblical Humanists; in the final chapter we will need to enlarge on the historical context of the Lutheran Reformation in order to substantiate the claim that Luther shared in a general shift of interest away from Scholastic philo-sophy and towards Humanist scholarship, so that for him the proper place for the exercise of 'reason' was in scholarship rather than philosophy.

It is of course to Luther's work as an exegete that we must turn if we are to estimate his debt to the Biblical Humanists.

---

[1] No. 4915: 'Si quis in consilium adhibet rationem, non potest assentiri nostris articulis fidei. . . . Nos manebimus etiam cum istis articulis contra rationem.'

And here, as so often, we are immediately struck by a certain tension in the Reformer's thinking. For his principles of exegesis reveal a subtle interweaving of at least two motives: the scholar's desire to interpret the text accurately and faithfully by means of the best tools of the grammatical sciences, and the believer's desire to search the text for further illumination of his own decisive experience. Needless to say, these two principles are not always easy to harmonize: on the contrary, they frequently run into conflict. But it is precisely this tension which illuminates Luther's relation to the Biblical Humanists, showing at once his indebtedness and his independence.

The grammatical sense of scripture

Luther's insistence on the primacy of the *sensus literalis, grammaticus*, or *historicus*, is clearly stated in the treatise 'against the Heavenly Prophets' (1525):

Natural speech is queen: it is superior to all subtle, clever, sophistic inventions; from it we must not retreat unless an obvious article of faith compels us. Otherwise not one letter of Scripture would withstand spiritual jugglers.[1]

Luther's objection to Carlstadt's 'spiritual interpretation' is that there is no true basis for it if we look honestly at the text: it is mere clowning. Literal meaning is first and foremost. If it could be shown to Luther that his interpretation of a passage was grammatically untenable, he made no effort to cling to it, however edifying. He did not fall back upon the evasion that he was offering a special, spiritual sense which the words concealed in addition to the literal sense: 'In translating I always observe this rule: we must not fight against the grammar.'[2] And again: 'I have not disregarded literal meanings too freely, but with my helpers I have been very careful to see that when a passage is important I have kept the literal meaning and not departed freely from it.' Sometimes it is necessary to keep close to the Hebrew form of words even when the German language would prefer a less literal rendering.[3] This predilection for plain,

[1] W.A. 18. 180. 17.
[2] 'In vertendo semper hanc regulam servo, ne pugnemus contra grammaticam.' TR. no. 2382; 2. 439. 19.
[3] *Open Letter:* W.A. 30². 640. 19; P.E. v. 19. Cf. *Summarien über die Psalmen:* W.A. 38. 13. 22.

undressed-up language even leads Luther on occasion to make disparaging remarks about the writings he is discussing. On the Apocalypse he remarks:

The apostles have nothing to do with visions, but prophesy in clear, plain words, as do Peter, and Paul, and Christ in the Gospel; for it belongs to the apostolic office to tell clearly and without images or visions about Christ and His work.[1]

Here is one of the reasons which led Luther to doubt the apostolicity of the Apocalypse. And it also led him to abandon the 'fourfold sense' of Scripture.

In his early expositions of the Psalms (*Dictata super Psalterium,* 1513–15) Luther still, as we would only expect, adopts the fourfold exegesis as a matter of course, explicitly defending it in his preface. Indeed, he goes further than this, drawing a distinction between 'spirit' and 'letter', which he apparently applies to each of the four senses. To be sure, even in these very early writings Luther shows himself to be fully conscious of the dangers of this kind of exegesis. Explicitly he lays down the principle that nothing in Scripture is to be interpreted allegorically, tropologically, or anagogically, which is not elsewhere expressly stated historically.[2] Further, he does use honorific epithets in speaking of the grammatical sense. It is the 'foundation' of the rest, it is *magister et lux et author et fons atque origo.* This, however, cannot alter the fact that Luther's insistence on the literal sense is not at this time taken seriously in practice, and he was not, of course, being original in giving it theoretical precedence: both his theory and his practice in the *Dictata super Psalterium* reflect the generally accepted opinions of his day.[3] Besides, we should not too readily assume that a defence of the literal sense is automatically a word in favour of twentieth-century methods of exegesis. Most of the Psalms, in Luther's opinion, referred *literally* to Christ, and could even be used to supplement the Passion-narratives of the Four Gospels.

In the *Seven Penitential Psalms* (1517) Luther is no longer making use of the fourfold sense, whilst in his exposition of the Decalogue (1518) he openly mocks the 'Scholastics' who 'play with' the manifold meaning of Scripture as though it were all

[1] W.A. DB. 7. 404. 7.   [2] W.A. 3. 11. 33.
[3] Cf. Karl Holl, op. cit., p. 545.

a game.[1] By the time he came to write the *Resolutions* of 1518, Luther has begun to see the traditional exegesis as an evil to be cut out, since his enemies are using it to justify many practices and beliefs which Luther himself regards as un-Biblical.[2] The same point arises in his *Defence against Eck* in connexion with the words 'Thou art Peter', which can only have 'one primary and proper meaning' (*unum, primum, principalem et proprium sensum*).[3] He sees in the manifold sense of Scripture the entire crux of his dispute with Eck, and says so explicitly in his letter to Dungersheim of December, 1519.[4] The 'simple sense' is again stressed in the later expositions of the Psalms, the *Operationes in Psalmos* (1519–21);[5] and in his reply to Emser of Leipzig, in a close and careful discussion of the entire problem, Luther utters the famous: 'The Holy Spirit is the most simple author and speaker in heaven and on earth; therefore, his words cannot have more than the one most simple sense.'[6] In his later years Luther allowed no place for allegorical exegesis, save as what he termed 'flowers' or 'ornaments'.[7]

It was all but inevitable that with his growing conviction of the primacy of the literal sense Luther should become more and more absorbed in matters of philology. He found the tools of scholarly philological research already available—or, at least, becoming more available almost every month—in the publications of the Humanists.

In the first place, Luther began to distrust the Vulgate Bible and to make more use of the Humanists' efforts to establish reliable texts of the Scriptures in Hebrew and Greek. 'Jerome's Bible' had come under heavy fire from Laurentius Valla, who had pointed out many discrepancies between the Vulgate and the Greek original in his *Annotations* (published by Erasmus in 1505, some years after Valla's death). Similarly Faber Stapulensis had drawn attention to the errors of the Vulgate in his

[1] W.A. 1. 507. 35.
[2] Purgatory is one such un-Biblical belief. See W.A. 1. 563. 40 ff. (esp. 564. 8). Trans. in the American edn., XXXI. 139.
[3] W.A. 2. 628. 22; cf. 2. 628. 18, 2. 641. 15.
[4] W.A. Br. 1. 603. 2; trans. in Smith, *Luther's Correspondence*, I. 255.
[5] See, for example, W.A. 5. 280. 36, 644. 2, 647. 2.
[6] W.A. 7. 650. 21 ff. Cf. further *Von dem Papsttum zu Rom* (1520): W.A. 6. 307. 6; Christmas Postil of 1522: W.A. 10[1, 1]. 169. 2.
[7] See esp. the *Genesisvorlesung*: W.A. 42. 173. 30 (on Gen. iii) and 377. 20 (on Gen. ix).

Epistles of Paul, and so did Erasmus in the Annotations to his New Testament. Luther began to doubt the Vulgate as early as his lectures on the Psalms (1513–15), and it is possible to trace the steady movement of his mind away from the hallowed version in his subsequent expositions of the Epistle to the Romans (1515–16) and of the Penitential Psalms (1517).

In the second place, quite obviously, Luther became more and more acutely aware of the need for acquiring the linguistic tools, without which the original text was of no use whatever to him. By the time he came to write his address *To the Council-men of All Cities* (1524),[1] advising them to establish Christian schools throughout the land, Luther was prepared to affirm without qualification that the preservation of the Gospel depended upon a knowledge of the original tongues. True, he says, the Gospel comes 'through the Holy Spirit'. But we cannot deny that it has come 'by means of the languages'. Here is the answer to the question: Granted that we must have schools, what is the use of teaching dead languages in them?[2] We cannot keep the Gospel without the languages.

They are the sheath in which the sword of the Spirit is encased; they are the casket in which this jewel is carried; they are the vessel which contains this wine; they are the cupboard in which this food is stored; and, as the Gospel itself says, they are the baskets in which these loaves and fishes and fragments are kept.[3]

If we lose the languages through our neglect, we lose the Gospel also. Unless the languages remain, the Gospel must ultimately perish.[4] Luther was not one to sentimentalize about the 'simple preacher of the faith': 'expositors' are what is needed, therefore languages also.[5]

In the third place, as Luther acquired a greater facility in the Biblical languages,[6] so he made more extensive use of the

---

[1] W.A. 15. 27–53. Trans. in P.E. IV. 103 ff.
[2] W.A. 15. 36. 6.
[3] Ibid. 38. 7.
[4] Ibid. 38. 12; 38. 30.
[5] Ibid. 40. 14; 40. 23.
[6] The actual details of his learning the languages need not detain us, since they are recounted in all the standard biographies. Fife's account is carefully documented: op. cit., esp. pp. 150–1. More detailed is Scheel, op. cit. II. 413 and 649 f. (Hebrew); 416 ff. (Greek). Luther seems to have begun Hebrew earlier than

Humanists' lexicons, commentaries, and critical editions. Indeed, these in turn stimulated his work on the languages. In particular, we know that he made diligent use of Reuchlin's *Rudimenta Linguae Hebraicae* (1506), which contained a lexicon (in the first two volumes) and a grammar (in the third); Faber's *Psalterium Quincuplex* (1509) and *Epistolae Pauli Apostoli* (1512); Reuchlin's *Septem Psalmi Poenitentiales* (1512); Erasmus's *Novum Instrumentum* (1516); and Melanchthon's *Greek Grammar* (1518).[1] In short, it was Carlstadt, not Luther, who advised the Wittenberg students to leave their books.[2] Luther himself valued 'letters' both for their own sake and for their aid to the student of the sacred text: of this his letter to the German councillors leaves us in no doubt.

Further evidence of Luther's indebtedness to the Humanists is hardly necessary. His gradual emancipation from the influence of the philosophers was paralleled by a growing dependence upon the labours of the Humanists. Not that he was ever slavish in his dependence: on the contrary, it was partly from the Biblical Humanists themselves that Luther acquired a certain freedom in dealing with the sacred text. As Reinhold Seeberg remarked, 'Luther employed "criticism" in the widest variety of forms. Almost all the criteria employed at the present day were applied by him in his own way.'[3] One of the most striking features of Luther's German New Testament[4] is the remarkable freedom with which he judges the relative worth of the various books.[5] In the list of New Testament books which immediately

Greek: Reu op. cit., pp. 96–97, 114–15, and 118–19. But by the time of the Leipzig Debate (1519) his knowledge of both languages was sufficient to attract notice: Boehmer, *Road to Reformation*, p. 288.

[1] Further details in the works cited in the preceding note. See also Kurt Aland, 'Luther as Exegete', *Expository Times*, LXIX. 2 and 3 (1957), 45–48, 68–70. M. Reu in his study, *Luther's German Bible*, offers a striking list of Humanistic 'helps' which Luther employed in making his translation of the New and Old Testaments.

[2] Cf. W.A. 40¹. 105. 22: 'Plerique vero non solum sacras literas, sed etiam omnes alias literas fastidiunt et contemnunt'—certainly an 'allusion to Carlsdadt', as the Weimar edn. comments. See also W.A. 18. 100. 27 ff. and 167. 5 ff. (In the last passage Luther makes his famous remark about the fanciful exegesis of Carlsdadt's *geystreichen und schrifftlosen kopffs*.)

[3] *Lehrbuch der Dogmengeschichte*: Eng. trans. II. 300 f. See also the present writer's article, 'Biblical Authority and the Continental Reformation', *Scottish Journal of Theology*, x. 4 (1957), 342 ff.

[4] The Gospels and Acts will be found in DB., vol. 6; the Epistles and Apocalypse, in vol. 7.

[5] See the 'Instruction' on 'which are the best and finest books of the New

follows his prefatory 'Instruction' four of the books appear un-numbered, and are set apart from the others by a blank space: Hebrews, James, Jude, and the Apocalypse. This is precisely the way in which Luther marks off the canonical from the apocryphal books of the Old Testament.[1] The individual pre-faces to the four degraded books afford an explanation and justification for this severe judgement, providing perhaps the best illustration of Luther's 'critical methods'. Nobody would pretend that he is always right; but his judgements are always interesting.[2] To some extent it can be shown that his critical judgements were suggested to him by the Humanists: in the Annotations to his Greek New Testament Erasmus expressed opinions very similar to Luther's on these four problem-books. And yet even where Luther is apparently leaning most heavily on Erasmus we can detect, at the same time, his genuine inde-pendence. In the last analysis, Luther's downgrading certain books of the New Testament must be taken as evidence of his theological convictions, not merely of his confidence in scholarly criticism.

Scripture and theological interpretation

However highly Luther valued the tools of scholarly labours, he nevertheless was quite sure that they alone were not enough. The literary skills of the Humanists were merely 'forerunners of the Gospel', as John the Baptist was forerunner to Christ.[3] 'Languages in themselves do not make a theologian: they are only a help. Before a man can speak on anything, he must first know and understand the subject (die Sache).'[4]

Testament': this concludes the prefatory remarks in the 1522 N.T. (DB. 6. 10): it was omitted in subsequent edns.

[1] DB. 6. 12 and 8. 34–35.

[2] For example: (1) Hebrews cannot have been written by Paul, since the writer admits that he received the Gospel second-hand (from 'them that heard': ii. 3; contrast Gal. i. 12). (2) The brother of our Lord could not possibly be the James who wrote the 'Epistle of James', since in ch. v the writer cites sayings from Peter and Paul, whereas we know from Acts that the brother of our Lord was put to death by Herod *before* Peter and Paul. (3) Jude has the appearance of being a copy taken from 2 Peter, 'so very like it are all the words'. Besides, Jude the Apostle went to Persia, and we therefore would hardly expect him to be writing an epistle in Greek. These are but a few of Luther's absorbing comments.

[3] W.A. Br. 3. 50. 24 (to Eoban Hess; 29 Mar. 1523); trans. in Smith and Jacobs, *Luther's Correspondence*, II. 176.

[4] W.A. TR. 1, no. 1040 (524. 38). Cf. 1, no. 1183; 3, no. 3271.

Again and again we find Luther asserting: 'It is not enough to know grammar. One must also take account of the sense.' And the sense can only be decided by one who has experience of the subject-matter. 'It is understanding the matter that provides understanding of the words.'[1] Hence, in reading Virgil's *Eclogues* you cannot understand the words until you know to whom they refer. Once you know the poet is speaking of Augustus, translation is easy. In another of Luther's sayings (the famous words he wrote on a slip of paper two days before his death)[2] he makes a somewhat different point in referring to Virgil's *Eclogues* and *Georgics,* but one which still indicates the necessity for knowledge of the subject-matter (*cognitio rerum*): no one can understand Virgil's *Eclogues* and *Georgics* unless he has been a shepherd or farmer for five years. In short, it is the matter which gives the sense: when we think we have the matter —the reference of the words (as Augustus) or the area of human experience which forms their setting (as farming)—then all we need to ask is whether grammar will allow the sense which the matter suggests.[3]

Hence, Luther would defend his exegesis and even his text by appeal to his own experience. Münzer attacked his rendering of Jonah ii. 5, since it demanded the insertion of a negation in the *textus receptus*; Luther retorted: 'You, dear Münzer, have not experienced those trials!'[4] Thus he does add, in a way, to the principle *scriptura sola*: 'Not Scripture only . . . but also experience. . . . Therefore, together with the Scripture I have the matter (*rem*) and experience.'[5] Translating, indeed, is not everybody's art: 'It requires a right pious, faithful, diligent, God-fearing, experienced, practiced heart.'[6] What W. Schwarz calls Luther's own 'inspiration' (meaning, of course, the decisive illumination by which he was led to a fresh understanding of God's righteousness) became regulative for his exegesis all the days of his life.[7] For Luther perceived that the Gospel revealed

---

[1] 'Non satis est nosse grammaticam, sed observare sensum, nam cognitio rerum affert cognitionem verborum.' W.A. TR. 4, no. 5002. (The reading *grammatica* is probably an error.)   [2] TR. 5, no. 5468 (168. 27).

[3] *Potestne grammatica hunc sensum pati?* TR. 4, no. 5002 (608. 14).

[4] TR. 3, no. 3503 (363. 4). Cf. the note ad loc. in DB. 4. 244.

[5] TR. 1, no. 701.   [6] *Open Letter on Translating,* P.E. v. 19.

[7] Schwarz, *Principles and Problems of Biblical Translation,* ch. vi. This is the best treatment of Luther's exegetical principles known to me, clearly stating the 'polarity and interdependence of the two elements which alone could lead to an

a 'justice by which God justifies us through faith'. His new understanding of Rom. i. 17 showed him the meaning of his own fearful struggle in the monastery, and then, in turn, experience illumined the meaning of the Scriptures. The Gospel reveals a God who justifies us by His grace; but first we must be humbled by His law. This is what Luther now read in the Scriptures and in his own experience as an Augustinian friar. Experience and philology went hand in hand.[1]

The familiar exegetical principle *scriptura sui ipsius interpres* ('Scripture is its own interpreter') also, in the last analysis, is closely bound up with Luther's 'experience'. In part, no doubt, it was a corollary of the *scriptura sola*: if the authority of God's Word is not to be supplemented, neither is interpretation to be governed and determined by some further authority. The principle *scriptura sui ipsius interpres* is inseparable from the principle *scriptura sola*. The Scriptures must rule in fact; not merely in theory. Luther would have the Scriptures interpreted neither by his own understanding nor by anyone else's. They must stand by themselves (*per sese*).[2] Again, when Luther challenges Eck for collecting passages from all over the Bible without regard for logical order or context, there is a remarkably modern ring about his words.[3] But one should be cautious of assuming too hastily that Luther here shows himself as careful a scholar as our conventions demand. The principle *scriptura sui ipsius interpres* does not mean just that you must consider a passage from Scripture in its proper context. Fortunately, it *did* mean this sometimes for Luther. But generally it meant more also: it meant that each individual passage had to be understood in the light of the Biblical message as a whole.[4] And this means: in the light of Luther's doctrine of 'justification by faith', which was at the heart of his evangelical experience.

understanding of God's word' (p. 200). Schwarz adduces many more references than is possible here.

[1] In addition to Schwarz's work, see Warren A. Quanbeck, 'Luther's early exegesis', *Luther Today* (essays by R. H. Bainton, *et al.*), pp. 37–103; and E. Harris Harbison, *The Christian Scholar*, pp. 119 ff.

[2] *Assertio omnium articulorum M. Lutheri per bullam Leonis X novissimam damnatorum* (1520): W.A. 7. 97. 23, 98. 40, 99. 18.

[3] *Disputatio Eccii et Lutheri* (W.A. 2. 361. 16).

[4] This is apparent in the same passage just referred to where Luther assails Eck for taking Scriptures out of context, for he goes on immediately to say that the theologian must keep in mind 'the whole of the Scriptures'. Cf. also W.A. 2. 302. 1.

The evangelical experience was, then, the key which illumined for Luther the *whole* of Scripture, not just the Pauline Epistles. And since the essence of that experience was what Luther likes to call 'a laying hold upon Christ', in whom alone God is seen as the gracious one who 'makes us just through faith', therefore Luther is only saying the same thing in a different way when he tells us that *Christ* is the key to Scripture. The evangelical experience is experience of Christ.[1]

In short, what is really characteristic of Luther's method as a Biblical scholar is his reliance upon neither grammar alone, nor experience alone, but a kind of dialectic of the two. Hence his relation to the Biblical Humanists manifests both indebtedness and independence. If we glance again, for a moment, at Luther's approach to the problem of the four disputed books of the New Testament, we could perhaps say that Luther was an exponent of that kind of criticism which P. T. Forsyth called 'neither literary nor scientific but evangelical'.[2] The exercise of 'evangelical criticism' demanded, so Luther thought, a revision of the canon. This he says explicitly in his preface to James and Jude:

> The true test by which to judge all books is to see whether they deal with Christ or not (*ob sie Christum treiben*). . . . What does not teach Christ is not apostolic, even though St. Peter or Paul taught it. Again, what preaches Christ would be apostolic, even if Judas, Annas, Pilate, and Herod did it.

And, of course, to 'preach Christ' means to set him forth as the centre of that Gospel which Luther rediscovered in the monastery. The same principle also determines Luther's interpretation of those books which constitute the remaining canon. As Luther put it, the whole Scripture has to be understood 'according to the analogy of faith': that is to say, faith in Christ (in

---

[1] Probably the unity of Scripture rests upon three facts in Luther's mind: its *author* was God, the Spirit; its *content* is Christ; and its *message* is justification by grace. But I do not wish to be deflected from my main purpose by devoting further space to these interesting points. Some remarks are made on Luther's 'Christo-centrism' in the article in *The Scottish Journal* referred to above. See also Luther's *Preface to the Old Testament* (P.E. VI. 379–80) and the preface to the *Last Words of David* (W.A. 54. 29–30).

[2] *Positive Preaching and the Modern Mind* (London: Independent Press, 1949), p. 12.

effect, justification by faith) becomes the touchstone of correct exegesis.[1] No doubt, such a methodological principle has its dangers.[2] But it could well be argued that Luther's evangelical principle, so far from hampering his judgement, lent him a freedom which Protestantism soon lost and did not recover until forced to by another kind of Biblical criticism. Nor should it be assumed that Luther's recognition of the place of 'experience' in exegesis is in itself unscholarly; for, as Harbison rightly observes, 'In the humanities, unlike the natural sciences, great scholarship is the result not of "objectivity" alone but of a balance between objectivity and sympathy.'[3] Only with respect to religion does the strange notion prevail that a scholar's safest equipment for his task is indifference, or even hostility, towards his subject. Perhaps, after all, there is something to be said— even from the standpoint of scholarship—in favour of Luther's bluff denial that anyone can interpret the Scriptures without a certain feeling for 'the matter'.

Be that as it may, sufficient has been said to substantiate the point that the exercise of 'scholarly' (as distinct from 'philosophic') reason led Luther into a close alliance with the Biblical Humanists: the fact that his own methodology contained more than theirs qualifies, but does not invalidate, the point. More, no doubt, could be said on this theme.[4] But we must now go on

---

[1] See esp.: W.A. 24. 549. 18; 42. 368. 35, 377. 20. The *analogia fidei* (which Luther based on Rom. xii. 6) was invoked chiefly as a check upon the use of allegorical exegesis. It will be seen from the passages cited (esp. W.A. 42. 377. 20) that Luther could interpret the principle quite broadly in theory ('Make your allegories fit Christ, the church, faith, the ministry of the Word'); but in actual practice it is the peculiarly Lutheran understanding of *the Gospel* that affords the hermeneutic touchstone.

[2] Mackinnon, indeed, speaks of the *analogia fidei* as the 'Lutheran equivalent of the allegoric method' (op. cit. IV. 298). That is to say, the analogy of faith was the device Luther could employ to find in Scripture what he wanted to find. Hence, ironically enough, the very principle which Luther introduced to combat allegorical extravagance came to be employed by himself in an equally extravagant way. Of course, it could be replied that 'faith in Christ'—'forgiveness', or however it be expressed—actually *is* the basic motif of Biblical religion, so that, even if Luther's exegesis of a particular passage is sometimes far-fetched, his understanding of the total significance of the Bible is correct and his insistence on interpreting the part by the whole might be said to have led him into a very pardonable error.

[3] Op. cit., p. 131.

[4] Perhaps the best evidence of Luther's capacities as a scholar is afforded by the Weimar volumes of the *Deutsche Bibel*. It is hardly too much to say that nobody knows the whole Luther unless he has perused the protocols and *Niederschriften* from which the Wittenberg Bible was finally brought into being—as the Weimar

to underscore the significance of Luther's leaning towards Humanism. Certainly, it has already become clear enough that Denifle's 'crass ignoramus' and Maritain's creature of passion ('wholly and systematically ruled by his affective and appetitive faculties') belong as much to the domain of mythology as the sainted Martin of early Lutheranism, whose advent was predicted in Holy Writ, and whose home in Wittenberg afforded relics that could miraculously relieve the toothache. But there is a further, perhaps more important, reason for associating Luther with the Humanists: namely, that they could speak no less forcefully than he against the corruption of theology by Aristotelianism, and the question therefore arises whether a part at least of his attitude towards reason and philosophy may not link him less with the Nominalists than with their Humanistic opponents.[1]

editor (Reichert) justly comments, *'ein Werk sorgfältiger, wissenschaftlicher Methode'* (DB. 4. xxxi). It is certainly not hard to believe Luther's own claim (in his *Open Letter on Translating*) that he sometimes wrestled with the text for two, three, or four weeks just to find a single *mot juste*.

[1] It is interesting to note that John Wesley linked Luther's attack on reason with neither Nominalism nor Humanism, but Mysticism. Watson, from whom I first learnt of Wesley's judgement (see Introduction, p. 1, n. 3, above), does not quote the whole passage. Wesley says: 'How does he [Luther] (*almost in the words of Tauler*) decry reason, right or wrong, as an irreconcilable enemy to the gospel of Christ' (*Journal*, 15 June 1741; the words in italics were omitted in Watson's citation). So far as the present writer is aware, very little has been said about the possibility that Luther's views on reason may have been influenced by Mysticism, though much has been written in general about Luther and the Mystics. It is commonly assumed that we should look to Occam, rather than Tauler, for the background of Luther's views on faith and reason.

X

HUMANISM AND SCHOLASTICISM

THE conclusion to our last chapter suggests the possibility that perhaps Luther may be, indeed, should be, classed with the so-called 'Biblical Humanists'. The name 'Humanist' by itself is, of course, a singularly ambiguous one, and there were many varieties of Humanist in the age of the Renaissance. What bound them all together was a characteristic *Heimweh*, a 'homesickness' for the distant past.[1] For the Biblical Humanists this homesickness was directed towards a 'primitive Christianity', recoverable only through the instrumentality of a new mastery of the Biblical languages. Without any doubt we may, broadly speaking, link Luther's name with this group. Trained in the dialectic of later Scholasticism during his youth, the conviction steadily grew upon him that it was the Humanists, not the Schoolmen, who came nearest to possessing the keys for unlocking the Gospel. The change in his thinking was reflected in a change of exegetical practice, whereby the literal sense of Scripture came to have primacy in actual fact, not merely in theory. Once this step was taken, the conclusion was, indeed, inevitable: 'What then is the basis for Scriptural interpretation in this literal sense? Luther's answer is: knowledge of the original tongues in which the Bible was written.'[2]

It was Calvin, not Luther, who spoke about 'sudden conversion'.[3] The German Reformation began with a new[4] interpretation of a Biblical text: it began with a fresh philological insight, and it developed into an academic debate. The man behind it all was a Doctor of Theology and a Professor of Bible; his first converts were taken from amongst his colleagues in the

[1] See Schwiebert, *Luther and His Times*, p. 275, and the references there cited. The whole chapter on 'The Triumph of Biblical Humanism in the University of Wittenberg' is germane to our present theme.

[2] Kurt Aland, 'Luther as Exegete', *Expository Times*, LXIX. 2 (1957), 47.

[3] See the autobiographical preface to Calvin's exposition of the Psalms: *Corpus Reformatorum*, XXXI. 21; trans. in Calvin's *Commentary on the Book of Psalms*, I. xl.

[4] 'Luther discovered the saving Righteousness of God afresh. It was something new for himself.' Lortz, cited by Rupp, *Righteousness of God*, p. 27.

University's faculties; and what proved to be the bugle-call for revolt had been in Luther's own intention only an invitation to scholarly dispute. One of the reasons why the Pope and his advisers were so slow in taking counter-measures was their initial assumption that they had no more than another monks' squabble on their hands, motivated, in part, by rivalry between the orders.

Amongst the immediate effects of the 'new theology' was a sweeping curricular revision in the University of Wittenberg. Luther's approach to his professional duties soon forged a link between himself and the humanistically-inclined members of the faculty. Lang began to give Luther lessons in Greek, and was himself soon drawn into theology. After the return of Trutvetter to his old university, the *via moderna* was no longer represented at Wittenberg; but the *via antiqua* still had no less than eight champions, four Thomist and four Scotist, headed by Carlstadt and Amsdorf respectively. Both Carlstadt and Amsdorf were won over to Luther's theology, very largely because of the disputations held under Luther's auspices in 1516–17 (including the ninety-seven theses *Against Scholastic Theology*, written for Guenther's disputation on 4 September 1517). Not only the theologians were won over: it is a remarkable tribute to Luther's powers of leadership that professors in other faculties were converted to his persuasion also: the lawyers, Schurff and Stehelin, and a Greek and Hebrew instructor, Thiloninus Philymnus. Writing to Lang on 18 May 1517, Luther elatedly announced that 'our theology and Augustine' were prospering, whilst Aristotle and the Lombard were on the way out.[1] Mainly through the instrumentality of Spalatin, the Elector's personal secretary and an ardent admirer of Luther, curricular reforms were proposed by Luther and carried through.[2] Hence, by 21 March of the same year, Luther could report to Lang that new courses of lectures were to be offered in languages, Pliny, Quintilian, mathematics, and other subjects; whilst certain of the old courses, including some on Aristotle, were to be dropped.[3] Lectures on Aristotle were henceforth based directly on the latest texts which the Humanists could provide. And not the

---

[1] W.A. Br. 1. 99. 8; Currie, p. 15.
[2] Luther to Spalatin, 11 Mar. 1518: W.A. Br. 1. 153–4.
[3] W.A. Br. 1. 155. 40.

least important consequence of the curricular revisions was the
addition of Philip Melanchthon to the University's faculty.[1]

Nor was there anything very unusual in this pattern of events.
Up to a point, the English Reformation also was academic in
its origins, and the emphasis on political aspects is sometimes
overdone. The reform of the English Church was not merely a
matter of expediency in the game of power politics between the
Crown and the Papacy. Other factors were at work to transform
a mere revolt into a religious renewal. Initially, the impulse
to reform came, not from the German Reformation, but from
the Renaissance. John Colet returned from Italy an ardent
convert to the Humanist cause and in 1496 began to lecture
on St. Paul's Epistles in the University of Oxford. Erasmus came
under Colet's influence, and through him the kind of policy
which the 'Oxford Reformers' stood for was passed on to Cambridge. It would be hard to overemphasize the importance of
the little group of 'Grecians' who met in St. John's College,
Cambridge, or of like-minded scholars in other colleges, for
these were the men who fashioned the English Reformation—
amongst them Cranmer, Latimer, Ridley, and Tyndale, to
mention only four. All of them were convinced that the only
way back to an unadulterated Christianity lay through a fresh
examination of the original sources, and that meant only through
an intensive study of New Testament Greek. Not a very exciting
or colourful programme: but here were the beginnings of
reformation. That Erasmus laid the egg from which the reformation was hatched, was certainly true in England and, as Conyers
Read remarks, 'It was at Cambridge...that the egg was laid.'[2]

The actual contacts between the Lutherans and the 'Oxford
Reformers', as they are called,[3] are of no immediate interest to

---

[1] The curricular revisions at Wittenberg from 1518 to 1523 are discussed in most
of the textbooks. Especially good at this point is Schwiebert, op. cit., pp. 293 ff.; cf.
also ibid., pp. 328–9, where Bucer's report on the Heidelberg Disputation is translated. Bucer comments: 'He [Luther] has brought it about that at Wittenberg the
ordinary textbooks have all been abolished, while the Greeks and Jerome, Augustine and Paul, are publicly taught.'

[2] *Social and Political Forces in the English Reformation*, p. 22. It is a merit of Read's
book that, whilst being primarily concerned with social and political aspects of the
English Reformation, he does full justice to the 'academic' origins of the movement
as well.

[3] The appellation apparently owes its currency largely to Seebohm's work, *The
Oxford Reformers: Colet, Erasmus, and More.*

us here. But a comparison between the types of reform which each party stood for is instructive. For the remarkable thing is that both revolted strongly against Scholasticism and that the revolt, in each case, was the direct result of the feeling that the Christian scholar's proper business must be sought elsewhere, namely, in the unravelling of the historical sense of Holy Scripture. Inevitably, one asks the question whether a part, at least, of Luther's estrangement from Scholasticism may not be accounted for by the trends of the times. In other words, the purpose of this final chapter is to see Luther's revolt against Scholasticism—which is so obviously integral to our enquiry— in its historical setting, and especially in relation to the undoubted shift of interest from Scholasticism to scholarship. For if it can be shown that Luther was, in fact, caught up in the current of this movement, then his revolt against philosophy will appear less as a *rejection* of reason, more as the *transference* of rationality from one sphere of exercise to another.

Luther and Humanist scholarship

That the fifteenth and sixteenth centuries witnessed a gradual shifting of interest from philosophy to scholarship, can hardly be doubted. The historical causes are complex, but they need not be discussed in detail here. In a pithy summing-up of the decline of Scholastic theology Williston Walker observes: it was 'discredited by nominalism, despised by humanism, and supplanted by mysticism'.[1] The day of the great Schoolmen was long past, and it was the Christian scholars who received the respect and admiration of the Church at large. Erasmus, the prince of them all, was courted by almost every nation in Europe: all desired the honour of being his host and of winning him for their own universities. And so the 'flitting Dutchman' (as Rupp calls him)[2] was able to wander from country to country, earning his living by something suspiciously close to begging, and yet more than 'paying his keep' simply by gracing his hosts with his presence.

There are many historical factors involved in this triumphant elevation of the Renaissance scholar. The so-called 'Revival of Learning' was more than a purely academic affair. It was,

[1] *A History of the Christian Church* (New York: Charles Scribner's Sons, 1918), p. 334.   [2] *Luther's Progress to the Diet of Worms*, p. 79.

indeed, closely bound up with the momentous social and economic upheavals of the times, for these afforded the scholar opportunities for the exercise of his talents—in the courts of princes or the homes of wealthy merchants—such as never existed in the High Middle Ages. Much could be written, and has been written,[1] about the social changes of the day; but what mainly concerns us is the effect of the Humanist learning upon Christian thought. Without any doubt, the heart of the Humanists' quarrel with Scholasticism lay in a dawning 'sense of history'.[2] The Humanists became aware of the dimension of historical distance; they acquired a temporal perspective which the Schoolmen conspicuously lacked. The consciousness of a vast distance between the Ancient World and the World of the Renaissance led to a new method of dealing with the literature of the past and to the fashioning of new tools for the job— philology, archaeology, and history itself.

The change in method was a shift within the *trivium*, from dialectic and towards grammar. Whereas Abelard had expressed anxiety lest theology be corrupted by grammar, Erasmus's opinion was that theology had already been corrupted by dialectic. The one demanded, 'What has Horace to do with the Psalter, Virgil with the Gospel, Cicero with the Apostle?' And the other demanded, 'What has Christ to do with Aristotle?'[3] All three of the sermonical arts are, of course, found necessary by both Abelard and Erasmus. But in Abelard dialectic has dominance; in Erasmus, grammar. Abelard culls isolated propositions from Scripture, Fathers, and philosophers, and weighs them one against another, without any conscious-

---

[1] See esp. Gilmore, *The World of Humanism* (1952); P. S. Allen, *The Age of Erasmus* (1914); Preserved Smith, *The Age of the Reformation* (1920).

[2] Gilmore, op. cit., pp. 201 ff.

[3] Cited by Richard McKeon in an essay on 'Renaissance and Method in Philosophy', *Studies in the History of Ideas*, III. 62 and 79. In this paragraph I have followed McKeon closely, who speaks of a 'shift in the emphasis in the three arts' (ibid., p. 87, &c.). His comparison of the methods of Scholasticism, Renaissance, and Reformation (exemplified respectively by Abelard, Erasmus, and Luther) is, in general, very discerning. But his judgements on Luther are not always sound, partly because he relies exclusively on Scheel's *Dokumente zu Luthers Entwicklung* and a few of Luther's early letters. From what we have had occasion to say already, it is clear that some of McKeon's statements could not stand without considerable qualification: e.g., that Luther 'considers the use of reason in the interpretation of the Bible ... a fatal error' (p. 46); or that in his exegesis individual insight 'crowded out reason' (p. 105).

ness of dealing with statements from the past and without any sense of difficulty in ascertaining what they mean. Erasmus takes an ancient writing *in toto*, and applies his historical and philological tools precisely to the task of elucidating the writer's meaning in relation to his original readers. Just how startling the new method could be is amply illustrated by the response to John Colet's lectures on the Pauline Epistles, delivered at Oxford.[1]

Clearly, then, Luther was not alone in turning from Scholastic exegesis to an exegesis based on an earnest attempt to let the whole Paul speak, and to let him speak with his own original meaning. It is not surprising, therefore, that parallels to Luther's invective against the Schoolmen are not hard to find in what are often regarded as sober Humanists. Erasmus's biographical sketches of Jehan Vitrier and John Colet afford examples of Colet's aversion to the Scholastic philosophers.[2] Colet, Erasmus informs us, felt only contempt for those whom most men thought particularly sharp ('quibus hominum vulgus ceu peculiare tribuit acumen'), since he considered it the mark of a poor and barren intellect to be forever 'quibbling about opinions and sayings of others, carping first at one thing and then at another and analysing everything so minutely'.[3] This was his opinion of the Scotists: of the Thomists he thought not one whit more highly, as Erasmus immediately proceeds to show. Concerning his friend's dislike of Aquinas himself, Erasmus was totally nonplussed. But the reason is not really so very hard to divine, even from Erasmus's own record. Colet thought Aquinas's definitions of matters theological an indication of gross presumption (*arrogantia*), and he considered that the Prince of the Schoolmen 'had polluted the whole doctrine of Christ with his profane philosophy'. How like Luther this sounds! And when Colet calls the Scotists 'dull and stupid', we may wonder what was new in Luther's outbursts.

[1] On John Colet's Oxford lectures, see the appreciative comments of Harbison, op. cit., pp. 58 ff. In his interpretation of the intellectual trends of the Reformation era, Harbison also is indebted to McKeon. He speaks of an 'interim' between the age of Scholasticism and the rise of science, during which 'the interests of scholars in general turned from what we would call philosophy and logic to philology and history' (p. vii).

[2] *Opus Epistolarum Des. Erasmi Rotterdami*, ep. 1211 in vol. IV: contained in a letter to Jodocus Jonas of 13 June 1521. There is a translation by J. H. Lupton.

[3] *Op. Epist.* IV. 520; Lupton, p. 32.

The views on Scholasticism which Erasmus attributes to his friend, he fully shared himself. Again, it could be Luther speaking when Erasmus protests against the corruption of pure, Biblical Christianity by Aristotelian philosophy.[1] And the statement: 'I am not averse to philosophy, provided the mixture is made with prudence and moderation (*modo sobrie moderateque admisceatur*)'[2] echoes Luther's own: 'Es gehört Bescheidenheit dazu.'

Edward L. Surtz, to whom I owe these references,[3] names four charges which the Humanists levelled against Scholasticism: its 'pretensions', its 'adulteration of the true teaching of Christ', its 'cold barren intellectuality', and its inability to 'make the student and the teacher better men'. These four charges the Humanists have in common. All that differentiates them is that some are prepared to allow for exceptions, e.g. St. Thomas. Hence, Erasmus could write of St. Thomas: 'He was wholly worthy to have had the knowledge of languages and other equipment of fine literature to grace him. . . .'[4] And Sir Thomas More could rise to Aquinas's defence against Tyndale—and, indeed, against Luther himself. But he 'keeps silent about Duns Scotus'. Against Tyndale's charge that the Pope and clergy 'medle philosophye with the thynges of God', More replied cautiously: this 'is a thynge that maye *in place* bee verye well done'. Wimpfeling makes the point that Aristotle's philosophy, logic, and metaphysics 'are not altogether useless to younger men of active intellect for the exercise of mental sharpness . . .'. Again, some of Luther's characteristic utterances come to mind; and even where the Oxford Reformers and their friends seem to allow more to Scholasticism than Luther did, there is still a definite restraint, a careful delimiting of legitimate spheres of exercise.[5]

---

[1] 'Sic Aristotele, sic humanis inventiunculis, sic prophanis etiam legibus est contaminatum [sc. hoc genus theologiae], ut haud sciam an purum illum ac syncerum Christum sapiat. . . . Quaeso, quid commercii Christo et Aristoteli?' Ep. 337 (to Martin Dorp; May 1515): *Op. Epist.* II. 101.

[2] *Apologia in Dialogum Jac. Latomi*; in *Opera omnia* (ed. by J. Le Clerc) IX. 103. Cf. *Annotationes* on I Timothy i. 6: *Op. Om.* VI. 928; *Ratio verae theologiae*: ibid. V. 83, 136.

[3] '"Oxford Reformers" and Scholasticism', *Studies in Philology*, XLVII. 4 (1950), 547, 556.

[4] *Annotationes* on the N.T. (Rom. i. 4) in *Op. Omnia*, VI. 654.

[5] The refs. to More, Tyndale, and Wimpfeling are also to be found in Surtz's article.

It is also noteworthy that Erasmus—and, indeed, the Humanists generally—in large measure shared Luther's admiration for Cicero. Here again Luther appears as a child of the Renaissance. The reasons for Luther's admiration and for Erasmus's, if not identical, certainly overlap. Both of them had been profoundly influenced by what can perhaps be described as the pragmatism (or utilitarianism) of the Revival of Learning.[1] To Luther Cicero seemed so much more the practical man of affairs than Aristotle; and Erasmus made a similar comparison of Cicero and Scotus, preferring the Latin because he was concerned with 'good manners'.

So that I had rather lose *Scotus*, and twenty more such as he, than one *Cicero* or *Plutarch*. Not that I am wholly against them neither; but because, by the reading of the one, I find myself become better; whereas, I rise from the other, I know not how coldly affected to Virtue, but most violently inclin'd to Cavil and Contention.[2]

No doubt Luther might detect in Erasmus's way of putting things a certain tendency towards 'moralism' (and to this point we will return); but the concern with practical utility he fully shared, and this concern underlies the fourth of Surtz's charges against Scholasticism. The same emphasis on 'practical wisdom' appears in Melanchthon, characteristically joined with praise for rhetoric as the art of pleasing and persuasive speech;[3] and in Calvin it appears as a refusal to be concerned with any 'doctrine' which would not promote the ends of 'piety'.[4]

There can be found in Colet statements which go beyond any of Erasmus's utterances against Scholasticism and which do, indeed, seem to approach an 'irrationalism' such as Luther himself never dreamed of. Some of Colet's utterances agree almost verbally with Luther's. 'Human reason is the enemy and opponent of grace (*inimica et adversaria graciae*)', he exclaims in one place. And he flatly denies that by the faculty of reason

[1] 'The test of truth with many Humanists became its utility, here, now, in this life.' Harbison, op. cit., p. 161.

[2] Colloquies of Erasmus, translated by N. Bailey, 1. 182: from 'The Religious Treat'.

[3] See Quirinus Breen, 'The Subordination of Philosophy to Rhetoric in Melanchthon', *Archiv für Reformationsgeschichte*, XLIII (1952), 13 ff. 'To Melanchthon philosophical wisdom is merged with prudence' (p. 17), so that even the garrulous old Nestor is ranked above Thomas and Scotus as a philosopher.

[4] See esp. *Institutes*, 1. ii.

man could 'soar to the designs and acts of God'.[1] Colet also, like
Luther, speaks of a *ratio* which is renewed by grace. But apparently he goes beyond Luther in denying the competence of
reason even to deal with *naturalia*, the affairs of human com-
munity-life. Hence Rice speaks of Colet's 'annihilation of the
natural': the natural is mere chaos without the 'spiritual reason'
(*ratio spiritualis*).[2] These and other signs of 'Augustinianism' in
John Colet have led some to deny categorically that he was
a Humanist at all: the mistaken opinion that he was in all
essentials an Erasmian was due, it is said, to Erasmus himself.
Erasmus's life of Colet is accordingly 'little more than a crystal-
lization of Erasmus's own religious attitudes', and the Dutchman was profoundly influenced only by 'a biographical portrait
which he himself has sketched'.[3]

If, however, such a radical Augustinianism really does accurately characterize Colet's outlook, if *all* rationality must, in his
view, be preceded by the illumination of faith, our central thesis
in this part of our essay is not greatly affected. The fact remains
that in many respects Luther was close to the Erasmians,
whether Colet was an Erasmian or not. Indeed, should we wish
to accept Rice's revision of Seebohm's picture of Colet, we can
still see Luther and all three 'Oxford Reformers' united in the
point at issue: the key to a renewal of Christendom is the
recovery of 'primitive Christianity' by means of improved
linguistic techniques. Here the spirit of the Renaissance and the
spirit of the Reformation agree: 'Both were animated by a
desire for a return to antiquity, a nostalgia for the golden age.
. . .' So Preserved Smith rightly observes, and here, at least in
part, is the reason why 'both were revolts against the mediaeval
scholasticism'.[4]

Luther against Humanist scholarship

Yet, for all this, Luther was himself miles apart from Erasmus.
Using the same tools as the Humanist, and using them on the
same sources, Luther nevertheless found a quite different Gospel.

[1] Cited by Eugene Rice, Jr., in an article on 'John Colet and the Annihilation
of the Natural', *Harvard Theological Review*, xlv. 3 (1952), 155–6.
[2] Ibid., esp. p. 162.
[3] So Rice, p. 142. Rice claims to be following A. Hyma in his interpretation of
Colet—and, of course, deliberately combatting Seebohm.
[4] *Erasmus*, p. 321.

If Erasmus laid the egg which Luther hatched, he was still quite right in his sardonic affirmation: 'I laid a hen's egg: Luther hatched a bird of quite different breed.' Some account must be taken of this remarkable divergence, by way of qualifying somewhat our association of Luther with the Humanists. Luther may be distinguished from Erasmus in three respects: exegetical method, reforming policy, and theological standpoint.

Enough has already been said in explanation of Luther's own method. It is only necessary to enquire where his exegetical principles departed from those of Erasmus. Broadly speaking, the answer is not obscure: whereas Luther holds philology and inspiration in balance, Erasmus relies upon philology alone. Luther agreed with Erasmus sufficiently to follow him very closely in his own exegesis. 'Indeed there is hardly a page in Luther's lectures where Erasmus's influence is not felt.'[1] Yet one cannot but perceive that Luther only *uses* Erasmus, and Schwarz is clearly right when he goes on to assert that 'Luther's notes begin at the point where Erasmus's end.'[2] Luther was often utterly infuriated as he turned the pages of Erasmus's *Annotationes* on the New Testament. For the Humanist seemed to him to be strangely indifferent to the religious significance of the text. Instead of grammar's laying the foundations for theological interpretation, grammar was everything—foundation and superstructure as well. Indeed, such comments on 'doctrine' as Luther found in the *Annotationes* only confirmed his impression that fundamentally Erasmus was not interested in the things which mattered: Luther searched in vain for 'the Gospel', as he understood it.[3]

Even when Luther and Erasmus were agreed on the reforms to be desired, their notions on the best policy for attaining them were different. Erasmus had a profound horror for *tumultus*, as

[1] Schwarz, op. cit., p. 189; pp. 187 ff. give some valuable evidence for the assertion.
[2] Ibid., p. 190.
[3] 'To read Erasmus's two lengthy notes on Rom. 1: 17 is to gain some inkling of what Luther meant.' So Harbison, op. cit., p. 105. The first note lists the meanings of *pistis* (*fides*), and gives its cognates in various compounds. The second demonstrated by numerous examples that *zesetai* is a genuine future and should be translated by *vivet*, not *vivit*. Finally, Erasmus concludes with the somewhat thin theological comment: 'Vita enim ex hoc habet initium, quod submittentes humanum sensum credimus verbis divinis' (*Op. Om.* VI. 563).

has so often been pointed out. He was not prepared to become embroiled in conflict, and the very suggestion of a breach with Rome was sufficient to make him shrink from what, to others, seemed the logic of his position. Nothing stands out so clearly in the story of Luther's relations with Erasmus as this basic contrast—partly, no doubt, a matter of temperamental differences—between the fighter and the cautious neutral.[1] Erasmus tried desperately hard to approve Luther's protests against ecclesiastical abuses without identifying himself with the Lutheran party. He was convinced that the Ninety-five Theses would 'please everyone'.[2] But as soon as he saw the storm-clouds gathering, he began hotly denying that he had so much as read Luther's writings.[3]

Of course, Luther thought Erasmus a coward, who had pulled his neck from the noose at the last moment.[4] Possibly he was right. And yet Erasmus was quite sincere in preferring his way to Luther's: he believed that a barbed pen could remove abuses without splitting the Church. And here, perhaps, Erasmus was right: it is hardly possible to say. But to Luther this policy seemed to border on the blasphemous. Luther 'felt the times demanded tears rather than laughter'.[5] Erasmus only mocked at God and religion. He was too good a pupil of Lucian. Luther

[1] See bibliography, under 'Erasmus', esp. the works of Huizinga, Smith, and Zweig. Zweig's somewhat journalistic style leads him to overdo the personality-conflict between Luther and Erasmus—even to make some downright errors (e.g. in describing Luther as enjoying an 'overplus of health' (p. 134); and one can hardly say without query that Luther, on the second day of the Diet at Worms, 'uttered his famous, "Here stand I"' (p. 171)). Indeed, his caricature of Luther is at points almost as crude as Denifle's: 'Of all the men of genius who have lived upon this earth, Luther was, perhaps, the most fanatical, the most unteachable, the most intractable, and the most quarrelsome' (p. 137). Yet, for all this, Zweig does, I think, conjure up something of the atmosphere of the fascinating conflict—and makes some discerning comments as well.
[2] *Op. Epist.* III. 409; letter to Lang, 17 Oct. 1518.
[3] See his letter to Melanchthon, 22 Apr. 1519 (*Op. Epist.* III. 540); to Wolsey, 18 May (ibid., p. 589); and to Luther himself, 30 May (ibid., p. 605). The letter to Luther is translated in full by Huizinga (op. cit., pp. 229 ff.) and in part by Smith, op. cit. I. 192–3. To Luther he does admit that he had 'tasted' (*degustavi*) the *Operationes in Psalmos*; but he still insists that he had not yet read Luther's books (*libros tuos nondum esse lectos*: i.e. he had not yet read them through). The whole letter is very revealing of Erasmus's standpoint, with his earnest desire to remain neutral.
[4] W.A. 31². 399. 17; W.A. DB. 3. 65. 22; TR. 2. 459. 7.
[5] Rupp, *Luther's Progress to the Diet of Worms*, p. 76. See also the same author's fuller discussion of 'Luther and Erasmus' in *The Righteousness of God*, pp. 259 ff.

calls him a veritable 'Momus', and, in another place, likens him to Democritus, the laughing philosopher of Ancient Greece.[1] Of course, Luther readily grants that Erasmus makes fun of certain ceremonies for the very good reason that they really are silly; but his sense of reverence is offended when Erasmus seems to treat even the Trinity and the Sacrament as laughing-matters. When it comes to theology he does nothing in earnest. Indeed, even the assault on ceremonies, however justified, is ineffectual.[2]

It is, then, manifest that deep-seated emotional differences underlay the conflict between the two reformers. Erasmus is reported as saying: 'I am averse to any action which might lead to commotion and uproar.' And again: 'Everything which Luther is demanding I, too, have taught, but not so vociferously.' And: 'We must not invariably tell the whole truth. Much depends upon how the truth is made known.'[3] But this is certainly not the whole picture, nor really the most important part of it: to affirm that 'method alone [what I have called "policy"] divided these two men', is a mistake.[4] Seebohm is much nearer the truth in his repeated assertion that what divided the two men was Luther's 'acceptance of the Augustinian system'.[5] For, although both rejected Scholasticism, Luther went behind the Scholastic theology to another 'dogmatic' brand of Christianity, which he found in the pages of St. Augustine. No doubt, there is plenty of Augustine in Scholasticism, indeed, in the New Testament itself (if the anachronism may be pardoned). But the general contrasts are valid between Luther, who sought insight from Augustine; and the Schoolmen, who sought it in Aristotle; and Erasmus, who supposed that he was portraying the Christ of the Gospels without any 'touching up' at all.

That this is the heart of the issue between the two men, that it is what ultimately explains both their exegetical practice and

[1] TR. 2. 41. 2, 410. 24; 1. 390. 13, 195. 15.
[2] TR. 1. 185. 22, 212. 30 (cf. 2. 289. 15, where Erasmus is quoted as saying that the theologians first invented (*invenerunt*) the Father and the Son, then added the Spirit to make it a pretty number); W.A. 40². 508. 36; 31². 305. 12. Many other judgements of Luther upon Erasmus will be found in the Weimar-index.
[3] Zweig, op. cit., pp. 157–60.
[4] Ibid., p. 158. Note that on p. 137 this interpretation is qualified by the words 'at the outset'.
[5] Op. cit., pp. 404 ff. and 492 ff., &c.

their difference of policy, could be demonstrated at length from the course of their growing conflict. Luther's standpoint is made clear in his letter to Spalatin of 19 October 1516, explaining what 'displeased' him in Erasmus's *Annotationes*.[1] Luther fondly imagines that a perusal of Augustine's anti-Pelagian writings would set Erasmus right. And Erasmus's standpoint could be illustrated from his letter to the Bohemian Slechta.[2] All through the letter, Erasmus's longing for an undogmatic religion is laid open to view. The *ecclesia universalis* (dare we say 'the Oecumenical Church'?) could only be established peacefully in the factious situation of Bohemia if the number of essential dogmas were drastically reduced. The world cried out, not for an exclusive Church, but for one whose boundaries were wide enough to include all the rival parties in Bohemia. The snag is, of course, that whilst Erasmus found everything requisite in the simplified Christianity of his 'philosophy of Christ', Calvin considered the entire *Institutes* a mere 'summary' of what was needful for true godliness. And Luther put his finger on another weakness in Erasmus's position: it tended to treat the Christian religion as a prop for the institutions of 'Christendom'.[3]

Luther was, in fact, surprisingly indifferent to matters of organization, ritual, and even (in a sense) morals—precisely the things which preoccupied Erasmus. To him the corruption of the Papacy lay deeper, in its loss of the Gospel. He was quite willing to accept the Papacy—even to 'kiss the Pope's feet'—so long as the Pope left him the Gospel.[4] 'We should not, therefore, give our attention to the wicked lives of the Papists so much as to their impious doctrine.'[5] In the final analysis, Luther's

---

[1] W.A. Br. 1. 70. 4. Both Luther's letter to Spalatin and Spalatin's to Erasmus (passing on his friend's criticisms) are translated in Smith, 1. 42–46. Luther's objections were (1) to Erasmus's restriction of *iustitia legis* to 'ceremonial' law; (2) to Erasmus's refusal to see any doctrine of original sin in Rom. v.

[2] *Op. Epist.* iv. 113–19.

[3] See Smith and Gallinger, *Conversations with Luther*, pp. 112–13.

[4] W.A. 40[1]. 177. 22 and 181. 11.

[5] W.A. 40[1]. 686. 28. The Weimar editor rightly comments: 'Hierin lag der fundamentale Unterschied zwischen Luther und Erasmus.' It is unfortunate that in what promises to be a widely-read book Will Durant utterly misrepresents Luther's views at this point. 'He seemed willing to accept medieval theology if he might disown the Renaissance Church' (*The Reformation*, p. 375); his rebellion was against 'Catholic organization' (p. 371). Hence Luther retained the 'old picture of God as the avenger' (p. 372); so far as his teaching was new, he merely left out the elements of 'tenderness' in medieval Christianity (p. 935). I can only imagine

objection to Erasmus is that he says nothing of the fundamental doctrine of faith in Christ.[1] Erasmus's 'philosophy of Christ' is sheer moralism: he makes Christ a Lawgiver. As far as Erasmus is concerned, the things described in the Christian religion need be no more than fables invented for the sake of moral training. Therefore, he does nothing but afflict consciences.[2] Luther perceived that the conflict between Erasmus and himself was a renewal of the conflict between Jerome and Augustine. For if it was Luther's distinguishing mark that he accepted the system of Augustine, then we can characterize Erasmus as one who made Jerome his mentor. So we find the same Luther who affirmed the primacy of the historical sense, attacking Jerome and Erasmus because for them the historical sense was all.[3] Luther's final verdict on Erasmus is: 'He has damaged the Gospel just as much as he has advanced grammar.'[4]

It could perhaps be said that our inquiry into Luther's views on philology and Humanism present, in some respects, a parallel to his views on philosophy and Scholasticism. In each case his attitude is ambivalent. It is all a question of what you *do* with your philosophy or your philology. Just as he finds a place in theology for at any rate the 'sermonic disciplines' of the philosophers, so also he perceives the value of the grammatical arts of the Humanists. And yet he could be no less brusque in his dismissal of Erasmus than of Thomas. Of course, philology hardly constitutes a threat to divinity in the same fashion as does philosophy, since the linguistic skills, though they also are an exercise of reason, in themselves offer no more than formal instruments for the theologian's use, not a positive world-view. If, in the end, Erasmus is guilty of the same theological failing

that what has misled Durant is Luther's retention of the Catholic Creeds: upon the essential doctrinal controversy (concerning justification) the Creeds have scarcely any bearing at all.

[1] TR. 1. 186. 7, 204. 19; 3. 316. 6.

[2] TR. 2. 149. 24; Smith and Gallinger, p. 108; TR. 1. 408. 3; W.A. 40¹. 259. 8, 30. Cf. Kooiman, *Martin Luther*, p. 172: 'Für Erasmus blieb das Evangelium ein neues Gesetz. Die reine religiöse Leidenschaft war ihm fremd. Er was mehr ein Sittenlehrer als ein paulinischer Theologe.'

[3] Letter to Spalatin, 19 Oct. 1516: W.A. Br. 1. 70. 17; Smith, 1. 43. Cf. Letter to Lang, 1 Mar. 1517; W.A. Br. 1. 90. 15; Smith, 1. 54–55. 'Jerome with his five languages did not equal Augustine with his one.'

[4] *Quantum promovit grammaticam, tantum nocuit evangelio* (TR. 5. 310. 15).

as the 'sophists'—namely, the moralistic attitude of mind that turns Christ into a Lawgiver—this is not because he carried his philology over into theology, but because (so Luther thought) he was a sorry theologian. Yet, in a sense, Luther *is* saying of grammar what he says of reason: without the leading of the Holy Spirit, neither is of any avail.

CONCLUSION

IN conclusion, it may be as well to state briefly our principal findings. We have discovered at each step of the way that Luther's thinking is far too complex and many-sided to be summed up in a neat formula or two. Reason is never, as Wesley imagined, condemned by him 'in the gross'. Of course, plenty of unguarded utterances are thrown out here and there; and we should not expect to produce a perfect harmony out of works dealing with a great variety of different topics, penned over a period of some thirty-five years, not always directed in scholarly style to academic readers, and, last but not least, very often dashed off in great haste. It may well be, indeed, that Luther would not wish us to make an entirely consistent system out of his great wealth of ideas; for he took a malicious joy in giving the 'contradictionists' something on which to exercise their misguided ingenuity.[1]

In the main, however, Luther's attitude towards reason does rest upon careful distinctions. 'Distinguenda enim est res ab abusu.' Here is his attitude in a nutshell. It explains the at first sight disturbing ambivalence of his statements concerning reason, philosophy, and philology alike. Reason may certainly be used against the interests of faith, but we do not therefore 'condemn it in the gross'—any more than Job condemned the female sex simply because his own wife said a few stupid things. What must be done is to draw a distinction between the 'substance' of reason and its 'vanity'.[2] There *is* a place for reason in Luther's theology, but not for reason corrupted by the presuppositions of the natural man—least of all, by the natural man's common-sense assumption that a righteous and holy God can only look with favour upon the righteous and the holy. Reason's standpoints are taken from the Earthly Kingdom with which it has to deal day by day. And the opinion of the world is that the unrequited lover is not merely a tragic figure, but a fool. As the poet says:

---

[1] See, for instance, the preface to Luther's *Fourteen of Consolation*, Phila. edn. 1. 109.
[2] TR. 3, no. 2938a (105. 3).

He that can love unloved again
Hath better store of love than brain.[1]

To transfer these presuppositions into theology, the Heavenly
Kingdom, is to make forgiveness unthinkable. And Luther fully
accepted this consequence, gladly admitting the folly of God's
love. To be God is to return good for evil: that is God's glory.[2]
What God requires of men is that they give Him His glory.
Reason cannot, because it is blinded by legalism. Only faith
gives God His glory; for faith is the correlative of grace, and
God's grace *is* His glory.[3]

This is, I believe, Luther's most characteristic usage: 'reason',
not in its strict sense as signifying man's reasoning capacity,
but in a special and derivative sense as signifying a particular
conclusion to which man's capacity for reasoning leads him.
The notion of 'reason', when Luther's remarks about it are
pejorative, is (so to speak) not merely formal, but also material:
ratio is a positive attitude rather than the bare possibility or
structure of reasoning.[4] It is not *thinking*, but a certain *thought*,
that Luther objects to. When, on the other hand, Luther's
remarks are more complimentary, 'reason' is generally being
understood precisely as the formal capacity to make inferences,
definitions, distinctions, and the like; for this rationality is what
sets man in a class of his own, above the brute beasts. As
rationality, reason has its place in both the Earthly and the
Heavenly Kingdoms, in dealing, that is, with both mundane and
spiritual matters; only, we must add, in dealing with spiritual

---

[1] Sir Robert Ayton, 'To an Inconstant One'.

[2] W.A. 4. 269. 25; 56. 520. 20.

[3] Cf. W. A. 40¹. 360. 24. I have come across only one passage in which Luther
seems to place reason on the side of grace: 'Reason', he says in the *Bondage of the
Will*, 'praises God when He saves the unworthy . . .' (W.A. 18. 731. 2). And even
here Luther goes on to make qualifications which are more in line with his usual
viewpoint, for he says: (1) that reason's praise for a God who crowns the undeserving arises out of self-interest, not out of genuine adoration for 'God as God';
(2) that in the judgement of men God's free forgiveness transgresses the bounds of
equity (He is considered *iniquus apud homines*), and His action remains 'incomprehensible'.

[4] 'Reason . . . denotes man's perverted attitude to things divine', as Hägglund
puts it: *Concordia Theological Monthly* (June 1957), p. 449. Luther uses *humana natura*
and *ratio naturalis* virtually as synonyms (e.g. in the Latin version of the *Treatise on
Christian Liberty*: W.A. 7. 73. 1 ff.); and he makes it quite clear that his quarrel with
ratio lies not in its reasonableness, but in its superstitiousness! What he has in mind,
in fact, is the naturalness of what Nygren has taught us to call 'Nomos-piety' (cf.
Nygren, op. cit., p. 72).

matters reason must take its premisses from 'the Word', and this is what Luther chiefly has in mind when he speaks of reason being 'illuminated'. Hence, the threefold distinction which we drew at the end of chapter one has been found to stand throughout our discussion as the framework within which all Luther's utterances concerning reason move. We have to maintain a clear-cut distinction between (1) natural reason ruling within its own proper domain of worldly matters, (2) natural reason illegitimately carrying over into the domain of spiritual matters certain presuppositions derived from 'the world', and (3) regenerate reason working legitimately within the domain of spiritual matters by humbly adopting presuppositions derived solely from 'the Word'. The natural reason which deals with mundane affairs is, as Luther's language often seems to suggest, a 'practical reason', approaching at times our own notion of 'common sense'; and to this extent natural reason, even within its proper boundaries, may appear to be a material as well as a formal conception, since it implies the adoption of certain concrete attitudes of mind. When the natural reason trespasses on the domain of spiritual matters, it is unambiguously a concrete, material attitude of the unregenerate man: here, we have seen, *ratio* is a certain definite *opinio*. The regenerate reason, finally, is in the main a formal conception: reason here is a tool, an instrument, an organ. But since regenerate reason tends to coalesce with the notion of faith, in this context also *ratio* may sometimes take into itself a certain material content.

If we are correct in regarding Luther's attack on reason as belonging mainly to the second of these three contexts (namely, where *ratio* stands for the legalistic standpoint of the natural man), then his alleged 'revolt against reason' must be viewed, however oddly this may sound in our ears, as a defence of the Reformation principle, *sola gratia*. It is, however, a further testimony to the many-sidedness of Luther's thinking that his 'anti-rationalism' does sometimes extend from this soteriological sphere into epistemology. And here we glanced briefly at his debt to Occamism. Yet it became clear that, however much Luther may have owed to Occamism for the purely formal opposition of 'faith and reason', he filled the antithesis with such content that he finally stood, not with the party of Occam, but over against it.

Lastly, we pointed to the necessity for comparing Luther's opinions on reason and philosophy, not only with late Scholasticism, but also with the Humanism of the Renaissance Era; and we saw the complexity of his thought similarly revealed in his ambiguous attitude towards Erasmus. Without the Humanists, Luther well knew, there could have been no Reformation, no revival of the Word.[1] To this extent we may regard Luther's revolt against Scholasticism as an indication of his share in a general shifting of the Church's academic interests from philosophy to scholarship, each of which in its own way is an exercise of 'reason'. The law-student who sold all that he had, save only his books of Plautus and Virgil; the Biblical professor who won the admiration of Bucer, Melanchthon, and Oecolampadius; the scholar who produced the massive Wittenberg Bible—surely this man was no stranger to the *bonae literae* of the Humanists. Luther fully shared Erasmus's longing to unite *bonae literae* with *sacrae literae*; and Luther's German Bible was the fulfilment of a dream which Erasmus himself had dreamed.[2] But just as David *used* his bow, neither trusting in it nor casting it away, so Luther *used* both the arts of the Humanists and the dialectic of the Schoolmen.[3] They were not, in his opinion dispensable, but still less dispensable was the guidance of the Spirit of God. And if mysteries remain—even to reason illuminated by the Spirit— Luther's last word is that all apparent irrationalities in God's dealings with us will one day become clear. Now we see in a glass darkly, but the light of glory will reveal to us plainly much that is still shrouded in mystery, even in the age of the Gospel. The light of grace, Luther reminds us, solved many problems that puzzled reason, the light of nature: to the question, 'Why do the wicked prosper?', for instance, the Gospel has replied, 'There is a life after this life. . . .' Just so, questions that seem unanswerable to those who are still pilgrims, even after the light of the Gospel has shone upon them, will be finally solved when they reach their homeland.[4]

---

[1] W.A. Br. 3. 50. 23. The Reformation also profited enormously, of course, from the negative labours of the Humanists—e.g. from Valla's exposing the forged 'Donations of Constantine'.

[2] In the 'Paraclesis' to his *Novum Instrumentum*. See Hajo Holborn's edn. of Erasmus's *Ausgewählte Werke*, p. 142.

[3] TR. 3, no. 2938b (105. 27).

[4] W.A. 18. 784 ff. (pp. 314 ff. in the translation by Packer and Johnston).

SELECT BIBLIOGRAPHY

I. SOURCES AND TRANSLATIONS

ANSELM, ST., OF CANTERBURY. *Proslogium, Monologium,* and *Cur Deus Homo.* Trans. by Sidney Norton Deane. Reprint edn. La Salle, Illinois: Open Court Publishing Co., 1954.

ARISTOTLE. *Aristotle's Psychology.* (Greek and English with Introduction and Notes.) Ed. and trans. by Edwin Wallace. Cambridge: University Press, 1882.

—— *The Ethics of Aristotle.* With Essays and Notes by Sir Alexander Grant. 3rd revised edn. 2 vols. London: Longmans, Green & Co., 1874.

CALVIN, JOHN. *Calvini Opera Selecta.* Ed. by P. Barth, G. Niesel. 5 vols. Munich, 1926–36.

—— *Commentary on the Book of Psalms.* Trans. by James Anderson. 5 vols. Grand Rapids, Michigan: Wm. B. Eerdmans Publishing Co., 1949.

—— *Institutes of the Christian Religion.* Trans. by Henry Beveridge. London: James Clark & Co., 1953.

—— *Iohannis Calvini Opera Quae Supersunt Omnia.* Ed. by G. Baum, E. Cunitz, E. Reuss. 59 vols. (*Corpus Reformatorum,* vols. XXIX ff.) Brunswick, 1863–1900.

ERASMUS, DESIDERIUS. *The Colloquies of Erasmus.* Trans. by N. Bailey and ed. by E. Johnson. 2 vols. London: Reeves & Turner, 1878.

—— *Desiderius Erasmus Roterodamus. Ausgewählte Werke.* Ed. by Hajo Holborn. München, 1933.

—— *The Lives of Jehan Vitrier and John Colet.* Trans. and ed. by J. H. Lupton. London: George Bell & Sons, 1883.

—— *Opus Epistolarum Des. Erasmi Roterodami.* Ed. by P. S. and H. M. Allen. 11 vols. Oxford, 1906–47.

—— *Desiderii Erasmi Roterodami Opera Omnia.* Ed. by Jean Le Clerc. 10 vols. in 11. Lugduni Batavorum, 1703–6.

LUTHER, MARTIN. *A Commentary on St. Paul's Epistle to the Galatians.* Trans. by Erasmus Middleton. Revised edn. by P. S. Watson. London: James Clarke & Co., 1953.

—— *A Compend of Luther's Theology.* Ed. by H. T. Kerr. Philadelphia: The Westminster Press, 1943.

—— *Conversations with Luther: Selections from recently published sources of the Table Talk.* Ed. and trans. by Preserved Smith and Herbert Percival Gallinger. Boston: The Pilgrim Press, 1915.

—— *D. Martin Luthers sämtliche Schriften.* Ed. by Johann Georg Walch. 24 vols. Halle, 1740–53.

—— *D. Martin Luthers Werke. Kritische Gesamtausgabe.* Vols. 1 ff. Weimar, 1883 ff.

—— *Dokumente zu Luthers Entwicklung bis 1519.* Ed. by Otto Scheel. Zweite Auflage. Tübingen, 1929.

LUTHER, MARTIN. *The Familiar Discourses of Dr. Martin Luther*. Trans. by Henry Bell. New edn., revised by Joseph Kerby. London, 1818.

—— *The Letters of Martin Luther*. Ed. and trans. by Margaret A. Currie. London: Macmillan & Co., Ltd., 1908.

—— *Letters of Spiritual Counsel*. Ed. and trans. by T. G. Tappert. (Library of Christian Classics, vol. xviii.) London and Philadelphia, 1955.

—— *Luther's Correspondence and Other Contemporary Letters*. 2 vols. Vol. I (1507–1521) ed. and trans. by Preserved Smith. Philadelphia: The Lutheran Publication Society, 1913. Vol. II (1521–1530) ed. and trans. by Preserved Smith and C. M. Jacobs. Ibid. 1918.

—— *Luther's Works: American Edition*. (55 vols. planned.) Ed. by Jaroslav Pelikan and Helmut T. Lehmann. St. Louis and Philadelphia, 1955 ff.

—— *Martin Luther on the Bondage of the Will*. Trans. by J. I. Packer and O. R. Johnston. London: James Clarke & Co., Ltd., 1957.

—— *The Precious and Sacred Writings of Martin Luther*. (Standard edition of Luther's Works.) Trans. and ed. by J. N. Lenker. 14 vols. Minneapolis, Minnesota: Lutherans in All Lands Co., 1903–10.

—— *Reformation Writings of Martin Luther*. Trans. by B. L. Woolf. 2 vols. London: Lutterworth Press, 1952 and 1956.

—— *The Table-Talk of Martin Luther*. Trans. and ed. by William Hazlitt. (Bohn's Standard Library.) London: George Bell & Sons, 1902.

—— *Works of Martin Luther: Philadelphia Edition*. 6 vols. Philadelphia: Muhlenberg Press, 1915–43.

THOMAS, ST., OF AQUINO. *Nature and Grace: Selections from the Summa Theologica of Thomas Aquinas*. Trans. and ed. by A. M. Fairweather. (Library of Christian Classics, vol. xi.) London and Philadelphia, 1954.

—— *On the Truth of the Catholic Faith: Summa Contra Gentiles. Book One: God*. Trans. and ed. by Anton C. Pegis. (Image Books.) New York: Doubleday & Co., Inc., 1955.

—— *St. Thomae de Aquino Ordinis Praedicatorum Summa Theologiae*. Cura et studio Instituti Studiorum Mediaevalum Ottaviensis ad textum S. Pii pp. V. iussu confectum recognita. Editio altera emendata. 5 vols. 1943–5.

WILLIAM, OF OCCAM. 'The *Centiloquium* Attributed to Ockham'. Ed. by Philotheus Boehner in Franciscan Studies, vols. xxii (1941) and xxiii (1942).

—— *The De Sacramento Altaris of William of Ockham*. Ed. by T. Bruce Birch. Latin text and English trans. Burlington, Iowa: The Lutheran Literary Board, 1930.

—— *Philosophical Writings*. A Selection ed. and trans. by Philotheus Boehner. London: Thomas Nelson & Sons, Ltd., 1957.

II. LUTHER'S LIFE AND THOUGHT

ABBOTT, E. S., *et al. Catholicity: A Study in the Conflict of Christian Traditions in the West*. London: Dacre Press, 1938.

ALAND, KURT. 'Luther as Exegete'. *Expository Times*, vol. LXIX, no. 2 (Nov. 1957), pp. 45–48; and no. 3 (Dec. 1957), pp. 68–70.

ALAND, KURT. ed. *Hilfsbuch zum Lutherstudium*. Berlin, 1957.

ALTHAUS, PAUL. *Evangelium und Leben. Gesammelte Vorträge*. Gütersloh, 1927.

AULEN, GUSTAV. *Christus Victor*. Trans. by A. G. Herbert. London: S.P.C.K., 1931.

BAINTON, ROLAND. *Here I Stand: A Life of Martin Luther*. Mentor Books edn. New York: The New American Library, 1955.

—— et al. *Luther Today*. Lectures by Roland H. Bainton, Warren A. Quanbeck, and E. Gordon Rupp. Decorah, Iowa: Luther College Press, 1957.

BILLING, EINAR. *Our Calling*. Trans. from the Swedish by Conrad Bergendoff. Rock Island, Illinois: Augustana Book Concern, 1950.

BOEHMER, HEINRICH. *Luther in Light of Recent Research*. Trans. by Carl F. Huth, Jr. New York: The Christian Herald, 1916.

—— *Martin Luther: Road to Reformation*. (Eng. trans. of *Der Junge Luther*.) New York: Meridian Books, 1957.

BORNKAMM, HEINRICH. 'Faith and Reason in the Thought of Erasmus and Luther'. *Religion and Culture: Essays in Honor of Paul Tillich*, ed. by Walter Leibrecht. New York: Harper & Brothers, 1959.

—— 'Luthers Lehre von den zwei Reichen im Zusammenhang seiner Theologie'. *Archiv für Reformationsgeschichte*, vol. XLIX, no. 1/2 (1958), pp. 26–49.

—— *Luther's World of Thought*. Trans. by Martin H. Bertram. St. Louis, Missouri: Concordia Publishing House, 1958.

CARLSON, EDGAR M. 'Luther's Conception of Government'. *Church History*, vol. XV, no. 4 (Dec. 1946), pp. 257–70.

—— *The Reinterpretation of Martin Luther*. Philadelphia: The Westminster Press, 1948.

CARTER, C. SYDNEY. *The Reformers and Holy Scripture*. London, 1928.

CAVE, SYDNEY. *The Doctrine of the Work of Christ*. London: Hodder & Stoughton, 1937.

CRANZ, F. EDWARD. *An Essay on the Development of Luther's Thought on Justice, Law, and Society*. (Harvard Theological Studies, XIX.) Cambridge: Harvard University Press, 1959.

DENIFLE, HEINRICH. *Luther und Luthertum in der ersten Entwicklung, quellenmässig dargestellt*, vol. I. 2nd edn., revised by Albert Weiss. Mainz, 1906.

DILLENBERGER, JOHN. *God Hidden and Revealed: The interpretation of Luther's deus absconditus and its significance for religious thought*. Philadelphia: Muhlenberg Press, 1953.

FIFE, R. H. *The Revolt of Martin Luther*. New York: Columbia University Press, 1957.

FLEW, R. N., and DAVIES, R. E., eds. *The Catholicity of Protestantism*. London: Lutterworth Press, 1950.

FORELL, GEORGE WOLFGANG. *Faith Active in Love: An Investigation of the Principles Underlying Luther's Social Ethics*. New York: The American Press, 1954.

FULLERTON, KEMPER. 'Luther's Doctrine and Criticism of Scripture'. *Bibliotheca Sacra*, vol. LXIII (1906), pp. 1–34 and 284–99.

GERRISH, B. A. 'Biblical Authority and the Continental Reformation'. *Scottish Journal of Theology*, vol. x, no. 4 (Dec. 1957), pp. 337–60.

GRANT, R. M. *The Bible and the Church.* New York: The Macmillan Co., 1948.

GRISAR, HARTMANN. *Luther.* Trans. by E. M. Lamond and ed. by Luigi Cappadelta. 6 vols. London: Kegan Paul, Trench, Trübner & Co., Ltd., 1913–17.

HÄGGLUND, BENGT. *Theologie und Philosophie bei Luther und in der occamistischen Tradition. Luthers Stellung zur Theorie von der doppelten Wahrheit.* Lund, 1955.

—— 'Was Luther a Nominalist?' *Concordia Theological Monthly*, vol. XXVIII, no. 6 (June, 1957), pp. 441–52.

HECKEL, JOHANNES. *Lex charitatis. Eine juristische Untersuchung über das Recht in der Theologie Luthers.* (Abh. der Bayer. Akad. d. Wissensch., phil.-hist. Klasse. Neue Folge, Heft 36.) München, 1953.

HILLERDAL, GUNNAR. *Gehorsam gegen Gott und Menschen. Luthers Lehre von der Obrigkeit und die moderne evangelische Staatsethik.* Stockholm, 1954.

HOLL, KARL. *Luther.* (*Gesammelte Aufsätze zur Kirchengeschichte*, vol. I.) 6th edn. Tübingen, 1932.

KOOIMAN, WILLEM JAN. *Martin Luther. Doktor der heiligen Schrift, Reformator der Kirche.* Aus dem Holländischen übersetzt. München, 1949. (Eng. trans.: *By Faith Alone.* London: Lutterworth Press, 1954.)

KÖSTLIN, JULIUS. *The Theology of Luther in its Historical Development and Inner Harmony.* Trans. from the 2nd German edn. by Charles E. Hay. 2 vols. Philadelphia: Lutheran Publication Society, 1897.

LAU, FRANZ. '*Äußerliche Ordnung' und 'Weltlich Ding' in Luthers Theologie.* (Studien zur systematischen Theologie, hrsg. von Arthur Titius und Georg Wobbermin, Heft 12.) Göttingen, 1933.

—— *Luthers Lehre von den beiden Reichen.* (Luthertum, Heft 8.) Berlin, 1953.

LEHMANN, PAUL L. 'The Reformer's Use of the Bible'. *Theology Today*, vol. III (1946–7), pp. 328–44.

LINK, WILHELM. *Das Ringen Luthers um die Freiheit der Theologie von der Philosophie.* Hrsg. von E. Wolf und M. Mezger. Berlin, 1954.

LOHSE, BERNHARD. 'Luthers Antwort in Worms'. *Luther. Mitteilungen der Luthergesellschaft*, 1958, no. 3, pp. 124–34.

—— *Ratio und Fides. Eine Untersuchung über die ratio in der Theologie Luthers.* Göttingen, 1958.

LÖWENICH, WALTHER v. *Luthers Theologia crucis.* 4. durchgesehene Auflage. München, 1954.

LUNN, ARNOLD. *The Revolt Against Reason.* London: Eyre & Spottiswoode, 1950.

MACKINNON, JAMES. *Luther and the Reformation.* 4 vols. London: Longmans, Green & Co., 1925–30.

MARITAIN, JACQUES. *Three Reformers: Luther, Descartes, Rousseau.* New York: Charles Scribner's Sons, 1932.

McGIFFERT, A. C. *Martin Luther: The Man and His Work.* New York, 1911.

—— *Protestant Thought Before Kant.* New York: Charles Scribner's Sons, 1913.

McNeill, J. T. 'History of the Interpretation of the Bible: Medieval and Reformation Period'. *Interpreter's Bible*, vol. I, pp. 115–26.
—— 'Natural Law in the Thought of Luther'. *Church History*, vol. X, no. 3 (Sept. 1941), pp. 211–27.

Meinhold, Peter. *Die Genesisvorlesung Luthers und ihre Herausgeber.* (Forschungen zur Kirchen- und Geistesgeschichte, herausgegeben von Erich Seeberg, Erich Caspar, Wilhelm Weber. 8. Band.) Stuttgart, 1936.

Mueller, William A. *Church and State in Luther and Calvin: A Comparative Study.* Nashville: Broadman Press, 1954.

Nitzsch, F. *Luther und Aristoteles.* Kiel, 1883.

Nygren, Anders. *Agape and Eros: A Study of the Christian Idea of Love.* Trans. by P. S. Watson. One-vol. edn. London: S.P.C.K., 1950.

Paquier, J. 'Luther'. *Dictionnaire de théologie catholique*, vol. IX, part I, cols. 1146–1335.

Pauck, Wilhelm. *The Heritage of the Reformation.* Boston: Beacon Press, 1950.

Pelikan, Jaroslav. *From Luther to Kierkegaard: A Study in the History of Theology.* St. Louis, Missouri: Concordia Publishing House, 1950.

Prenter, Regin. *Spiritus Creator.* Trans. by John M. Jensen. Philadelphia: Muhlenberg Press, 1953.

Preuss, Hans. 'Was bedeutet die Formel "*Convictus testimoniis scripturarum aut ratione evidente*" in Luthers ungehörnter Antwort zu Worms?' *Theologische Studien und Kritiken*, vol. LXXXI, no. 1 (1908), pp. 62–83.

Reid, J. K. S. *The Authority of Scripture: A Study of the Reformation and Post-Reformation Understanding of the Bible.* New York: Harper & Brothers, 1957.

Reu, M. *Luther and the Scriptures.* Columbus, Ohio: The Wartburg Press, 1944.
—— *Luther's German Bible: An Historical Presentation Together with a Collection of Sources.* Columbus, Ohio: The Lutheran Book Concern, 1934.
—— *Thirty-Five Years of Luther-Research.* Chicago, Illinois; Wartburg Publishing House, 1917.

Rupp, Gordon. *Luther's Progress to the Diet of Worms.* Greenwich, Connecticut: The Seabury Press, 1951.
—— *The Righteousness of God: Luther Studies.* London: Hodder & Stoughton, 1953.

Saarnivaara, Uuras. *Luther Discovers the Gospel.* St. Louis: Concordia Publishing House, 1951.

Scheel, Otto. *Martin Luther. Vom Katholizismus zur Reformation.* 2 vols. Vol. I (1st edn.), Tübingen, 1916; vol. II (3rd and 4th edns.), ibid. 1930.

Schwarz, W. *Principles and Problems of Biblical Translation: Some Reformation Controversies and their Background.* Cambridge: The University Press, 1955.

Schwiebert, E. G. *Luther and his Times: The Reformation from a New Perspective.* St. Louis, Missouri: Concordia Publishing House, 1950.

Seeberg, Reinhold. *Die Lehre Luthers* (Lehrbuch der Dogmengeschichte, vol. IV, part I). 4th edn. Leipzig, 1933. (Eng. trans. of the 1st German edn.

by Charles E. Hay. One-vol. edn. Grand Rapids, Michigan: Baker Book House, 1954.)

SMITH, PRESERVED. 'Luther's Development of the Doctrine of Justification by Faith'. *Harvard Theological Revue*, vol. VI (1913), pp. 407–425.

—— *Luther's Table Talk: A Critical Study*. New York: Columbia University Press, 1907.

STROHL, HENRI. *L'Épanouissement de la pensée religieuse de Luther de 1515 à 1520*. Strasbourg, 1924.

—— *L'Évolution religieuse de Luther jusqu'en 1515*. Strasbourg, 1922.

STÜRMER, KARL. *Gottesgerechtigkeit und Gottesweisheit bei Martin Luther*. (Heidelberg Dissertation.) Mannheim, 1939.

TÖRNVALL, GUSTAF. *Geistliches und weltliches Regiment bei Luther. Studien zu Luthers Weltbild und Gesellschaftsverständnis*. (A German trans. of the Swedish *Andligt och världsligt regemente hos Luther*, 1940.) München, 1947.

VAJTA, VILMOS. *Luther on Worship*. (Eng. trans. of *Die Theologie des Gottesdienstes bei Luther*.) Philadelphia: Muhlenberg Press, 1958.

VIGNAUX, P. *Luther commentateur des Sentences*. Paris, 1935.

—— 'Sur Luther et Occam'. *Franziskanische Studien*, vol. XXXII (1950), pp. 21–30.

WATSON, PHILIP S. *Let God Be God! An Interpretation of the Theology of Martin Luther*. London: Epworth Press, 1947.

WHALE, J. S. *The Protestant Tradition*. Cambridge: The University Press, 1955.

WINGREN, GUSTAF. *Luther on Vocation*. Trans. by Carl C. Rasmussen. Philadelphia: Muhlenberg Press, 1957.

WOOD, A. S. 'The Theology of Luther's Lectures on Romans'. *Scottish Journal of Theology*, vol. III (1950), pp. 1–18 and 113–26.

III. MOVEMENTS RELATED TO LUTHER

1. *Scholasticism: St. Thomas and William of Occam*

ADDIS and ARNOLD. *A Catholic Dictionary*. 15th edn. London, 1951.

BOEHNER, PHILOTHEUS. '*In Propria Causa:* A Reply to Professor Pegis' "Concerning William of Ockham".' Reprinted from *Franciscan Studies*, vol. XXVI (new series, vol. V), no. 1, March 1945.

BURNABY, JOHN. *Amor Dei: A Study in the Religion of St. Augustine*. London: Hodder & Stoughton, 1947.

COPLESTON, FREDERICK. A History of Philosophy, vols. I–III. London: Burns Oates & Washbourne, Ltd.; vol. I (revised), 1947; vol. II, 1950; vol. III, 1953.

FARRELL, W. *A Companion to the Summa Theologica*. 4 vols. New York: Sheed & Ward, 1939–49.

FISHER, G. P. *History of Christian Doctrine*. (International Theological Library.) 7th impression. Edinburgh: T. & T. Clark, 1949.

GARRIGOU-LAGRANGE, R. *Grace: A Commentary on the Summa Theologica of Thomas Aquinas 1a–11ae Q. 109–114*. Eng. trans. St. Louis: B. Herder Book Co., 1952.

GARRIGOU-LAGRANGE, R. *La Synthèse thomiste.* Paris, 1946.

GILSON, ETIENNE. *History of Christian Philosophy in the Middle Ages.* New York: Random House, 1955.

—— *Reason and Revelation in the Middle Ages.* New York: Charles Scribner's Sons, 1954.

GUELLUY, ROBERT. *Philosophie et Théologie chez Guillaume d'Ockham.* Louvain et Paris, 1947.

HARNACK, ADOLF. *History of Dogma.* Eng. trans. of the *Dogmengeschichte* (3rd German edn.) by Neil Buchanan. 7 vols. Boston, 1895–1900.

HAURÉAU, B. *Histoire de la philosophie scholastique.* 2 vols. in 3. Paris, 1872–80.

HEIM, KARL. *Das Gewißheitsproblem in der systematischen Theologie bis zu Schleiermacher.* Leipzig, 1911.

—— 'Zur Geschichte des Satzes von der doppelten Wahrheit'. *Studien zur systematischen Theologie* (Theodor von Haering zum 70. Geburtstag von Fachgenossen dargebracht), pp. 1–16. Tübingen, 1918.

McGIFFERT, A. C. *A History of Christian Thought.* 2 vols. New York: Charles Scribner's Sons, 1932–3.

MOODY, E. A. *The Logic of William of Ockham.* New York: Sheed & Ward, 1935.

RUCH, C. 'Biel.' *Dictionnaire de théologie catholique,* vol. II, part 1, cols. 814–25.

TORNAY, STEPHAN CHAK. *Ockham: Studies and Selections.* La Salle, Illinois: The Open Court Publishing Co., 1938.

VIGNAUX, P. 'Nominalisme'. *Dictionnaire de théologie catholique,* vol. XI, part 1, cols. 717–84.

WULF, MAURICE DE. *History of Medieval Philosophy.* Trans. by Ernest C. Messenger from the 5th French edn. 2 vols. London: Longmans, Green & Co., 1926.

2. *Humanism and the Reformation: Erasmus*

ALLEN, P. S. *The Age of Erasmus.* Oxford: Clarendon Press, 1914.

—— *Erasmus: Lectures and Wayfaring Sketches.* Oxford: Clarendon Press, 1934.

BAINTON, ROLAND H. *The Reformation of the Sixteenth Century.* (Paperback edn.) Boston: Beacon Press, 1956.

BEARD, CHARLES. *The Reformation of the Sixteenth Century in its Relation to Modern Thought and Knowledge.* (Hibbert Lectures, 1883.) London: Williams & Norgate, 1885.

DURANT, WILL. *The Reformation.* (Story of Civilization, Part VI.) New York: Simon & Schuster, 1957.

FROUDE, J. A. *Life and Letters of Erasmus.* New York: Charles Scribner's Sons, 1896.

GILMORE, MYRON P. *The World of Humanism 1453–1517.* New York: Harper & Brothers, 1952.

HARBISON, HARRIS. *The Christian Scholar in the Age of the Reformation.* New York: Charles Scribner's Sons, 1956.

HUIZINGA, JOHAN. *Erasmus and the Age of the Reformation.* (Harper Torch-books. Originally published as *Erasmus of Rotterdam.*) New York: Harper & Brothers, 1957.

LINDSAY, T. M. *A History of the Reformation.* 2nd edn. 2 vols. Edinburgh: T. & T. Clark, 1953.

MCKEON, RICHARD. 'Renaissance and Method in Philosophy.' *Studies in the History of Ideas* (ed. by the Department of Philosophy of Columbia University), vol. III, pp. 37–114. New York: Columbia University Press, 1935.

READ, CONYERS. *Social and Political Forces in the English Reformation.* Houston: The Elsevier Press, 1953.

RICE, EUGENE F., Jr. 'John Colet and the Annihilation of the Natural.' *Harvard Theological Review,* vol. XLV, no. 3 (1952), pp. 141–63.

SEEBOHM, FREDERIC. *The Oxford Reformers: Colet, Erasmus and More.* 3rd edn. London: Longmans, Green & Co., 1887.

SMITH, PRESERVED. *The Age of the Reformation.* New York: Henry Holt & Co., 1920.

—— *Erasmus: A Study of his Life, Ideals and Place in History.* New York: Harper & Brothers, 1923.

SURTZ, EDWARD L. '"Oxford Reformers" and Scholasticism.' *Studies in Philology,* vol. XLVII, no. 4 (1950), pp. 547–56.

SYKES, NORMAN. *The Crisis of the Reformation.* London: Geoffrey Bles, 1950.

ZWEIG, STEFAN. *Erasmus of Rotterdam.* Trans. by Eden and Cedar Paul. New York: The Viking Press, 1956.

INDEX OF PERSONS

Abbott, E. S., 115 n.
Abel, 93 n., 105.
Abelard, Peter, 157.
Abraham, 16, 19, 78 f.
Adam, 23, 24, 30, 124.
Adam, Karl, 120 n., 134 n.
Ailly, Pierre d', 48, 54, 55, 95, 121.
Aland, Kurt, 146 n., 153 n.
Albert the Great, 49.
Althaus, Paul, 83 n.
Amsdorf, Nicholas von, 154.
Annas, 150.
Anselm, 49.
Aristotle, 1 f., 11, 29, 31, 32 ff., 44, 46 n., 75 n., 92, 95 f., 126 n., 128, 129 n., 131, 134, 136, 154, 157, 159, 160, 164.
Arnold, of Usingen, 37, 41, 44.
Augustine, Augustinian, ix, 43, 56, 95, 124 n., 125 n., 126, 129 n., 132, 132 n., 133, 154, 155 n., 161, 164, 165, 166.
Augustus, 148.
Aulen, Gustav, 4 n.
Averroes, 35, 53 n.
Ayton, Sir Robert, 169.

Bailey, N., 160 n.
Bainton, R. M., 98, 149 n.
Beard, Charles, 24, 28, 140.
Bell, Henry, 10 n.
Bernard, of Clairvaux, 109.
Biel, Gabriel, 44, 44 n., 49, 54, 55, 95, 121.
Billing, Einar, 8 n., 58.
Birch, T. Bruce, 48 n., 51 n.
Boehmer, Heinrich, 8, 43 n., 45 n., 47 n., 49 n., 138, 139, 146 n.
Boehner, P., 46 n., 50 n., 51.
Bornkamm, Heinrich, 8 n., 32 n.
Bouyer, Louis, 121 n., 125 n., 128 n.
Breen, Quirinus, 160 n.
Brunner, H. Emil, 83 n., 98.
Bucer, Martin, 63 n., 155 n., 171.
Bullinger, Heinrich, 63 n.
Bultmann, R., 69 n., 108 n.
Burnaby, John, 127 n.

Caiaphas, 20 n.
Cain, 93 n.
Calvin, John, ix, 8, 57, 69 n., 93 n., 132 n., 133 n., 153, 160, 165.
Carlson, E. M., 2 n., 8 n., 97.
Carlstadt, Andreas, 28, 142, 146, 154.

Cave, Sydney, 57.
Cicero, 34, 40 f., 67 n., 157, 160.
Colet, John, 155, 158, 160 f.
Copernicus, 32.
Copleston, F., 51 n., 52 n., 75 n.
Cornelius, 104.
Cranmer, Thomas, 155.
Cranz, F. E., 8 n., 13 n., 16 n., 35 n., 53 n., 113 n., 120 n., 126 n.
Cruciger, Caspar, 63.
Currie, Margaret A., 154 n.

David, 171.
Davies, R. E., 104 n.
Deane, S. N., 49 n.
Democritus, 164.
Denifle, Heinrich, 2, 3, 20 n., 43, 45, 52, 53 n., 138, 139, 152, 163 n.
Dietrich, Veit, 11 n., 63.
Dillenberger, John, 9 n.
Dorp, Martin, 159.
Drescher, R., 59 n.
Dungersheim, Hieronymus, 144.
Duns Scotus, 36, 39 n., 48, 50, 95, 97, 159, 160.
Durant, Will, 165 n.

Eck, John, 144, 149, 149 n.
Egranus, John, 39 n.
Elijah, 109.
Emser, Hieronymus, 144.
Engelland, Hans, 129 n.
Erasmus Desiderius, 5, 7, 22, 32 n., 79 n., 139, 144, 145, 146, 147, 155, 156 ff., 171.
Eve, 24, 30, 93.

Faber, Stapulensis, 144, 146.
Farrell, Walter, 125 n.
Fife, R. H., 34 n., 38 n., 44 n., 46 n., 145 n.
Flew, R. N., 104 n.
Forell, G. W., 102 n.
Forsyth, P. T., 98, 150.
Freitag, A., 59 n.

Gallinger, H. P., 10 n., 30 n., 32, 165 n., 166 n.
Garrigou-Lagrange, R., 108 n., 130 n., 131 n.
Gerrish, B. A., 146 n., 150 n.
Gilmore, Myron P., 157 n.
Gilson, Etienne, 51 n., 52 n.
Graebner, Th., 59.
Grant, Sir Alexander, 35 n.

Grisar, Hartmann, 2, 5, 43, 47, 48 n.
Grobel, Kendrick, 69 n.
Guelluy, Robert, 51 n.
Guenther, Francis, 154.

Hägglund, Bengt, vii, 37, 49 n., 53 n., 55 n., 98, 169 n.
Harbison, E. H., 149 n., 151, 158 n., 160 n., 162 n.
Harnack, Adolf von, 134.
Hastings, Cecily, 121 n.
Hauréau, B., 52 n.
Hazlitt, William, 10 n.
Heckel, Johannes, 113 n.
Heim, Karl, 49 n., 53 n., 95.
Herbord of Lippe, 44 n.
Herod, 20 n., 147 n., 150.
Hess, Eoban, 147 n.
Hill, Charles Leander, 129 n.
Hillerdal, Gunnar, 14 n.
Holborn, Hajo, 171 n.
Holcot, Robert of, 49, 52, 53, 54.
Holl, Karl, 5 n., 35 n., 45 n., 55 n., 97, 143 n.
Horace, 157.
Huizinga, Johan, 163 nn.
Hutchison, John A., 4 n.
Hyma, A., 161 n.

Isaiah, 129 n.

Jacob, 78.
Jacobs, C. M., 147 n.
James, 147 n.
Jerome, 144, 155 n., 166.
Job, 167.
John the Baptist, 19, 147.
John the Evangelist, 129 n.
Johnston, O. R., 171.
Jonas, Jodocus, 158 n.
Joshua, 32.
Judas, 75 n., 150.
Jude, 147 n.

Katie von Bora, 62.
Koehler, W., 139.
Kooiman, Willem Jan, 5 n., 166 n.
Köstlin, Julius, 26, 28 n.

Lang, Johannes, 154, 163 n., 166 n.
Latimer, Hugh, 155.
Lau, F., 8 n., 13 n., 14 n.
LeClerc, J., 159.
Leibrecht, Walther, 32 n.
Lenker, J. N., 10 n.
Lewis and Short (Latin Dictionary of), 67 n., 84.
Lightfoot, J. B., 127 n.
Link, Wilhelm, vii, 133 n.
Littledale, A. V., 121 n.

Lohse, Bernhard, viii, 4 n., 15 n., 16 n., 25 n., 98 n., 102 n.
Lombard, Peter, 154.
Lortz, J., 153 n.
Löwenich, Walter von, 83 n.
Lucian, 163.
Lunn, Arnold, 2 n.
Lupton, J. H., 158 n.

Mackinnon, James, 111 nn., 151 n.
Maritain, Jacques, 2 ff., 152.
Mary (Sister of Martha), 89.
Mary (Mother of Jesus), 18, 19.
McGiffert, A. C., 125 n.
McKeon, Richard, 157 n., 158 n.
McNeill, J. T., 113 n.
Meinhold, Peter, 11 n.
Melanchthon, Philip, 11 n., 32, 47, 116, 129, 129 n., 146, 155, 160, 163 n., 171.
Middleton, Rev. Erasmus, 59.
Milton, John, 45 n.
Momus, 164.
Moody, E. A., 38.
More, Sir Thomas, 155 n., 159.
Moses, 77, 107.
Mueller, William A., 35 n.
Müller, A. V., 97.
Münzer, Thomas, 28, 148.

Nathin, Johann, 44, 44 n.
Nestor, 160 n.
Nicodemus, 18, 93.
Nitzsch, F., 32 n.
Nygren, Anders, 2 n., 103 n., 114, 115 n., 129 n., 133 n., 169 n.

Oecolampadius, John, 171.
Oman, John, 93.
Otto, Rudolf, 9.
Owen, John, 59.

Packer, J. I., 171 n.
Palladius, Petrus, 53 n.
Paltz, Johann, 44, 44 n.
Paquier, J., 55.
Paton, H. J., 4 n.
Pauck, Wilhelm, 109 n.
Paul the Apostle, 22, 35, 36, 47, 53, 57, 62, 66 n., 69, 70 n., 76, 80–81, 82 n., 88, 89, 96, 99 n., 104, 107, 112, 115, 116, 118, 123, 127, 128, 129 n., 140, 143, 147, 150, 155 n., 157, 158.
Pegis, Anton C., 49 n.
Pelikan, Jaroslav, 11 nn.
Peter the Apostle, 87 n., 104, 129, 136, 143, 144, 147 n., 150.
Petrus, Hispanus, 46 n.
Petrus, Pomponatius, 53 n.
Philymnus, Thiloninus, 154.

Pilate, 20 n., 150.
Plato, 35, 40, 41 n.
Plautus, 171.
Pliny, 154.
Plutarch, 160.
Porphyry, 46 n.
Prenter, Regin, viii, 133 n.
Preuss, Hans, 24 n., 25 n.

Quanbeck, Warren, 149 n.
Quintilian, 154.

Read, Conyers, 155.
Reichert, O., 152 n.
Reu, M., 5 n., 146 n.
Reuchlin, Johannes, 146.
Rice, Eugene, 161.
Ridley, Nicholas, 155.
Rörer, George, 4 n., 63 ff.
Ruch, C., 49 n.
Rupp, E. G., 5 f., 44 nn., 45 nn., 49 n.,
    71 n., 109 n., 110 n., 111, 111 nn.,
    153 n., 156, 163 n.

Saarnivaara, Uuras, 120 n., 126 n.
Sarah, 79.
Scheel, Otto, 37 n., 44 n., 145 n., 157 n.
Schmidt, O. G., 138.
Schurff, Jerome, 154.
Schwarz, W., 5 n., 148, 149 n., 162.
Schwiebert, E. G., 153 n., 155 n.
Seeberg, Reinhold, 48 n., 121 n., 146.
Seebohm, Frederic, 155 n., 161, 164.
Slechta, John, 165.
Smith, Preserved, 10 n., 30 n., 32,
    144 n., 147 n., 161, 163 nn., 165 nn.,
    166 nn.
Spalatin, George, 39 n., 154, 165, 166 n.
Stehelin, Wolfgang, 154.
Staupitz, Johann von, 64 n., 115.
Strohl, Henri, 44 n.

Stürmer, Karl, 4 n., 99 n.
Surtz, Edward L., 159, 160.

Tauler, Johann, 152 n.
Tawney, R. H., 7.
Taylor, A. E., 41 n.
Tertullian, 127 n., 135.
Thomas, Aquinas, 36, 38, 39 n., 41 n.,
    45, 49, 49 n., 114, 120, 121, 121 n.,
    123 ff., 158, 159, 166.
Tilemann, 53 n.
Tornay, S. C., 50 n.
Törnvall, G., 8 n.
Trutvetter, Jodocus, 34, 44, 44 n., 154.
Tyndale, William, 155, 159.

Vajta, Vilmos, 102 n.
Valla, Laurentius, 144, 171 n.
Vignaux, P., 45 n., 52, 55 n.
Virgil, 148, 157, 171.
Vitrier, Jehan, 158.

Walch, Johann Georg, 11 n., 29 n.
Walker, Williston, 156.
Wallace, Edwin, 41 n.
Watson, P. S., 1 n., 2 n., 59 ff., 71 n.,
    97, 100 n., 101 n., 103 n., 104 n.,
    108 n., 110 n., 152 n.
Wesley, John, 1, 152 n., 167
Whale, J. S., 98, 109 n.
William of Occam, 6, 38, 42, 43 ff.,
    75 n., 95, 97, 114, 121, 121 n., 139,
    152, 170.
Wimpfeling, James, 159.
Wingren, Gustaf, 7, 16 n., 113 n., 137 n.
Wolsey, Thomas, 163 n.
Wood, A. S., 71 n., 111 n.
Wulf, Maurice de, 50 n., 51 n.

Zweig, Stefan, 163 n.
Zwickau, Prophets of, 28.
Zwingli, H., 59.

INDEX OF SUBJECTS

Acceptation, 47 f., 121 n., 130 n.
After-life, 30, 171.
Allegorical interpretation, 143, 144, 151 nn.
Anabaptists, 28 n., 64 n.
Anagogical sense, 143.
Analogy, 80 f.
 analogia fidei, 150 f.
Antinomianism, vii, 22, 102, 117, 120 n., 123, 136.
Apocrypha, 147.
Apostles, 17.
Archaeology, 157.
Arianism, 28, 80.
articulus stantis et cadentis ecclesiae, 99 n.
Ascension, 79.
Astrology, 31 f., 38 n.
Astronomy, 32, 38 n., 44.
Atonement, 48, 49, 79 n., 82.
Authority, 48, 50, 93 n.
auxilium Dei, 124, 125, 131 n.

Baptism, 20 n., 70, 79.

Calling, *see* Vocation.
Canon, 147, 150.
Causes, 19, 30, 47.
Ceremonies, 100, 104, 105, 112, 117, 118, 164.
Christ, 12, 17, 18, 19, 31, 39, 49 n., 53, 57, 59, 60, 60 nn., 71, 76, 91, 100, 109, 110, 112, 116, 117, 123, 143, 147, 151 n., 164.
 as content of Bible, 150.
 as God, 80, 112.
 as Lawgiver (Example), 90, 107, 166, 167.
 as revelation of God, 15, 60 n., 78, 102, 150.
 as Saviour, 48, 90.
 as wisdom, 82.
 merits of, 133 n.
 ousted by Aristotle, 33 ff., 129 n., 158 f.
 righteousness of, 112, 119.
 two natures, 20 n., 24, 30.
Christian, 89.
Church, 16 n., 33, 48, 49, 50, 59, 81, 115, 151 n., 156, 162, 171.
Circumcision, 20 f.

Commandments, the Ten, 14, 24, 108, 109, 122, 123, 143.
Common Sense, 31, 73, 170.
Concupiscence, 70 f.
Conditionalism, 133 n.
Conscience, 78, 86, 98, 106, 108, 118, 137, 166.
Conversion, 153.
Copernican Revolution, Luther's, 2.
Councils, 18.
Creation, 20 n., 40 n., 124.
Creeds, 166 n.
Criticism, Biblical, 146, 150 f.
Crucifixion, 20 n., 79, 106, 113.
Curiosity, 30, 32.
Curricular revisions (at Wittenberg), 154 f.

Death, 18, 86, 90.
Devil, 19, 22, 30, 36, 39, 60, 74, 100, 141.
 the White, 114 ff., 136, 137, 138.
DeMorgan's Laws, 46 n.
Dialectic, 38, 40, 46 f., 66, 73, 78, 81, 153, 157, 171.
Disputations, 11.
Doctrine, 165.
Dogma, 165.
Double-truth theory, 21, 49 ff.

Election, 95.
Epicurean, 41.
epieikeia, 35.
Erasmians, 79 n.
Eternal life, 95, 124, 125, 130 n., 132, 134, 135 n.
Ethical categories, 114, 117, 128, 134.
Ethics, vii, 34, 37, 75, 96 n., 118, 123, 134, 135 n.
Evangelical experience, 141, 142, 148 ff.
Exegesis, 141 ff., 153, 158, 162, 164.
Experience (*erfarung*), 29, 31 f., 141, 148, 151.
ex puris naturalibus, 121.
eyn mal, 120, 126, 134.

facere quod in se est, 72 ff., 95, 122.
Faith, 21, 39, 62, 72, 73, 74, 87, 100, 112, 117, 118, 119, 129, 149, 151 n., 162 n., 168, 169.
 and despair, 115.

Faith (contd.)
  and love ('charity'), 61 n., 126 ff.,
    134.
  and reason, 20 ff., 58, 81 f., 93, 97,
    99 n., 110, 135 f., 170.
  and the four causes, 47.
  and the Word, 20, 78.
  and works, 16, 62, 105, 118, 123, 134.
  ante, post fidem, 22 f.
  articles of, 20, 41, 50, 51, 52, 79, 85,
    141, 142.
  as hearing, 89, 90, 104 f.
  as humility, 110 ff.
  as knowledge, 32, 58, 82.
  as virtue, 127.
  gives God glory, 78, 103.
  historic (acquired), 127.
  in Christ, 62, 85, 86, 87, 166.
  saving (justifying), 57 f., 127.
  sola fide, 104 n., 115, 120, 126, 128,
    134.
Fall, 17, 21 n., 30, 124 n.
Fanatics, 19, 70, 77, 79 n., 116.
Fathers, 18, 139, 157.
Flesh, 18, 69 ff., 76, 85, 113, 118 n.
Forgiveness, vii, 8, 9, 47, 58, 90 ff., 112,
    117, 119, 129 n., 130, 131 n., 135 n.,
    151 n., 169.
Fourfold sense, 143 f.
Freedom, Christian, 71.

Galatians, Luther's Commentary on, 4,
    10, 24, 39, chap. iv passim, 69, 84,
    92, 94, 97, 100, 104, 106, 111, 115,
    118, 119.
  Middleton edn., 59 ff.
  Shorter Commentary, 4 n., 62 n.
Genesis, Luther's Lectures on, 10–11.
Geometry, 44.
German Bible, Luther's, 151 n., 171.
Gift and example, 118.
Glory, the light of, 171.
Glory of God, 59, 77, 78, 90, 103, 106,
    113, 169.
Glosses, 61.
God, 30, 38, 40, 59, 67, 76, 85, 88, 94,
    95, 112, 129 n., 140, 161.
  accepts sinners, 114 ff., 123, 130 f.,
    169.
  active, not passive, 19.
  and idolatry, 14.
  as Author of Scripture, 150 n.
  as Creator, 101.
  as Debtor, 122.
  as First Cause, 51, 52, 131.
  as 'Hidden (Naked) God', 9, 77, 83 n.
  as Highest Good, 133 n.
  as Judge, 90, 94, 101.
  care for men, 19, 41.
  existence of, 15, 18, 19, 41, 101.

  foreign work of, 110, 137 n.
  justice of, 132, 149.
  man wants to be, 95.
  natural knowledge of, 52, 100 ff.
  nature of, 15, 29, 77, 112.
  not placated by works, 105 f.
  of works-righteousness, 97.
  proofs of, 50 f.
  quod, quid sit Deus, 15.
  reason's knowlege of, 14 f., 18 f.
  sole Author of salvation, 113.
  unity of, 51, 52.
  will of, 18, 77, 101, 129 n., 130 n.
  works against reason, 20.
Gospel, vii, 12, 19, 22, 29, 62, 85, 87,
    91, 92, 98, 109, 110, 111, 112, 114,
    115, 134, 143, 145, 150, 151 n., 153,
    161, 162, 165, 171.
Government, civil, 8 n., 9, 13, 17.
Grace, 22, 34, 36, 70, 76, 87, 91, 94, 95,
    112, 117, 118, 119, 135 n., 136, 140,
    149, 150 n., 169, 170.
  and reason, vii, 98, 135, 136, 160.
  in Luther, 129.
  in Melanchthon, 129.
  in Occam, 47 f., 95, 121 ff.
  in Thomas, 121, 123 ff., 129 ff., 132,
    133, 134.
  preparation for, 95.
Grammar, 37, 44, 60, 66, 73, 148, 150,
    157, 162, 166, 167.
Grammatical sense, 142 ff., 153, 156,
    166.
Grecians, the, 155.
Greek authors, 139.
Greek language, 145 n., 154, 155.
Greek terms, 46 f.

habitus (= hexis), 86, 96, 125 n.
Heaven, 120 n., 125.
Hebrew, 145 n.
Heretics, 28.
Hierarchies, the three, 16 n.
History, 139, 157, 158.
  Church, 139.
Hope, 82.
Humanism, chaps. ix and x passim.
  and Aristotelian philosophy, 158 ff.
  and 'primitive Christianity', 153, 159,
    161.
  and the English Reformation, 155.
  as forerunner to Gospel, 147, 171.
  Biblical helps of, 146.
  Luther's debt to, 5, 43, 151, 153, 171.
  meaning of name, 153.
  pragmatic outlook of, 160.
Humility, 19 f., 110 ff., 119.

Idealism, 133 n.
Idolatry, 77, 93.

Illumination of reason (*see also* Re-
    generation), 18, 22 ff., 73, 81, 140 f.,
    161, 170, 171.
Immortality, 36, 41, 50.
Impanation, 48.
Imputation, 47 f., 111, 129.
Incarnation, 14, 20 n., 49, 79 n.
incurvatus in se, 71.
intellectus agens, 41 n.
Irrationalism, vii, 65, 66, 79, 98, 135,
    136, 138, 160.
Israel, 123.

Jews, 19, 77, 85, 118.
Judgement, 94, 109.
Justification by faith, 9, 26, 30, 47 f., 58,
    62, 65 n., 74, 75, 76, 78, 85, 86, 87,
    88, 89, 91, 93 n., 94, 95, 96, 97, 98,
    104, 105, 108, 110, 111, 112, 115,
    117, 118, 123, 149, 150 n., 151,
    166 n.
    — Luther's doctrine of, 119 f., 125 f.,
    135 n.
    Occam's, 47 f., 120 ff.
    Thomas's, 123 ff., 130, 131 n., 132,
    134.

Kingdom of Christ, 26, 69, 71, 82, 106,
    126, 137 n.
    — of grace, 94.
    — of reason, 25 f., 35 n., 72, 73, 80.
    — of world, 69, 76, 82.
Kingdoms, the Two, 25 f., 119 f., 137,
    168 ff.
    and civil righteousness, 75.
    and ethics, 34.
    and law, 113 n.
    and philosophy, 41.
    and *politia, economia*, 13 n.
    and reason, chaps. I and V *passim*, 69.
    confusion of, 120, 134, 137.
    structural principle of Luther's theo-
    logy, 8 f., 97.

Ladders of Scholasticism, 103.
Languages, 22, 145, 147, 153, 159, 161,
    166.
Latin authors, 139.
Law, 74, 76, chap. VI (*passim*), 87, 98,
    100, 101, 117, 118, 119, 122, 134,
    136, 149, 165 n.
    and grace, 95
    and reason, *see* reason.
    as a method of salvation, 107.
    ceremonial and moral, 107 f.
    civil, 22.
    demands inwardness, 106.
    Divine, 18.
    does not justify, 89, 104.
    ecclesiastical, 33, 34.

how performed, 122 n.
illustrations of, 108 f.
natural, 9, 13 n., 107, 113 n.
of Moses, 77, 107.
Paul's descriptions of, 88.
third use of, 113 n.
twofold office (use), 100, 108 ff.,
    137 n.
Legalism, legalists, 83 n., chap. VI
    passim, 101, 102, 107, 108, 110, 113,
    114, 138, 169.
    in the Nominalists, 120 ff.
    in St. Thomas, 123 ff., 133.
Legalistic assumption, 86, 88, 93, 95,
    100, 102, 117, 134, 168, 170.
Light of nature, 12, 33.
Literature, secondary (on reason), vii f.,
    4, 96 ff.
Logic, 37, 40, 44, 46, 66, 73, 159.
    logica fidei, 53, 54, 55 n.
Love, 74, 76, 95, 119, 121, 128, 128 n.,
    129, 130 n., 134, 169.
Lutheri Dialectica, 11 n.

Magi, 31.
Majesty of God, 77 f., 79 n., 113.
Manichaeism, 28.
Mass, 92, 94.
Mathematics, 32, 38 n., 44, 54 n., 154.
Merit, 47, 79, 101, 125, 126, 128,
    131 ff., 134, 135 n.
    merita de congruo, condigno, 121 ff., 132.
Metaphysical categories, 114, 128, 131,
    159.
Metaphysics, 38 n.
Method of present work, viii, 4, 6 f., 57.
Ministry, 151 n.
Miracle, 17, 80.
Mohammedans, 85.
Monasteries, monastic vows, monks, 9,
    15, 16, 62, 76, 77, 79, 89, 93, 106,
    136, 149, 150, 154.
Moralism, 160, 166, 167.
Moral philosophy, 34, 40 n., 41.
Morals, 129 n., 134, 165.
    Reason's capacity in, 14.
Music, 44.
Mystics, 43, 139, 152 n., 156.

naturalia, 23, 73, 161.
Natural knowledge (of God), 52.
Natural philosophy, 30 ff., 34, 36,
    38 n., 41.
Natural theology, 50.
Nature, 15, 17, 19, 95, 124 n., 134 n.
Nominalism, Nominalists, 21, 114, 133,
    152, 156.
    and *habitus*, 96.
    and the 'original Aristotle', 38.

Nominalism (*contd.*)
division of philosophy and theology, 42.
doctrine of salvation, 121 ff., 126.
empiricism, 52.
epistemology, 6, 55.
faith and reason, 49 ff.
interest in sermonic disciplines, 37.
legalism in, 120 ff.
literature on, vii, viii.
Luther's education in, 3, 43 ff., 138, 141, 170.
Luther's Nominalist professors, 7, 44.
on the indemonstrability of God, 50 ff.
Pelagianism, 6, 55, 95, 126.
present state of scholarship, 4 f.
Nomos-piety, 169 n.
numinous, 9.

Obedience, 20 n.
Occamism, *see* William of Occam, Nominalism.
Occam's Razor, 50.
oeconomia, 14 n.
ordinatio, 132 n.
Origin of mankind, 40.
Oxford Reformers, 155, 161.

Papists, 28, 29, 35, 39, 47, 64 n., 73, 85, 93.
Pelagianism, 6, 55, 95, 123, 126.
Perseverance, 125.
Philology, 144, 149, 153, 157, 158, 162, 166, 167, 168.
Philosophy, 20, 21, 53, chap. II *passim*, 95, 135, 140, 141, 156, 166, 168, 171.
in Nominalism, chap. III *passim*.
philosophia Christi, 165, 166.
Physics, 37, 38 n., 41, 134.
Piety, 160.
politia, 14 n.
Pope, 18, 34, 49, 117, 118, 136, 153, 159, 165.
Postils, 10 f., 29.
Pride, 19 f., 88, 103, 106 f., 109, 110, 116, 158.
pro me, 94.
Promise, 118 n.
Protestantism, viii, 115, 120, 132 n., 135 n., 151.
Psalter, 62.

quadrivium, 44.

Reason (*see also* 'Faith', 'Kingdoms', &c.):
ambivalence of Luther's attitude towards, 4.

and argument, 65, 66.
and grace, vii, 9.
and law, 13, 35 n., 67, 68, 87 ff., 102, 137.
and life of Church, 16 n.
and nature, 17, 20.
and obedience, 20.
and the True Light, 17.
and will, 55 f., 99 n.
and works, 92 f.
and world, 13, 18.
as a charisma, 14 n.
as a formal notion, 169 f.
as carnal (human, natural), 18, 69 ff., 73, 141, 168, 169 n., 170.
as Devil's Whore, Frau Hulda and Madam Jezebel, 1, 9, 19, 26, 28 n., 137, 138.
as God's gift, 15, 17.
as handmaid of faith, 26, 67, 82, 84, 140.
as light of nature, 33, 171.
as *opinio*, 56, 84 ff., 90, 95, 169, 170.
as organ of thought, 140.
as 'practical reason', 170.
as pride, 19, 20, 88, 103.
experiences only temporal things, 18.
fallibility of, 17.
false inferences of, 67, 84, 88 ff., 100 ff.
in captivity to Christ, 53, 99 n.
'inferior' and 'superior', 24.
Luther's abuse of, 1.
Luther's praise of, 16 f.
nova ratio, 72, 81.
ratio, 65 ff.
ratio spiritualis, 161.
recta ratio, 75, 81, 96.
sacrificium intellectus, 21, 79, 90.
'scholarly reason', 141, 151.
soteriological problem, 58, 62.
use and abuse of, 22 f., 140, 168.
Reformation, viii, 55, 120, 153, 161, 171.
the English, 155.
Regeneration, 72.
of reason, 22 ff.
Religion, 38, 67, 85, 88, 93, 94, chap. VII *passim*, 134, 141, 151.
Religious viewpoint, 117.
Renaissance, 139, 155, 156 f., 160, 161, 171.
Resurrection:
Christ's, 20 n., 79.
the saints', 20 n., 79.
of reason, 23 f.
Revelation, 18, 31, 48, 67, 91, 100 ff., 107, 140.
Revival of learning, 139, 156, 160.
Reward, 101, 125, 132, 132 n., 133, 134.

Rhetoric, 44, 46 f., 81, 160.
Righteousness, 64 n., 70, 74, 88, 90, 102, 109, 110, 112 f., 117, 118, 119 f., 129, 130, 134.
active and passive, 26, 86, 112.
by faith (grace), 26, 86, 87, 89, 112.
Christian, 75, 91, 100, 112.
civil, 26, 29, 74, 75, 112, 118.
of law (works), 86, 87, 112.
Scholastic view, 47.
Rome, Roman Catholicism, viii, 120, 129, 130, 135 n., 136, 162.

Sacramentarians, 28 n., 47.
Sacraments, 81, 131 n.
Salvation, 18, 34, 56, 62, 77, 88, 93, 103, 104, 105, 106, 108, 109, 110, 111, 113, 116, 118, 121, 123, 125, 126, 129, 132, 133, 134, 135 n., 136.
Sanctification, 135 n.
Scholasticism, Schoolmen, viii, 5, 28, 33, 38, 39, 49, 67, 71, 73, 75, 94, 96, 97, chap. VIII passim, 139, 143, chap. X passim, 153, 171.
Scholia, 61.
Schwärmer, 28.
Science, 31 f., 37, 53, 140, 151.
Scriptures, the Holy, 5, 12, 17, 18, 19, 23, 29, 33, 35, 36, 48, 50, 60, 63, 80, 102, 105, 123, 132 n., 157.
Luther's attitude towards, chap. IX passim.
Scriptura sola, 148, 149.
Scriptura sui ipsius interpres, 149.
'Scripture and reason' (= Wormser Formel), 24 f., 28, 50 n.
Sense-perception, 29, 32, 52.
Sermonic disciplines, 36 f., 46, 157, 166.
Service of neighbour, 135 n.
Signs, 31.
simul iustus et peccator, 120 n.
Sin, sinners, 9, 18, 22, 70 f., 80, 85, 90, 91, 97, 108, 113, 114 ff., 124, 129, 135 n., 165 n.
Social morality, 7.
Sophists (see Schoolmen), 121 n.
Soul, 40, 41, 95, 113, 129, 131.
Sources (on reason), 4, 10 f.
Speculation, 9 n., 30, 32, 77 f., 82, 83, 95.
Spirit and body, 106, 118, 129 n.
Spirit and letter, 143.
Spirit, the Holy, 16, 17, 22, 60, 72, 81, 90, 91, 104, 121, 140, 144, 145, 150 n., 167, 171.

spiritualia, 73.
Substance and accidents, 30, 38.
superbia, 76, 111, 116.
Superstition, 76, 95, 169 n.
Supper, Lord's, 20 n., 48, 79, 164.

Table-talk, 10 f., 29.
Terminism, 45.
terminus conceptus, prolatus, 46.
Theological interpretation, 147 ff., 162.
Theology, 20, 21, 81, 84, 91, 114, 134, 136, 154, 164, 167, 169.
and philosophy, chaps. II and III passim, 74 f., 96, 118, 152.
Luther's, 7 ff., 57 f., 135.
of glory, 76, 83 n.
Tower of Babel, 103.
Transubstantiation, 48.
Trinity, 20 n., 24, 30, 45 n., 51, 52, 164.
trivium, 44, 157.
Tropological sense, 143.
tumultus, 162.
Turks, 77.

Universals, 45 f.
Universities, 33, 36, 96 n.

via antiqua, 154.
via moderna, see Nominalism.
Virgin Birth, 79.
viri heroici, 14 n.
Vocation, 7, 16, 76.
Voluntarism, 48.
Vulgate, 144 f.

Will, 55 f., 75, 76, 81, 96, 99 n., 119.
bondage of, 65, 106.
freewill, 80, 131 n., 132, 132 n.
Witchcraft, 59.
Word of God, 14, 16, 18, 19, 20, 23, 24, 25, 26, 26 n., 28, 30, 33, 76, 77, 80, 81, 91, 93, 94, 140, 141, 170, 171.
Works, 16, 47, 62, 74, 76, 82, 83, 87, 95, 100, 101, 103, 104 ff., 109, 111, 113, 117, 118, 119, 123, 125, 128, 130 n., 132.
'will-works', 77 f., 85, 86, 88, 89, 91, 93, 94, 99 n.
World, 13, 18, 86, 106, 117, 170.
eternity of, 41 n.
World-view, 36, 37, 166.
Worship, 79, 93, 100.
Wunderleute, 14 n.

Zwinglians, 64 n.

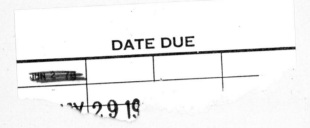